SLANTING I, IMAGINING WE

TransCanada Series

The study of Canadian literature can no longer take place in isolation from larger external forces. Pressures of multiculturalism put emphasis upon discourses of citizenship and security, while market-driven factors increasingly shape the publication, dissemination, and reception of Canadian writing. The persistent questioning of the Humanities has invited a rethinking of the disciplinary and curricular structures within which the literature is taught, while the development of area and diaspora studies has raised important questions about the tradition. The goal of the TransCanada series is to publish forward-thinking critical interventions that investigate these paradigm shifts in interdisciplinary ways.

Series editor:

Smaro Kamboureli, Avie Bennett Chair in Canadian Literature, Department of English, University of Toronto

For more information, please contact:

Smaro Kamboureli
Avie Bennett Chair in Canadian Literature
Department of English
University of Toronto
170 St. George Street
Toronto, ON M5R 2M8
Canada
Phone: 416-978-0156
Email: smaro.kamboureli@utoronto.ca

Lisa Quinn
Acquisitions Editor
Wilfrid Laurier University Press
75 University Avenue West
Waterloo, ON N2L 3C5
Canada
Phone: 519-884-0710 ext. 2843
Fax: 519-725-1399
Email: quinn@press.wlu.ca

SLANTING I, IMAGINING WE

Asian Canadian Literary Production in the 1980s and 1990s

Larissa Lai

WILFRID LAURIER
UNIVERSITY PRESS

Wilfrid Laurier University Press acknowledges the support of the Canada Council for the Arts for our publishing program. We acknowledge the financial support of the Government of Canada through the Canada Book Fund for our publishing activities.

Library and Archives Canada Cataloguing in Publication

Lai, Larissa, 1967–, author
    Slanting I, imagining we : Asian Canadian literary production in the 1980s and 1990s / Larissa Lai.

(TransCanada)
Includes bibliographical references and index.
Issued in print and electronic formats.
ISBN 978-1-77112-041-8 (pbk.).—ISBN 978-1-77112-042-5 (pdf).—
ISBN 978-1-77112-043-2 (epub)

    1. Canadian literature (English) —Asian Canadian authors—History and criticism. 2. Canadian literature (English) —20th century—History and criticism.
I. Title.

PS8089.5.A8L33 2014   C810.9'895   C2014-901721-9
                                                 C2014-901722-7

Front-cover image by Haruko Okano: *The Hands of the Compassionate One*, 1993 (acrylic on canvas, 5' wide by 9' high); photo by Al Reid Studio. Cover design by Martyn Schmoll. Text design by Angela Booth Malleau.

This book is printed on FSC recycled paper and is certified Ecologo. It is made from 100% post-consumer fibre, processed chlorine free, and manufactured using biogas energy.

Printed in Canada

Every reasonable effort has been made to acquire permission for copyright material used in this text, and to acknowledge all such indebtedness accurately. Any errors and omissions called to the publisher's attention will be corrected in future printings.

RECYCLED
Paper made from
recycled material
FSC® C103567

for my mother and father,
Yuen-Ting Lai and Tyrone Lai

It was all well and good to have a tragic story in the past, but what if it returns? What if it comes back with all it has stored up, to be resolved and decided, to be answered. She couldn't foresee an easy time, as Binh must have envisaged…. Would he be kind to her mother and father?

In the end that is what she meant, she realized, that is what she wanted. They deserved kindness, and Tuyen doubted whether this ghost could deliver it.

What We All Long For
Dionne Brand

I hold my culture in my hands and form it on my own,
so that no one else can shape the way
it lies upon my body

"The Body Politic"
Hiromi Goto

CONTENTS

PREFACE AND ACKNOWLEDGEMENTS

Of course this is a personal project. How could it be otherwise? The 1980s and 1990s appear to me as an extraordinary moment in Canadian cultural politics because they were also the moment of my own emergence from the sleep of invisibilization into a subject with a measure of public voice. The first anti-racist project I worked on was the 1990 exhibit *Yellow Peril: Reconsidered,* organized by the video artist and curator Paul Wong and his collaborator Elspeth Sage, through their production company On Edge, which Paul housed in his Main Street apartment on Vancouver's East Side. It was a national exhibition that travelled to six artist-run centres across the country, showcasing the works of twenty-five Asian Canadian artists working in contemporary media. Through a reclamation of the racist name "yellow peril," the show was, for me, a moment of inauguration into an oppositional politics of race that was both empowering and unsettling. I lived it out at work and at play, in intellectual and creative modes as much as personal ones. It drew me into a consciousness of my own subjectivity and agency (or lack thereof), in ways that I had not considered before, perhaps in ways that were not available for consideration until this cultural moment. For me, the "reconsideration" of the "yellow peril" occurred before its overt "consideration." The problem with race for the duration of my childhood growing up in Newfoundland in the 1970s was that it was a repressed but very much live force beneath the surface of Canadian cultural life. Both "consideration" and "reconsideration" were a huge relief, as though one could finally point out the tiger sleeping in the corner of the room.

In the years after the implementation of the Multiculturalism Act, so much was possible—not because of the act itself, but because community-based artists', writers', and activists' responses to its limitations added to an organic energy that was already there in racialized Canadian communities. It was a moment in which the Japanese Canadian Internment, the Chinese Head Tax and Chinese Exclusion Act, the Indian Act, and the *Komagata Maru* incident could be spoken of and interrogated for their social, cultural, and political effects as much as for their legal ones. Mainstream reaction and obfuscation were and continue to be tremendous. Nonetheless, with the reclamation of the racist name and the concept of "breaking the silence" as two of its major tools, Canadian anti-racist cultural communities opened up new possibilities for ethical practices, human relations, "self-fashioning," art, and writing. Some people embraced these possibilities inside the walls of the academy, some found it more productive to engage through artist-run centres, small collectives, spontaneous gatherings, organized gatherings, editorial committees, conference organizing committees, demonstrations, or purely within the context of their own art or writing practices.

I engaged through a combination of these strategies, working for a while as the administrative coordinator for SAW Video in Ottawa, organizing two small exhibitions—*Telling Relations* and *Earthly Pleasures*—for the grunt gallery in Vancouver, reading creative work for the exhibition and performance project *Racy Sexy*, working as a video technician for the Banff residency Race and the Body Politic, enjoying potlucks and video nights with Asian Lesbians of Vancouver (ALOV), briefly editing *Front* magazine, guest editing *Kinesis*, sitting on the organizing committee for the Writers' Union–sponsored conference Writing Thru Race, while writing my first novel *When Fox Is a Thousand*. This way of working was not so uncommon among anti-racist cultural workers of that decade. The cultural movements of the moment were saturated with love, joy, envy, competition, rage, horror, sorrow, and dismay. These emotions could be crushing, but they could also lead to generative acts of creation or critique.

With the question "How do I (or we) make (or remake) things/events/texts/selves in order to be free?" at its centre, this book explores a range of strategies engaged in by groups or individuals identified with the concept "Asian Canadian" in order to test the waters of liberation (variously defined, imagined, and/or produced). I am highly aware that this is a question that can be addressed through a range of discourses and practices; indeed, I have engaged those practices and languages in other ways at other moments.

In Western critical terms, this book's initial impulse is a Foucauldian one: What are the possibilities for "self-fashioning" through histories of the present, in the "present" of 1980s and 1990s Canada? Its concerns become quickly Marxist materialist, with a Deleuzian tinge as questions of subject construction veer quickly away from what linear history can offer. The subject itself is thrown into contention, and then variously (and always differently) reconstituted through collaboration, juxtaposition, active imagination, experiments in language, or an emphasis on relation that destabilizes the Cartesian subject altogether. This book, in a sense, tries out different kinds of liberatory practices by examining how different individuals or collectives have engaged in them. It asks who or what is produced through these engagements. The "personal" and the collective, then, enter into realms of re-vision and reconsideration in ways that remain lively and productively unfinished.

Questions of how to be and how to write are deeply intertwined. If I have done my job well, this book illustrates the mutual dependency of theory on practice and vice versa; or indeed, the continuity between modes that aren't nearly as discrete as we sometimes imagine them. My dream is that it will be taken up by artists, writers, cultural workers, and activists as much as by intellectuals.

This book would not have been possible without the support of Aruna Srivastava, who, as my Ph.D. supervisor, saw it through its first incarnation. I am so appreciative of the ideas, critique, and encouragement received from the original members of my dissertation committee: Pamela McCallum, Shaobo Xie, Clara Joseph, Rebecca Sullivan, and Heather Zwicker. In the rewriting and revision of this book, Smaro Kamboureli has been supportive far and beyond her role as editor of the TransCanada series. I most grateful to her. I would also like to thank the good people at Wilfrid Laurier University Press for the roles they played in guiding this book to publication, especially Lisa Quinn, Leslie Macredie, Rob Kohlmeier, and Wendy Thomas.

I have been incredibly fortunate in having strong communities that have supported me and my work. This project would not have been possible without the support, feedback, and encouragement of many friends and colleagues with whom I was in conversation while the book was being written: Rita Wong, Hiromi Goto, Ashok Mathur, Janet Neigh, Roy Miki, Fred Wah, Pauline Butling, Rebecca Sullivan, Bart Beaty, Malek Khouri, Mary Polito, James Ellis, Jacqueline Jenkins, Tom Loebel, Jay Gamble, Carmen Derksen, Nikki Sheppy, Camille Isaacs, Robinder Sehdev, Christopher Ewart, Jason Christie, derek beaulieu, Jill Hartman, Paul Kennett, Janice Grant, Myron Campbell, Michael Boyce, Sandra Dametto, Leonard Lee, Sandy Lam, Travis Murphy, and Jason Laurendeau. I am most appreciative of current friends and colleagues, who were so present and supportive during the rewrite: Lorraine Weir, Christopher Lee, Glenn Deer, Laura Moss, Sherrill Grace, Richard Cavell, Margery Fee, Jennifer Chun, David Chariandy, Sophie McCall, David Khang, Christine Kim, Daniel Heath Justice, Janey Lew, and Sneja Gunew. I would also like to thank the cultural workers, writers, artists, editors, curators, academics, and activists whom I knew and worked with through the 1980s and 1990s, too numerous to name here. Those people and those days are what inspire this work. A few of them are Monika Kin Gagnon, Shani Mootoo, Richard Fung, Lloyd Wong, Melina Young, Scott Toguri McFarlane, Viola Thomas, C. Allyson Lee, Fatima

Jaffer, Agnes Huang, Lynne Wanyeki, Lenore Keeshig-Tobias, Lee Maracle, jam ismail, Sadhu Binning, Ajmer Rode, Paul Wong, Elspeth Sage, Jim Wong-Chu, Kaspar Saxena, Susan Crean, Shamina Senaratne, Karlyn Koh, Charmaine Perkins, Mark Nakada, Phinder Dulai, Eden Robinson, Gregory Scofield, Andrea Fatona, Burcu Ozdemir, Rajinderpal S. Pal, Susanda Yee, Lily Shinde, Anne Jew, Windsor Jew, Cynthia Low, Chris Rahim, Sook C. Kong, Da Choong, Henry Tsang, Karin Lee, Lorraine Chan, Kathy-Ann March, Effie Pow, Kevin Louie, Jean Lum, Nadine Chambers, Deblekha Guin, Deborah O, Janisse Browning, Cheryl L'Hirondelle, Lillian Allen, Glenn Lowry, Sara Diamond, Glen Alteen, and Haruko Okano, whose beautiful artwork graces the cover of this book. Thanks especially to my family: Tyrone Lai, Yuen-Ting Lai, and Wendy Lai for believing I could do it. And finally, much gratitude to Edward Parker for his loving support of this work.

I am most grateful to have had the financial support of the Social Sciences and Humanities Research Council (2002–2005); a graduate research scholarship from the English Department, University of Calgary (2001–2002); and a Dean's Research Excellence Award (2002–2005). A version of Chapter 1 of this book was presented at Beyond Autoethnography: Writing Race and Ethnicity in Canada at Wilfrid Laurier University, Waterloo, in April 2005. A version of Chapter 4 was presented at Wild Words: 2005 Alberta Centennial Literary Celebration at the University of Calgary in October 2005. The first half of Chapter 6 was presented at Blurring the Boundaries: Transrealism and Other Movements, 26th International Conference on the Fantastic in the Arts in Fort Lauderdale, Florida, in March 2005. A version of the second half of Chapter 6 was presented at "No Language Is Neutral": A Conference on Dionne Brand through OISE and the University of Toronto in October 2006.

In earlier forms, parts of this book have been published in books and journals. A version of Chapter 1 is a chapter in Eleanor Ty and Christyl Verdun's *Asian Canadian Writing Beyond Autoethnography*. A version of the conclusion appears as an article in Sophie McCall and David Chariandy's special issue of *West Coast Line*, entitled *Citizenship and Cultural Belonging*. Finally, a version of Chapter 2 has been published in *Shifting the Ground of Canadian Literary Studies*, edited by Smaro Kamboureli and Robert Zacharias. I am most grateful to the editors of all these publications for their support of my work.

ASIAN CANADIAN RUPTURES, CONTEMPORARY SCANDALS

ASIAN CANADIAN RELATIONS

It is my contention that the formation of Asian Canadian literature as it was conceived in the 1980s and 1990s emerges as a rupture. This rupture comes about partly through the confluence of a number of factors—the growing acceptance of poststructural theory in Canadian universities, the passing of the Multiculturalism Act in 1988, and the Japanese Canadian achievement of apology from the Canadian government for wartime internment and the expropriation of Japanese Canadian property during World War II. It builds on the idea of "Asian Canadian identity" as it was imagined and practised through the 1960s and 1970s but problematizes earlier formations using recently arrived poststructural tools—a shift in form from one moment to the next, though not necessarily progress as such. But most importantly it arises in relation to a set of unpredictable contingencies and a great deal of energy arising from so-called Asian Canadian communities working beside other marginalized communities. It is thus also profoundly relational, built in coalition with broader anti-oppression movements in the arts, involving people who variously articulate the building movements as anti-racist, of colour, Black, First Nations, South Asian, Caribbean, queer, feminist, Japanese Canadian, Chinese Canadian, Korean Canadian, GLBTQ, working class, disability, and more. It emerges also in relation to a burgeoning Indigenous sovereignty movement as the terms and framework of that movement were growing and changing. These many movements sometimes overlap, sometimes work in conjunction with one another, and often work in contention with one another in ways that, in that period of fifteen or so years, produced a great deal of energy for autobiographies, conferences, special issues, anthologies, novels, poetry books, poetic experiments, and criticism.

While there has been a tendency, certainly at present, but also at various historical moments to posit a linear and heroic history for Asian Canadian literature, I argue that it is in rupture and coalition that the term has been most generative. Further, at each rupture or each coalitional moment,

1

different temporalities are invoked that produce both Asian Canadian literature and its relations differently. In this book, I articulate a small handful of those ruptures and/or coalitional moments and in so doing illustrate both its instabilities and its productivities. I contend that while its oppositional power matters a great deal, it is in paradox and contradiction that the term "Asian Canadian literature" is most generative.

If one wanted to posit a linear trajectory, one might locate the beginnings of Asian Canadian literature with Edith and Winnifred Eaton, also known as Sui Sin Far and Onoto Watanna. Or one might locate the first use of the term "Asian Canadian" in *Inalienable Rice*, an anthology of Chinese Canadian and Japanese Canadian writing produced by the Powell Street Society and the Chinese Canadian Writers' Workshop in 1979. Such a narrative, articulated most famously by Donald Goellnicht's "The Protracted Birth of Asian Canadian Literature," and productively critiqued and modified by Chris Lee, Smaro Kamboureli, and Guy Beauregard contributed to the blossoming of Asian Canadian cultural production in the late 1980s through the 1990s. However, the energy that fed this flowering was also profoundly coalitional. The rise of Asian Canadian literature as a concept and category coincided with Asian Canadian community-based activism and community-based activism in other marginalized communities, many of which overlapped or ran parallel with the framework "Asian Canadian," as I described above. As "Asian Canadian" overlapped with other racialized categories, so "literature" overlapped and interacted with other genres and organizational forms. Many who wrote fiction, shorts stories, essays, poetry, and criticism were also involved with film, video, photography, installation, community arts, social activist, and artist-run communities. Some of these writers, thinkers, and artists include Anne Jew, Monika Gagnon, Shani Mootoo, Richard Fung, Lloyd Wong, Lorraine Chan, Henry Tsang, and Karin Lee. There was much crossover and dialogue through these communities, which were often as activist as they were creative and critical. Numerous cultural events across the country addressed the conditions and problems of identifying as a racialized subject: the InVisible Colours Film and Video Festival, the exhibit *Yellow Peril: Reconsidered*, the exhibit and cultural festival *Racy Sexy*, the Desh Pardesh festival of South Asian Canadians and the arts, the Appropriate Voice conference, the Writing Thru Race conference, It's a Cultural Thing (the Minquon Panchayat gathering of artists and administrators involved in artist-run centres), the *First Ladies* exhibition at the Pitt Gallery in Vancouver, the Race to the Screen Festival at the Euclid Theatre in Toronto, the Race and the Body Politic artists' residency at the Banff Centre for the Arts, just to name and few. Though their formations varied, the dialogues that moved through them were deeply intertwined. Certain publications also became engaged in the struggles and celebrations of racialized people in that moment. I think in particular of *Kinesis: The Newspaper of the Vancouver Status of Women, Fuse Magazine,* and *West Coast Line*.[1]

Many special issues of journals were produced on the subject of race and racialization, involving writers, editors, and thinkers who also identified as Asian Canadian. I address two of these in this book—the *Awakening Thunder* special issue of *Fireweed* published in 1993, and *Colour. An Issue*, a special issue of *West Coast Line* published in 1994. There were, however, many others: the *Prairie Asians* special issue of *absinthe*, edited by Ashok Mathur in 1998; *Asian Canadian Writing*, a special issue of *Canadian Literature*, edited by Glenn Deer in 1999; and in 2001 a special issue of *West Coast Line* entitled *In-Equations: can asia pacific* edited by Glenn Lowry and Sook C. Kong. Important anthologies also emerged in the 1980s and 1990s, including *Many-Mouthed Birds, Swallowing Clouds, The Very Inside,* and *Piece of My Heart*.[2]

This was also a moment of important cultural protests, particularly concerning the 1993 staging of *Miss Saigon* and the purpose-built Princess of Wales Theatre (Tator et al. 141). Protests organized through Asian ReVision against racist stereotyping in *Miss Saigon* were tied intimately to protests organized through Black, African, and Caribbean Canadian communities against racist stereotyping in a production of *Showboat*, launched by Garth Drabinsky's company Livent the same year. I would suggest that energy and analysis from protests against the Royal Ontario Museum exhibit *Into the Heart of Africa* in 1989–90 influenced and supported these two 1993 actions, though certainly there is research to be done on the form and extent of the connections. The debates about both *Showboat* and *Miss Saigon* focused on the value of artistic freedom measured against the right of marginalized people not to be harmed by the circulation of negative stereotypes (Tator et al. 145). The idea that artistic freedom was available only to those who had privileged access to the avenues of public expression seemed never quite to hit the public arena, precisely because access to that arena was restricted to exclude those with this analysis. That both *Showboat* and *Miss Saigon* are stories acutely lacking in imagination and thus lacking in the exercise of artistic freedom also went unremarked and unnoticed. What I would like to emphasize here, however, is the collaborative relationships that must have existed among the activists working against both productions—Asian Canadian and Black Canadian cultural activists working and sharing analysis and strategy together. This is a history that is largely under-addressed in both the mainstream and community-based presses, but one that I suggest, attending to the many other collaborative projects that emerged in the late 1980s through the 1990s, took place en masse with very little discussion as a phenomenon and as intentional coalition-building work on the part of those involved. This book is intended to tell at least part of this missing story.

Coalition-building work has been ignored largely because the framework of understanding, at least at a mainstream level, was one that privileged the binary white versus colour and could not see any real difference within the marginalized side of the split, in spite of all the rhetoric of "diversity" in that historical moment. One of the few moments on the public record in which this coalitional work and its invisibilization is noted is in Scott Toguri McFarlane's 1995 *Fuse Magazine* article "The Haunt of Race," in which he notes the invisibilization of the organizing committee for the 1994 conference Writing Thru Race (1997–98), a very diverse group of "approximately sixty people including community activists, artists, filmmakers, critics, writers, curators, performance artists, students and teachers," many of whom were not members of the Writers' Union of Canada and who organized in direct challenge to it. Intelligent and powerful though his work was, that Roy Miki alone became the face of that committee in the public furor that unfolded, largely in the *Globe and Mail,* was a conflation and an erasure that few to this day note or remember. At Monika Kin Gagnon's prompting, McFarlane connects the organizing of Writing Thru Race and its "controversial" policy of limiting daytime events to writers of colour and First Nations[3] writers to earlier coalitional work, specifically the About Face, About Frame gathering of First Nations and "of colour" film and video producers (29). McFarlane writes:

> [T]hese national gatherings staged an aggregate of mass cultural producers, which in itself rhetorically staged processes of cultural difference and historical trajectories not directly referring to whiteness. It is as if these conferences produced a different ethnography (in the service of people of colour and First Nations people) operating within the national address. As such, they function as signs of cultural locations within the all inclusive nation that they cannot know. As a result, the nation cannot know itself. In this context the priority of the all-inclusive nation becomes secondary or, more accurately, postponed. The nation here functions as an event. (29)

In other words, the radical work of coalition building is the building of relation, and the production of narrative, theoretical, or poetic content at the site of relation—always a struggle and, until recently, largely invisibilized. Specific designations, including Asian Canadian, do matter, but they are produced relationally. In the context of the state and whiteness, relational dialogue is hegemonic, compulsory, and present on the surface. It occurs sometimes in the service of some measure of social justice, and sometimes in the service of entrenching racism. But more deeply and more invisibly, relational dialogue is also at work among cultural workers of colour and Indigenous cultural workers. This is also sometimes productive and sometimes not, but in either case it is less legible on the surface of national culture.

In all of these instances, then, the designation "Asian Canadian" is a porous one. It is genealogically produced and deeply relational. The power of the term comes not from a particular essence as such, but from the coalitional work it does. However, through a desire not to supply ammunition to a biological discourse concerning race or, worse, old colonial forms of racism, some thinkers of the moment called for strategic essentialism. Strategy was always contextual and contingent. Those contexts and contingencies were made, I suggest, collectively.

GENEALOGIES, SUBJECTS, STRATEGIES

In positing the late 1980s and the 1990s as a special time for Asian Canadian literature, I am aware that this book cannot escape linear time or the Gregorian calendar so easily. Further, I recognize that there are certain historical moments in which attachments to a linear notion of history can be useful. For me, the turn to a linear understanding of history with regard to Asian Canadian literature would be a kind of strategic essentialism in Gayatri Spivak's sense, as "a *strategic* use of a positivist essentialism in a scrupulously visible political interest" (*Selected Subaltern Studies* 13).

In working genealogically, I dance with narratives of progress. Progress is always a possibility, though not an inevitability. And its narrativizing is always ideological. I try here to be as attentive as possible to the ideological work progress does if and when I posit it.

For Foucault, to trace the linear history of a concept is utilitarian, but inaccurately so, because it assumes that "words ... [keep] their meaning, that desires still ... [point] in a single direction, and that ideas ... [retain] their logic" ("Nietzsche, Genealogy, History" 76). For him, such an assumption is naive because "the world of speech and desires has known invasions, struggles, plundering, disguises, ploys" (76). If this book has an approach, then, it is a genealogical one as Foucault encourages: "[I]t must record the singularity of events outside of any monotonous finality ... not in order to trace the gradual curve of their evolution, but to isolate the difference scenes where they engaged in different roles.... Genealogy ... rejects the metahistorical deployment of ideal significations and indefinite teleologies. It opposes itself to the search for 'origins'" (76–77). I also take up his call to recognize those moments when genealogical articulations are absent and chances are lost (76). Foucault's work is particularly important to a term like "Asian Canadian" because this term does profoundly different work in different historical moments, in spite of the fact that it may not appear to on the surface. I want to be clear that Foucault does not throw out the necessity to historicize in doing genealogical work. Rather he cautions us to be aware that the same word can mean different things or, at least, be valenced very differently depending on the historical moment. Further, as Sourayan Mookerjea notes, "Since the objects of investigation ... are, in fact, subjects ... hopes for ethico-political responsibility ... [are] pinned on various formulations of intersubjectivity and dialogue" (4).

As a discourse and a discipline emerging within the confines of a national discourse itself predicated on narratives of progress and a myth of origin, within a political, legal, and religious framework that values such myths, it is not surprising that Asian Canadian literature should, in its earliest iterations, seek out its own narratives of progress and myths of origin, and retroactively address the work of such writers as Sui Sin Far (Edith Eaton) and Onoto Watanna (Winnifred Eaton). The Chinese and Japanese Canadian anthology *Inalienable Rice* has also been important to narratives of progress, as the first text in linear Canadian history to use the term "Asian Canadian." Such narratives as narratives have contributed a great deal toward the production of Asian Canadian literature. Problematic and incomplete though they might be, gestures toward origin do form one aspect of the genealogical production of Asian Canadian literature. Donald Goellnicht's "A Long Labour: The Protracted Birth of Asian Canadian Literature" does not claim such narratives without problematizing them, though perhaps the claim is still implicitly there in his work. Goellnicht notes that Asian Canadian literature seems to be in a state of perpetual arrival (2). He is also very clear about limiting the frame of his argument to the emergence of Asian Canadian literature within the academy. (A deeper question, beyond the scope of this Introduction, might be this: Does the academy require a linear narrative in order to incorporate Asian Canadian literature? And further: Is the academic incorporation of Asian Canadian literature desirable? From which locations and to what ends?) Lien Chao's "Anthologizing the Collective" does overtly take up a progress narrative, one that emphasizes the need to "transform the community's hundred year silence into a resistant voice" (34). While these analyses may be problematic because of their tendency to produce Asian Canadian subjects as mimetic of mainstream subjects, and so open them to state incorporation, these are also empowering narratives without which the genealogical rupture of Asian Canadianness would not have been possible. Chris Lee, for instance, recognizes that such a narrative of progress can be empowering, but is nonetheless troubled by it because "what gets privileged is the completed act of emergence, which marks the culmination of a historical narrative of oppression and resistance, a narrative that finally functions to call into existence and justify the Asian Canadian" ("Enacting" 34).

Such a narrative, in other words, inadvertently denies the discontinuities, reversals, and aporias in experience, self-understanding, self-sameness, and writing, as well as the ongoing racisms and injustices that can so easily be erased then repeated through myths of origin and myths of arrival, which, as I argue in Chapter 1, quickly become national myths and are thus easily coopted as state strategies of assimilation. Indeed, it is precisely representations of past exclusions that, under narratives of progress, allow state apology to stand as a key turning point and a sign of incorporation—a second obliterating fantasy that hides a prior trauma. Mainstream Canadian citizens become, in a sense, melancholics in the way that the psychoanalysts Nicolas Abraham and Maria Torok describe them:

> To state that endocryptic identification is the work of fantasy alone means that its content amounts to maintaining the illusion of the topographical *status quo*, as it had been prior to the covert transformation. As for the *inclusion* itself, it is not a fantasy. Inclusion attests to a painful reality, forever *denied*: the "gaping wound" of the topography. It is therefore crucial to establish the following. The melancholic's complaints translate a fantasy—the imaginary suffering of the endocryptic object— as fantasy that only serves to mask the real suffering, the one unavowed, caused by a wound the subject does not know how to heal. (142)

Racialized subjects in this equation become those whose reality is forever denied, encrypted as it is, undigested, in the psyche of the consuming nation. It is denied, paradoxically, under the sign of its expiation—this is the paradox that, I argue, plagues the realist novels and autobiographies of the early 1990s, important and necessary though they were. Even as they do their silence-breaking work, they open themselves to state incorporation. There may, however, be a temporal gap that opens between silence breaking and state incorporation, one that can be experienced joyfully as the production of coherent selfhood and as a moment of arrival.

Scott McFarlane writes eloquently of this phenomenon in "The Haunt of Race." In relation to the conference Writing Thru Race, he posits the politics of multiculturalism as the site of encryption:

> The politics of cultural difference are shifting away from identity politics and the work of mourning and toward what I will call the politics of incorporation. As Judith Butler points out, in its psychoanalytic use incorporation "denotes a *magical* resolution of loss" wherein that list

> (originary/maternal) is maintained as unnameable or "other." Incorpo-
> ration encrypts the loss within the body as "a dead and deadening part of
> the body or one inhabited or possessed by phantasms of various kinds."
> The politics of incorporation act by staging that which is "encrypted" in
> the body politic and also in its phantasms. In the context of multicultur-
> alism, the politics of incorporation stage the haunting of race—its very
> "otherness"—as encrypted within the institutional, cultural and politi-
> cal bodies that ostensibly represent people of colour and First Nations
> people. (26)

What then of agency, subjectivity, and sense of self for those who must
occupy the site of haunting, those who, in essence, have no essence—we
incomplete ghosts? Homi Bhabha has famously recognized, through the
figure of Toni Morrison's *Beloved*, a subjectivity that flickers, that operates through a dance of presence and absence in representation: "[F]orcibly
entering the house of art and fiction in order to invade, alarm and dispossess,
they also demonstrate the compulsion to move beyond; to turn the present
into the past ... to touch the future on its hither side" (18). He calls the time
of such ghosts "an 'in-between' temporality that takes the measure of dwelling at home, while producing an image of the world in history" (13). This
in-between time, I would suggest, haunted, abject, and encrypted, is a violent and painful time but has nonetheless been necessary to give racialized
people in Canada back their history, or at least something like it. Bhabha's
in-between time swings between silence and voice, and also between being
and representation. And the 1980s and 1990s, as it was experienced, inhabited, and made by racialized subjects, was that kind of in-between time.

Roy Miki's work, particularly his essay "Asiancy" in *Broken Entries*, has
been useful for countering progress narratives and questioning the coherence
of the Asian Canadian subject. For Miki, "Asian Canadian" and its cousins
"Japanese Canadian," "Chinese Canadian," "Oriental," etc., are eruptions
in language that sometimes coincide with bodies, often uncomfortably. In
"Asiancy," Miki recalls a moment as a schoolboy in 1950s Winnipeg when
his teacher had the class read Ann Marriot's "The Wind Our Enemy":

> Though supposedly valorizing "our" local place, for me the tension in the
> class radiated from the single line "Japs Bomb China." Yes, of course,
> the day "we" read that poem out loud, the turn came for me at that line,
> and "i" could not—had not the terminological apparatus—to resist the
> act of voicing the word that was anathema at home. No one expected,
> except for the chuckle chuckle, this moment of linguistic anguish. The
> match between the word and "me" struck a chord but the unspoken
> fluttered out the (open) window. Even "i" was numbed by the evacuated
> words. (112)

In Miki's text, this anecdote is related in a call-out box, separate from the flow of his more properly "theoretical" text, itself a rupture that breaks the apparently coherent subjectivity of the "authoritative" writing self. The bourgeois self that might seem to have arrived with incorporation into state belonging is in fact fragmented and discontinuous. The histories of expulsion, exclusion, evacuation, internment, and incorporation produce Asian Canadian subjects not as the linear subjects of arrival but as discontinuous subjects for whom the possibility of speaking or writing the self is never easy or complete. Of such a subject, Miki asks, quoting and ghosting Gail Scott, "What if the surfacing unconsciousness stream finds void instead of code?" (qtd. in *Broken* 114).

If the breaking of silence was the important political labour carried out by activists, writers, and critics in the 1970s and early 1980s, then the late 1980s and the 1990s are marked by a recognition of the difficulty in speaking and writing, not because of any lack of ability or talent on the part of racialized writers, but because of problems inherent in racialized subject formations. In order to recognize such a difficulty, the Asian Canadian subject first needs a self. The need to "break the silence" is a crucial step—not necessarily a first step, but a "step forward" in the sense that Trinh Min-ha posits, in her own genealogical sense, as a step that moves at once both forward and back (*When the Moon Waxes Red* 15). We could understand "breaking the silence" as a historical *a priori* in Foucault's sense:

> [T]his *a priori* does not elude historicity: it does not constitute, above events, and in an unmoving heaven, an atemporal structure; it is defined not imposed from the outside on the elements that they relate together; they are caught up in the very things they connect; and if they are not modified with the least of them, they modify them, and are transformed with them into certain decisive thresholds. The *a priori* of positivities is not only the system of a temporal dispersion; it is itself a transformable group. (127)

"Breaking the silence" in other words, as an eruption of the opportunity to speak in the public arena, at once disrupts the subject formation of racialized subjects, and disrupts the public's ability to understand who and what such subjects are. Shut out of national history until the moment of rupture, Asian Canadian writers and critics suddenly and unexpectedly produce that history differently and, in so doing, produce another series of ruptures on the national plane that do not easily resolve and should not easily resolve.

Within the framework that Miki offers in "Asiancy," influenced by contemporary poetics, poststructural theory, and his own experience of being born and raised in the Japanese Canadian uprooting, a coherent self is no guarantee. In other critical texts, specifically Himani Bannerji's "Sound Barrier" and Lien Chao's "The Transformation from Silence to Voice," the self is, in a sense, spread across a range of cultural and linguistic locations, some of which are more powerfully experienced as "me" than others. Bannerji, in another essay entitled "Re: Turning the Gaze" (in *Thinking Through*) writes heartwrenchingly of her experience of dissociation while teaching in a racist classroom:

> The social relations of teaching and learning are relations of violence for us, those who are not white, who teach courses on "Gender, 'Race' and Class," to a "white" body of students in a "white" university.... I don't want to have to prove the obvious, to explain, argue, give examples, images from everyday life, from history, from apartheid, from concentration camps, from reserves.... My own voice rings in my ears, my anecdotes of the street feel hollow, I am offering up a piece of my experience, body, intellect, so others can learn. Unless I am to die from this violence of the daily social relations of being a non-white, South Asian woman in a white Ontario, Canada classroom—I have to dissociate. I hold a part of myself in reserve. All has not been offered up. A part is saved. That is mine. (102–03)

I have chosen this excerpt because it emphasizes a moment of self-preservation, but Bannerji largely addresses her own acts of dissociation in the face of everyday racism, the white cultural norms of the academy, and the demands placed upon her by these entities. Elsewhere, she writes eloquently of a connectedness at the level of the body to Bengali literature and culture and her association of it with her recently deceased mother ("Sound Barrier," 172). She calls on racialized people to remember that they have histories and cultures beyond the ones pushed on them by the state and mainstream society: "It is not as though our identities began the day we stepped on this soil!" (166).

However, the pressures of assimilation are not to be taken lightly. Lien Chao notes, in a rather unsettled way, that for Chinese Canadians to "break the silence" such breakage had to happen in English:

> In choosing English as their working language contemporary Chinese Canadian writers ... acknowledge the need to communicate with the rest of society. Although Chinese language still plays an important role in the community today, continuous enclosure in that language for contemporary Chinese Canadian writers would suggest a self-imposed and self-prolonged silence and isolation in Canadian culture. (23)

Here Chao validates the monolingual ideal that has been so much a part of the culture of assimilation in Canada. But something of her own truth as a native speaker of Chinese erupts here, in the sense that a desire and validation of Chinese language remains present in her text, even as she validates English as the language of "the rest of society." She also, however, speaks a material truth of existence for racialized people in this country. Indeed, as I argue in Chapter 1, it seems as though the English-speaking Chinese Canadian is perpetually stuck between the rock of needing to speak the master's tongue in order to break the silence and so enter into liberated "Canadian" subjectivity and the hard place of telling "the secrets of Chinatown" (Choy qtd. in Givener) and so betraying her ancestors. In Chapter 4, I discuss what it means to break the silence in one's mother tongue, as Rita Wong does in her poem "write around the absence."

There is something mimetic, then, at the very core of breaking the silence, that very thing that is apparently necessary for Asian Canadians to have a voice and a literature. When Roy Miki and Fred Wah write of the "muzak muzak muzak" that fills the corridors of power (5), they could be talking of the ambivalent, mimetic self-articulations of racialized subjects as much as the banalities of the white academy. It seems that the necessary breaking of silence can too easily become, paradoxically, the denial of the Asian Canadian subject. Indeed, Homi Bhabha notes, "[T]he visibility of mimicry is always produced at the site of interdiction" (89). Bhabha is talking about the work of irony in the production of racial stereotypes, which produce metonymies of presence for racialized people. The unsettling truth about breaking the silence is that it too can produce its own metonymy of presence, all the more potent because this metonymy represses the racialized subject while appearing to free her.

I want to argue, however, that there is still something productive about silence-breaking work for racialized subjects—that the excess Bhabha posits as erupting from metonymies of presence might offer a kind of empowerment, not the same kind that unmarked subjects take for granted, but empowerment that flares up and dies back as a kind of haunting in relation to master discourse. A great deal of cultural production is possible in such a flaring up, and it is such production that I articulate and analyze in this book.

The deep but productive paradox of the late-1980s, early-1990s moment was the recourse that marginalized people took to self-empowerment in the very terms of their marginalization. Monika Kin Gagnon, an important critic in that moment as at present, entitled her book *Other Conundrums* to highlight this problem as the definitive problem of the moment. Gagnon writes:

"[N]aming racism's operations means racializing oneself and others within the very terms and operations that have historically enabled racist discourse to proliferate" (22).[4] This is her elaboration of Albert Memmi's proposition that "[t]he term race already involves us in a dilemma."[5] Gagnon eschews the binary implications of the term "dilemma" in favour of jam ismail's coin "oolemma," which implies a problem with multiple facets.[6] Gagnon, in other words, favours an opening out of the term into many locations, in order to break away from the dualism that, unquestioned, the term "race" seems to set up.

This is the problem at the root of anti-racist politics, especially as they were conceived in 1990s Canada. To write from an always already racialized subject position is to be rootless. It is to write without an originary being. It is to write always in relation to a superiority one can never attain, precisely because the racialized subject is constructed and constructs herself in relation to it. This is what Hegel termed the master/slave dialectic, and what Frantz Fanon proposed as the black man's ontological difficulty:

> Ontology—once it is finally admitted as leaving existence by the wayside—does not permit us to understand the being of a black man. For not only must the black man be black, he must be black in relation to the white man.... His metaphysics, or, less pretentiously, his customs and the sources on which they were based, were wiped out because they were in conflict with a civilization that he did not know and that imposed itself on him. (110)

Himani Bannerji also addresses the issue in the groundbreaking anthology of essays on racism, feminism, and politics published by Sister Vision Press, *Returning the Gaze*:

> The presence and representation of non-white women moves from the margin to the centre only to be marginalized again. Boxed into an alien agenda in a feminist text as a variation on the theme of "woman", even when the non-white women express themselves, an effect of alienation sets in with the very act itself. Why? Because it is always on the borderline, judged by extrinsic and irrelevant standards, and serves another's cause; for example, as a tribute to pluralism, diversity or a tolerant form of difference. It is always contained within an adjectivized boundary, such as "black" poetry, "visible minority" prose writings, "women of colour" politics, "black" feminism, etc. This situates our "difference" or constructs it, as it were, through the very gestures of "inclusion" and multiculturalism. (xv)

This formulation is productive in that it pressures the mainstream to address the conundrum of its own racism. Both Bannerji and Gagnon recognize the deep difficulty that confronts the racialized subject in terms of her or his agented, articulated position in relation to a national politics that appears to include racialized subjects, but in fact radically shuts them/us down. The shutdown is radical, but not complete. Gagnon is more optimistic than Bannerji in the sense that she sees a possibility for self-articulation through the claiming of racialized positions. And Bannerji herself says later, "There would be no critique if we did not begin from our actual lives" (xix). The difficulty of talking about one's "actual life" from a raced position remains fraught, however, as I illustrate in Chapter 1.

The racialized subject darts in and out of the narratives that contain her. Further, as Smaro Kamboureli notes in her famous essay "Sedative Politics," the marked subject can respond to the Althusserian hail without necessarily accepting all of its content (*Scandalous Bodies* 105). The question of marked subjectivity then becomes a temporal question. If we cannot inhabit the positivist, linear history of the nation, then we must invent or imagine our own racialized times and places, or at least pay attention and make the most of their moments of eruption.

As I suggested at the beginning of this section, there are times and places, however, when a linear narrative is politically expedient. Perhaps there are times and places too when subjects marked "Asian Canadian" deeply desire such a narrative, even knowing its violent underpinnings. The idea of strategic essentialism as articulated by Gayatri Chakravorty Spivak was particularly productive for the time/space of 1980s to 1990s Asian Canada. For Spivak, the problem with what she calls "positivist historiography" is that it falsely locates the consciousness of the subaltern with that of the hegemonic subject. Seeing herself as that which she is not, the subaltern must then construct a linear history for herself from precisely that location at which she does not have a self. She produces herself not as a subject, but as a subaltern subject-effect (a problem taken up by both Dionne Brand and Margaret Atwood, as I discuss in Chapter 5):

> [T]hat which seems to operate as a subject may be part of an immense discontinuous network ("text" in a general sense) of strands that may be termed politics, ideology, economics, history, sexuality, language and so on.... Different knottings and configurations of these strands determined by heterogenous determinations which are themselves dependent on myriad circumstances, produce the effect of an operating subject. (*Selected Subaltern Studies* 12–13)

However, because history tends to be produced by hegemonic subjects—policemen, soldiers, bureaucrats, journalists, academics—the only way the subaltern can access her own history is through what Spivak calls "reading against the grain," that is, reading official documents for the truths that might emerge in their gaps, counter to their intended purpose and thus counter to their overt framing. Sometimes the subaltern subject-effect needs to be situated for the sake of her own political interest in the language of official documents and "capital H" History. This is what Spivak calls "strategic essentialism" (*Selected Subaltern Studies* 13). Writing in feminist terms, Diana Fuss argues that the "risk of essentialism" may sometimes need to be taken (18). For her, it is always a risk, since the outcome is unpredictable. The consequences of taking that risk could be revolutionary or could be reactive (19).

Since so much of the cultural work of the 1980s and 1990s took place outside the academy, in artist-run centres, editorial collectives, community groups, and ad hoc political organizations, these ideas—anti-racist, feminist, and poststructural—entered into different organizations at different times and in different ways. Many activists read them as "too academic" and did not take them on at all. The concept of "identity politics," for whatever reason, took hold much more intensely until it quickly fell out of favour. Some critics, most notably Monika Gagnon and Richard Fung took up Cornel West's notion of "cultural race politics" instead (19). Fung prefers the term "cultural race politics" because of its connections with the civil rights movement, various multiculturalisms, a range of ethnic and racial nationalisms, as well as what he calls the "Fourth World" nationalisms of First Nations and Aboriginal peoples, which involve geopolitical questions of land and political sovereignty (19). For him, "identity politics" can be neutral, but it can also get used dismissively to "conjure up a simplistic, single-issue politics of self-righteous rage and guilt mongering" (19–20). For Fung, "identity politics" does not make room for more complex discussions of the interactions among oppressions (20).

As the pitfalls of essentialism became clear, then, the ontological dangers of "identity politics" became apparent, productive as they were of what Rey Chow[7] has called "fascist longings in our midst." In her essay of that name, Chow posits a straw man, or rather, a straw woman, curiously named after Pauline Réage/Dominique Aury/Anne Desclos's masochistic heroine, "O." Chow's O is an upper-class woman from a Third World country who poses as coming from peasant stock. She finds her way into graduate school by brandishing slogans of solidarity with the downtrodden masses of the Third World and, without doing a stitch of work, is held up mostly by white academics as a brilliant and talented intellectual (28). Chow admits to caricaturing in her figure of O. She does it to hold white academics accountable to what she perceives as a new form of fascism predicated on a politics of the visual to produce O as a cipher, "an automaton performing the predictable notions of the 'third world' intellectual *they* desire [emphasis in original]" (Chow 29). Chow's articulation of O is daring because it breaks a taboo, one, I would suggest, that holds both white and racialized critics in its thrall. As a respected and politically committed thinker with a track record behind her, Chow is well placed to articulate this taboo figure, though such an articulation is still dangerous even for such a respected critic. She is aware of this, and makes the straw nature of her O very clear. Indeed, her writing of O is a new strategic essentialism in the aftermath of a more idealistic strategic essentialism. What she doesn't do is call other racialized thinkers to account in their holding up of the figure of O. For to do so would be to validate thinkers like Robert Fulford (in a Canadian context), who, reactionary though he is, is also intelligent and astute enough to see the aporia, the emperor without clothes, the empty ontology that racialized people must nonetheless sometimes call into being in order to seem to have a positivist history of their own, that is a visible history, one that the ideal subjects of national belonging can see in terms of sameness rather than difference. And politically, while it is all very well and fine for racialized writers, thinkers, and cultural workers to embrace a politics of the body as it is attached to history, the social labour that a figure like Chow's O might do among those who claim the Romantic individual and ahistorical, "universalist" ontological modes is potentially devastating to social justice movements. Chow's O is taboo in racialized communities precisely because she disguises a deeper aporia. That aporia is the aporia at the heart of national history itself—the fact the national subject is also naked—that nations are, as Benedict Anderson teaches us, imagined communities with carefully selected roots, (not so) secretly built on violence and the expropriation of land, culture, and identity from Indigenous peoples.

This is why Miki's insistence on the incompleteness of the evacuated Asian Canadian subject is so important. As Asian Canadian subjects and texts are increasingly drawn in to the academy, and as Asian Canadian Studies programs are produced within them, we need to be very aware of the gaps and aporias in the founding conditions of subjects, canons, programs, apologies, and other forms of incorporation. Strategic essentialisms do indeed cut both ways. If their productivity is the breaking of silence and the empowerment of racialized subjects at the level of speech, their danger is incorporation and the erasure of the social justice possibilities of racialized articulations. The paradox of laying claim to racialized identities has not gone away—the possibility of the racialized name "Asian Canadian" always already contains its erasure.

The power and possibility of this dynamic get played out in 1980s and 1990s Canada. These dynamics are, of course, never fully tied to their moment. We still live with the power that the production of linear history in the 1970s gave us. We still live too with the dynamics of strategic essentialisms of the 1980s and 1990s. Our current moment, for better or worse, is one of incorporation. But other moments of possibility always lie in wait to erupt at any moment.

TWENTY-FIRST-CENTURY SCANDALS

All of this matters because the histories and conundrums of the 1980s and 1990s are still with us in the second decade of the twenty-first century, as we can see in two scandals that erupted in the late 2000s: the publication of the article "Too Asian" in *Maclean's* magazine on November 20, 2010, and second, the lawsuit launched by SKY Lee, Wayson Choy, and Paul Yee regarding the publication of *Gold Mountain Blues* by Ling Zhang a year later. Smaro Kamboureli, in her well-known essay "Sedative Politics," understands media scandals as "the dramatization of multicultural conflicts ... that enact and mobilize the historically and psychologically rooted anxieties of the dominant society" (*Scandalous Bodies* 88). Kamboureli reads the scandal that revolved around the 1994 conference Writing Thru Race as one that reveals and produces mainstream anxiety about multiculturalism as an irresolvable site of trouble. At the same time, the hysteria produced functioned to obscure the long histories of oppression that marginalized subjects have endured (89). If media scandals dramatize mainstream anxiety about its others, then I want to ask what anxieties are dramatized by the two scandals I describe above. Further, I want to examine how the mainstream readership is imagined in each instance.

The "Too Asian" scandal pertains to the term "Asian Canadian" broadly, beyond the bounds of Asian Canadian literature. Later retitled "The Enrollment Controversy" by *Maclean's* after outrage from Asian Canadian students and their allies, the "Too Asian" scandal[8] predictably bemoans an excess of Asian students on Canadian campuses. The "Too Asian" article matters because it understands Asianness as a fixed and essential category, and because it deploys it in an overtly racist way. All of the nuanced debate that happened in the 1980s and 1990s concerning the instability of racialized categories, the ontological problems attached to that instability, and the democratic possibilities of the term vanish in this scandal. It makes it clear that the old racisms that were the founding conditions of the Canadian state remain fully in play, more or less intact, just beneath the surface of a cultivated civility. For those unfamiliar with the "Too Asian" scandal, the "Too Asian" article portrays Asian students as being academically focused at the expense of fun and freedom (Findlay and Kohler 76), and therefore as insufficiently "well-rounded." The outrage and scandal surrounding the publication of the article echoes the 1979 controversy over the "Campus Giveaway" episode of the CTV program *W5* in which the University of Toronto was portrayed as a site overrun by foreign students at the expense of whites. Both the *Maclean's* and the *W5* cases repeat the trope of the "yellow peril," which views Asians in numbers as a threat and contamination to ordinary and upright whiteness. These are, of course, tropes that date back to colonial-era Canada and the deliberately fabricated notion of Canada as a white country and white people as a superior race. While other models of the state[9] have emerged since Queen Victoria signed the British North America Act in 1867 (which constituted Canada as a Dominion of the United Kingdom), imagining Canada as a vertical mosaic, and then later as a bilingual state with two founding nations, and still later as a multicultural state, the old narratives remain alive beneath the surface available for access—constitutive in fact of the later narratives and ready to erupt in their ugliest form at any time.

These narratives, however, have their variations, and these variations and their critiques can tell us a great deal about the terms of race/power relations in any particular historical moment. Both the *Maclean's* piece and the *W5* piece begin with the portrayal of a young white woman who thinks that the presence of Asians at Canadian universities diminish her capacity to enroll in schools she might otherwise attend. The W5 "Campus Giveaway" program of 1979 misrepresented the racialized students it portrayed at the level of legal nationality. Images of Chinese Canadian students at orientation sessions for Chinese Canadian students were verbally described as "foreign" students taking over the pharmacy program at the University of Toronto. The critique mounted against CTV by the Council of Chinese Canadians emphasized the Canadianness of all the students portrayed in the program, and the racism of a society, or at least, a television program, that could not see the Canadianness of Canada's nonwhite citizens. By contrast, the *Maclean's* "Too Asian" article of 2010 makes no bones about the elisions it makes. Stephanie Findlay and Nicholas Köhler write: "[M]any white students believe that competing with Asians—both Asian Canadians and international students—requires a sacrifice of time and freedom they're not willing to make." The language is more nuanced here. There is no attempt to pass off local students as "foreign." Instead, local and international students are overtly conflated with the casual sweep of a hand as being equally threatening to white students. And while there is an apparent critique of the white students as being insufficiently studious in relation to the "Asians," local or international, the original title of the article and its subsequent pulling give the lie to whose difference is seen as contaminating and abnormal. Further, within the implicit framework of the article, the white students hold the trump card of valuing their freedom, that vaunted if nebulous characteristic that is supposed to mark Western democracy. In the thirty years since the *W5* "Campus Giveaway" program, journalistic language has become more nuanced, but the racist tropes that founded the nation have not gone away.

In a sense, the "Too Asian" scandal enacts the same ritual as the 1907 Anti-Asiatic Riots in Vancouver, in which white labourers rampaged through Chinatown and Japantown over four days, breaking windows, looting, and beating up any Asians they could find. The ostensible reason was resentment against Chinese Canadian workers for taking jobs that white workers believed should accrue to them. At the political level of the Canadian state, the 1907 riots, like "Campus Giveaway" and "Too Asian" function to reproduce white students' and workers' sense of legitimacy vis-à-vis access to the institutionalized privileges of national belonging that according to the narrative of the white settler nation are supposed to trickle down to them. Racialized others—"Asians" in the "Too Asian" case, "foreign students" in the "Campus Giveaway" case, and "Orientals" or "Asiatics" in the case of the 1907 riots—are understood as external to national belonging, and their construction as such is ritually reproduced through these acts of verbal or physical violence. In their reproduction, the founding conditions of the Canadian state are reproduced, and more importantly, since they are in fact so tenuous, revalidated. Beneath the surface of all three lies the unspoken crisis of white settler colonialism on land that at the time of its claiming for various European crowns—Portuguese, Spanish, French, and British—was inhabited by Indigenous peoples. The white desire to expel Asians in fact reveals the recognition of the illegitimacy of European colonialism in the Americas. One might even read a buried desire in white subjectivity for whites' own expulsion, projected on to those it deems its others. To enact such an expulsion ritually functions to reproduce white legitimacy, but only as a return of the repressed. As Judith Butler teaches us, such legitimacies, because they are arbitrary at their root, must be regularly and ritually repeated in order to retain their appearance as natural and right. The 2010 "Too Asian" article in *Maclean's* magazine is thus merely the most recent reiteration of the violence that founds the Canadian state.

The second "Asian Canadian" scandal, a more directly literary one, that marks the beginning of the second decade of the second millennium is the publication of the novel *Gold Mountain Blues* by Ling Zhang and the subsequent lawsuit launched against her on charges of plagiarism, by three Asian Canadian writers: SKY Lee, Wayson Choy, and Paul Yee. Ling Zhang might also be described as an Asian Canadian author. She was born in Hangzhou and has lived in Toronto since 1986. *Gold Mountain Blues* was initially written in Chinese and published in 2009 in the People's Republic of China. In the fall of 2011, the English translation came out in Canada, the United States, England, Ireland, India, South Africa, and Australia. As the controversy—begun on a blog in China—deepened, Penguin hired the novel's British translator, Nicky Harman, to conduct a study on whether plagiarism had occurred. Harman found that it had not. However, May Cheng, the lawyer representing Lee, Choy, and Yee, found Penguin's use of the novel's translator to judge the case to be lacking in impartiality (Canadian Press par. 12). The bases for the charge of plagiarism are plot parallels between *Gold Mountain Blues* and books by the three Chinese Canadian authors. In both *Gold Mountain Blues* and SKY Lee's *Disappearing Moon Cafe*, a young Indigenous woman of mixed heritage[10] rescues a young Chinese man and has a romantic encounter with him. In both novels, he abandons her, and at both novels' ends he contemplates that abandonment remorsefully. In both *Gold Mountain Blues* and Wayson Choy's *The Jade Peony* a young Chinese man is disfigured while working on the railway, rescues a white foreman, and much later is given a gift of great value by the foreman's child. And in both *Gold Mountain Blues* and Paul Yee's *The Bone Collector's Son*, a young Chinese houseboy is targeted by white bullies and later rescued by his white employer (T. Wong par. 37–46). There are parallels between *Gold Mountain Blues* and Denise Chong's *The Concubine's Children* as well (Samson par. 5). Chong, who does not want to see the discussion reduced to legal arguments (Taylor par. 17), has chosen not to take part in the suit but is watching it with interest and concern.

Zhang vehemently denies the charge of plagiarism (T. Wong par. 7), claiming that she hasn't even read any of the books in question except *The Concubine's Children* and *Ghost Train* (Samson par. 7), and further that the plot elements she is accused of plagiarizing belong to a common stock of plot possibilities that emerges from Chinese immigrant history (Canadian Press par. 10). In a statement to the *National Post* she said: "A hundred and fifty years of Chinese Canadian history is a 'common wealth' for all of us to share and discover" (Medley par. 3). Zhang has lived in Canada since 1986 and so was present for the debates on appropriation that raged through the 1980s and 1990s, the conference The Appropriate Voice in 1992 being a key moment. Nonetheless, she takes up the Eurocentric language of the post/neocolonial state in this argument. It must be noted that the notion of a "common wealth" after the repatriation of the Constitution still connotes cultural wealth that the former colonies of the British Empire share in common. It is a strange word to use for an author who may not have lived through the worst of Anglo-centric colonialism in Canada but who has researched it extensively and written a very big book about it. Her use of the word "discover" is also troublingly nativist. As many Indigenous activists and scholars have taught us, one can only be "discovered" when one is not perceived as having the agency of self-knowledge. Wayson Choy, writing in the *Globe and Mail* three weeks after Zhang's remarks calling Asian Canadian history a "common wealth" were published, has clearly attended to these discussions. He says: "It has to do with respect for our families who lived through this.... I have benefitted from their sacrifices. Their stories are not clichés. They are not common. It's insulting.... These stories are unique to my family" (Taylor par. 7).

The *Gold Mountain Blues* scandal is slightly complicated because it involves two loci of power, and complicated forms of otherness that reverberate through yet other forms of difference that are not apparent on the surface. The plot repetitions that Lee, Choy, and Yee claim are indeed present in Zhang's texts. Zhang's claim not to have read them seems terribly disingenuous. Whether her use of these plotlines constitutes plagiarism in the legal sense remains to be seen. Denise Chong may be right, however, when she says that the legal battle does not get at the real issues, which are about ethical practice in the age of the Internet (Taylor par. 18). The start of the scandal on an anonymous blog in China, however, gives the attentive reader a clue to the complicated anxieties about intellectual property that are reverberating in powerfully racialized ways through newly internationalized forms of both Chinese and Canadian cultures. The instigating blogger, who initially identified himself only as "Changjiang," was later identified as Robert Luo, a businessman with a degree from China's Fudan University (Schiller par. 19). He became a landed immigrant in Canada in 2001, and so, like Zhang, presumably has a stake in both countries. According to Bill Schiller at the *Toronto Star*, Luo is motivated by a desire for justice and for the intellectual property rights of Canadian writers to be respected (par. 20). If we can take these stated motivations at face value, then there is a very interesting form of identification going on here, in the sense that Luo would betray a fellow immigrant in favour of more deeply established (albeit after much hard work) Chinese Canadian writers. Schiller takes a perverse delight in calling Lee, Choy, and Yee "Canada's Chinese Canadian literary elite," a phrasing reiterated later the same day that Schiller's piece appeared, in a *Quill and Quire* headline for an article on the issue: "Chinese novel alleged to have stolen from Canada's 'literary elite'" (Woods n. pag.).

That Lee, Choy, and Yee all come from the history of hardship that Zhang appropriates and fictionalizes remains as subtext, except in the above quoted statement from Wayson Choy, which is overt in its critique.

For me, what is compelling about this case is the cultural context in which it unfolds. Zhang is a Chinese Canadian writer in the sense that she has lived in Canada since 1986. As I said earlier, she was born in Hangzhou. She writes in Chinese. In contrast, Lee, Choy, and Yee are all *loh wah kiu* descendants—children of the Gold Mountain sojourners whom all three write about in their books. Zhang is a relative newcomer and an outsider to the long-established and long-suffering communities she writes about. I offer this information not as judgement but as necessary background to an unfolding situation that calls the disagreements and analyses of the 1980s and 1990s back in ways that illustrate the incompletion of the appropriation debates and their relevance at present.

As a Chinese person who writes in Chinese and has a solid foot in the PRC, Zhang also has access to an audience hundreds of times the size that Lee, Choy, or Yee can access. Further, her novel was taken up by a large international press, Penguin, and has been translated and distributed all over the English-speaking world. Luo accuses her of taking advantage of the fact that Lee, Choy, and Yee don't read Chinese, while Chinese readers and critics don't read English (Schiller 1). By contrast, one might argue that the success that Lee, Choy, and Yee have achieved has been hard won, against the odds, in the sense that until the 1990s mainstream publishing venues were largely closed to Asian Canadians. The cultural activist work described in this book documents the struggles required at the broad level of community to make publishing opportunities possible. Nevertheless, they are now widely read and studied all over the country, though perhaps not so much beyond its borders. Chinese translations of their books, are, however, currently under way (Taylor par. 9). The English translation of *Gold Mountain Blues* was released in the fall of 2011.

Lee, Choy, and Yee all published their first books in the early 1990s, because they were talented writers certainly, but also because the time was right. All three had been active in the anti-racist movements of the 1970s. Both Lee and Yee, for instance, were contributors to *Inalienable Rice*. But it took a confluence of events, and a great deal of activist labour, beginning in the 1970s and picking up speed though the 1980s and 1990s to make their texts legible and available to the mainstream Canadian reading public. Their outrage at the ease with which Zhang has appropriated their stories and circulated them internationally for her own gain is understandable. We are living in a moment when the economic fortunes of China are rising rapidly, albeit after a terrible century of upheaval, violence, and suffering. For some

Chinese Canadians, there might be vindication and pride to be felt through
Zhang's success. However, although fortunes in China are rising rapidly, the
fortunes of Chinese people, including members of the diaspora, are not rising equally. Those Chinese Canadians who don't feel vindicated by Zhang's
success might feel that a writer who has neither experienced nor directly
inherited through family legacy the forms of suffering endured by the Gold
Mountain sojourners should not profit from the telling of their stories.

This is a tension that belongs directly to the appropriation debates that
took place in Canada in the 1980s and 1990s, but the form of embodiment it takes today and the historical background addressed are different. The appropriation debates of the 1980s and 1990s were led by Lenore
Keeshig-Tobias of the Chippewas of Nawash Unceded First Nation. In a
1990 article in the *Globe and Mail*, she asked white writers and filmmakers,
specifically Darlene Quaife and W.P. Kinsella, to "stop stealing Native[11]
stories" (A7). She was particularly critical of the fact that those stories were
appropriated in a neocolonial context in which Indigenous writers' stories
in their own voices did not circulate as widely as when white writers told
them, and also that in many cases Indigenous stories were meant for specific
contexts, and not the broad ones into which writers like Quaife and Kinsella
were publishing them. Tensions in that moment ran high because the stakes
were high, and also, I would suggest, because the public arena was just
open enough that the injustice of the founding conditions for the Canadian
state could be articulated and understood, but not necessarily accepted. In
the immediate aftermath of Keeshig-Tobias's request, an outraged Alberto
Manguel wrote: "No one, including Ms. Keeshig-Tobias, has the right to
instruct a writer as to what stories to tell. The idea of anyone, but especially
a fellow writer, forbidding someone to tread on what she considers private
turf, makes me sick" (D7). He cites other examples, somewhat arbitrary ones,
of appropriation: James Joyce's *Ulysses* and William Styron's *The Confessions
of Nat Turner*. What is elided in Manguel's critique is a recognition of the
embodied, historical conditions of Keeshig-Tobias's request, as a Chippewa
woman writing in a white settler colony that has not really reckoned with
the injustice that founded it, injustice that remains ongoing. For indeed
there is a politics of inherited experience at work here—what Judith Butler
would call the sedimenting of bodies through re-iterated practice in language. For Keeshig-Tobias, as an Indigenous woman, there is a politics of
connection to land, and a recognition that the Canadian state is a colonial
state that has enacted waves of injustice on the bodies of Indigenous peoples.

Another ubiquitous voice for an angry Romantic humanism espousing
ideals of universality even as it shut down the voices of First Nations writers
and writers of colour was that of Robert Fulford. In a piece entitled "The

Trouble with Emily" in *Canadian Art* published a year after Keeshig-Tobias's request, Fulford chastises those who criticize the early twentieth century West Coast Canadian painter Emily Carr for appropriation. His rage against "postmodern revisionism and retroactive social justice" only points to deeper and more contemporary repressions that the discourses of social justice and some forms of postmodern critique do in fact address. Fulford's arguments, however, might be useful in my querying here of Ling Zhang's context and culpability. Is Zhang, like Carr, a person who belongs to another history who thus cannot be held responsible for the way her actions read in a contemporary Canadian context? Fulford writes that Emily Carr could not have known what kinds of critiques might arise in relation to her work in the future, and that hers was a progressive vision for her time. She allied herself with Indigenous people, though she saw them through the same romanticized lens that other Victorians saw them. Fulford argues that we cannot retroactively judge her for this. This argument is not, however, incompatible with Keeshig-Tobias's request, which says in essence: "Now that you do know, stop."

Indeed, what Fulford and Manguel do not acknowledge is the state of exception that upholds their points of view and disposes of Keeshig-Tobias's by virtue of precisely those race, class, and gender privileges that Keeshig-Tobias addresses. There is a paradox at work in the fact that these men use the language of universality and freedom to, in practice, maintain their hold on hegemonic power.

What then can it mean when a parallel dynamic plays itself out between three *lo wah kiu* descendants (i.e., descendants of the pioneer/soujourner/settlers who came to Canada in the late 1800s and early 1900s to work in the gold rush, the Canadian Pacific Railway, Chinese laundries, and Chinese Canadian cafés) and a Chinese Canadian writer who belongs to a more recent wave of immigration to Canada, and who has one foot firmly planted in contemporary mainland China and one firmly planted on Canadian soil? My job here is not so much to pass judgement as to illustrate tensions. I would like to suggest that the old dynamics of racial hierarchy that founded the state are alive and well in contemporary Canada, as the "Too Asian" scandal illustrates, but that in addition new forms of power relations have emerged at the start of the millennium that recirculate the logic of colonialism in newly embodied forms. We see this at work in the way the drama of *Gold Mountain Blues* is playing out. On the one hand, Zhang appears to be a writer with a large profile making use of the work of writers with less access to the public arena while denying the originating claim of those less-empowered writers to the stories of old times, in the name of freedom of the imagination and universal right of access. On the other hand, she appears as a foreign writer taking something that rightfully belongs to (nativist) Canadians—but this time these Canadians are Chinese Canadians. Her position is sublime in the sense that Julia Kristeva describes it in *The Powers of Horror*, as both too much and not enough:

> [T]he sublime is a *something added* that expands us, overstrains us, and causes us to be both *here*, as dejects and *there*, as others and sparkling. A divergence, an impossible bounding. Everything missed, joy—fascination. (12)

Kristeva describes sublimation as that which keeps the abject—the fascinated, but unformed subject—under control (11). She opposes the sublime to the symptom, which is the nonassimilable alien that reveals itself as such (11).

The spectre of plagiarism that hovers around Zhang's case, if revealed as "truth" in a court of law, might roll her abject being over in to the place of symptom, but for now she seems to be "getting away with it"—able to use the language of universality to preserve her good name and the lucrative circulation of her novel. Indeed, Lee, Choy, and Yee have done the cultural labour of the symptom. Theirs were the marked bodies that were shut out of the public arena and then incorporated into it as a sign of the nation's benevolence to those it previously excluded. These were the authors who did the difficult work of silence-breaking, and who carry the troubling burden of the incorporation of the Asian Canadian subject into the contemporary state—the state that benefited from the exclusions, expulsions, and internments of Asian Canadians in the early twentieth century, and now benefits from including them.

In the years between the publication of *Disappearing Moon Cafe* and the publication of *Gold Mountain Blues*, the national and international publics into which these books were released have changed vastly. More importantly, the idea of what Asian Canadian literature can be and do has shifted, which brings me to my reason for these stories and their analysis. As the consequences of these two scandals continue to reverberate through cultural space, both nationally and internationally, it becomes important that we understand them in their historical contexts. The purpose of this book is to interrogate the ways in which the term "Asian Canadian" has been imagined, produced, and put to work between approximately 1985 and 2000, and to consider its implications and possibilities in the new millennium.

EMBODIED CULTURES, APPROPRIATE VOICES

It would be impossible to talk about the problem of racialized subjectivity without talking about the embodiment of race. As we have seen, Himani Bannerji and Roy Miki's articulations in particular have been important for recognizing the ways that racialized subjectivities are produced and experienced through the body. If there is something mimetic about breaking the silence, then difference erupts through the body, and it is the body that, in a sense, is put on the line, textually and experientially. This call to the body is a key element that I would like to tie here to the notion of strategic essentialism—it is the body and its experience that must sometimes be essentialized, but at great cost, in order for the politics of "identity politics" to work, when it works. Problematic though the concept is, its circulation did a lot of cultural labour in the late 1980s through the 1990s.

From a poststructuralist point of view, Judith Butler has been particularly useful for many critics needing to make sense of how such a body comes into being, comes to have an ontology that matters. For her, bodies come into being through the constant reiteration of regulatory norms. Located, in the first instance, in queer theory, Butler articulates the production of bodies as occurring through "sex" as a regulatory norm:

> The category of "sex" is, from the start, normative; it is what Foucault has called a "regulatory ideal." In this sense, then, "sex" not only functions as a norm, but is part of a regulatory practice that produces the bodies it governs, that is, whose regulatory force is made clear as a kind of productive power, the power to produce—demarcate, circulate, differentiate—the bodies it controls. Thus, "sex" is a regulatory ideal whose materialization is compelled, and this materialization takes place (or fails to take place) through certain highly regulated practices. In other words, "sex" is an ideal construct which is forcibly materialized through time. (*Bodies That Matter* 1)

Though the focus of her study is on "sex" as a regulatory practice, she does see that in contemporary Western society, "race" can also function as one, often, for her, in conjunction with "sex" (18). Now, whether what Bannerji means by "experience" and what Butler means by "regulatory practice" are the same thing needs to remain open to question, but certainly there is overlap. We can clearly see "regulatory practice" at work in Miki's description of his childhood encounter with the word "jap."

I wish here to emphasize an understanding of racialized subjectivity as both experienced and discursively sedimented over time in order to get at the difficulty of the appropriation debates which were so important to the historical/genealogical moment under consideration. What Butler gives us is an understanding of the subject as discursively produced, but radically so. There do exist bodies beyond their discursive construction, but since we cannot speak of them without language, language always determines how we understand them:

> To claim that discourse is formative is not to claim that it originates, causes or exhaustively composes that which it concedes; rather it is to claim that there is no reference to a pure body which is not at the same time a further formation of that body. In this sense, the linguistic capacity to refer to sexed bodies is not denied, but the very meaning of "referentiality" is altered. In philosophical terms, the constative claim is always to some degree performative. (*Bodies That Matter* 10–11)

Here, Butler acknowledges that there is a body that exists beyond discourse, but since discourse is our only means of talking about it, any understanding of the body is always discursively informed and constructed. Thus, while the idea of social constructedness offers those who make use of it a strong sense of agency with regard to the possibility to change that status quo, Butler reminds us how heavily the weight of regulatory norms bears down upon any social construction. She proposes repetition with a difference as a key strategy to erode regulatory norms.

So then, since the spectre of the cultural appropriation debates of the late 1980s and the 1990s hangs so ominously over the *Gold Mountain Blues* case it seems necessary to address them. Further, I suggest, these debates were deeply formative for racialized cultural producers in those years, including Asian Canadian writers, organizers, and critics. The notion of the racialized body as discursively sedimented and as produced through historical and contemporary experience was necessary to these debates. So too, as I explained earlier, was a sense of cross-racial alliance. In fact, the 1992 gathering The Appropriate Voice, organized through the Racial Minority Writers' Committee of the Writers' Union of Canada, beautifully exemplifies such cross-racial alliance at work. This was a three-day gathering of seventy writers of colour and First Nations writers in Orillia, Ontario, to talk about issues of common concern and to identify barriers to writing and publishing in Canada (Gagnon 66). It is also a key occasion at which many writers engaged in anti-racist work met, as writers, for the first time. As I briefly explained above, Lenore Keeshig-Tobias was one of the organizers, and her voice was key in leading the debates on the appropriation of voice, specifically, the appropriation of First Nations voices and stories by white writers with privileged access to publication and circulation. As I discussed at the beginning of this Introduction, Keeshig-Tobias is very clear that the appropriation of native stories constitutes theft. She understands deeply that narrative is ideological: "Stories are power. They reflect the deepest, the most intimate perceptions, relationships and attitudes of a people. Stories show how a people think. Such wonderful offerings are seldom reproduced by outsiders" (71). Indeed, whether an "outsider" can reproduce Indigenous stories is open to question, certainly at the level of whether that outsider is able to tell the story respectfully and well, but even if she or he is able to do so, the meaning of the story shifts. As Linda Alcoff explains:

> [W]here one speaks from affects the meaning and truth of what one says, and thus that one cannot assume an ability to transcend one's location. In other words, a speaker's location (which I take here to refer to their *social* location, or social identity) has an epistemically significant impact on that speaker's claims and can serve either to authorize or disauthorize one's speech. (6–7; emphasis in original)

Further:

> [T]he practice of privileged persons speaking on behalf of less privileged persons has actually resulted (in many cases) in increasing and reinforcing the oppression of the group spoken for. (7)

If, as Himani Bannerji insists, it matters who speaks, then it is crucial that the oppressed speak for themselves and tell their own stories. This is Keeshig-Tobias's decolonizing demand. Keeshig-Tobias says, quoting Leslie Marmon Silko, "[S]tories 'are all we have, you see—all we have to fight off illness and death'" (72).

Analytic philosopher James O. Young and writer Susan Haley have argued that cultures cannot own subject matters. For them, "Anyone may write about or otherwise represent what falls within his experience or within the ambit of his imagination" (270). They argue further that in representing another culture, outsiders to that culture take nothing from it, since the outside act of representation does not prevent insiders from making representations if they want to (270). They suggest further that appropriation may in fact benefit "insider" cultures by creating or augmenting audiences where none existed before (271). For example, Paul Simon's appropriations of South African music, they suggest, paved the way for the success of the Zulu choir Ladysmith Black Mambazo (271). Further, they argue, the work of Rudy Wiebe and James Houston "is at least partly responsible for the strong interest that has been awakened in the work of Native authors such as Thomas King, Thomson Highway and Robert Alexie" (271). In

articulating Paul Simon as a white musician who authorizes the work of
Black musicians, or Wiebe and Houston as white writers authorizing the
work of Native writers, however, Young and Haley miss the point of how
power works. While in his own book, *Cultural Appropriation and the Arts*,
Young recognizes in a limited way some of the harms of colonialism, his
search for and faith in a universal and rationalistic discourse to contain
accusations of cultural appropriation ultimately serves Eurocentric interests.
In articulating cultural appropriation in legalistic terms as different forms of
harm—theft, assault, or profound offence—he maintains the primacy of a
Western analytic framework that may serve Indigenous people and people
of colour in limited ways, but at the expense of a deeper analysis that values
Indigenous and other non-Western epistemologies.

Rosemary Coombe is helpful here in pointing out that a liberal legal
discourse of rights may fundamentally distort issues of cultural politics (74).
She argues, radically, that both sides of the debate, as it was framed and
played out in the *Globe and Mail* in 1992, embraced unproductive Western
ideological modes without acknowledging them as such. Those crying for
"freedom of the imagination" and accusing their racialized critics of "cen-
sorship," she suggests, are caught in the grip of a Romantic individualism
in which

> the writer is represented in Romantic terms as an autonomous individual
> who creates fictions with an imagination free of all constraint. For such
> an author, everything in the world must be made available and accessi-
> ble as an "idea" that can be transformed into his "expression" and thus
> becomes his "work." Through his labor, he makes these ideas his own;
> his possession of the work is justified by his expressive activity. As long
> as the author does not copy another's expression, he is free to find his
> themes, plots, ideas, and characters anywhere he pleases, and to make
> these his own. Any attempts to restrict his ability to do so are viewed
> as an unjustifiable restriction on freedom of expression. The dialectic of
> possessive individualism and liberal democracy is thereby affirmed. (77)

Coombe notes further that it is upon these principles that contemporary
laws of intellectual property, particularly copyright, are based (77).

However, she also she argues—quite controversially in progressive circles—that the claims to authenticity made by racialized groups adhere to a
kind of cultural nationalism that,

> however pluralistic in its intent, employs a European logic of possessive
> individualism when it claims objects as essential to identities and ele-
> ments of authentic traditions. Possessive individualism—the relationship

that links individuals to property as formulated in Locke's labor theory of value—increasingly dominates the language and logic of political claims to cultural autonomy.... [N]ational culture is envisioned as a kind of property and the nation is imagined as a property-owning "collective individual".... Modernity has extended these qualities to nation-states and ethnic groups, who are imagined on the world stage as "collective individuals." Like other individuals, these collective individuals are imagined to be territorially and historically bounded, distinctive, internally homogenous, and complete unto themselves. In this word view, each nation or group possesses a unique identity and culture that are constituted by its undisputed possession of property. Within cultural nationalism, a group's survival, its identity and objective oneness over time, depends upon the secure possession of a culture embodied in objects of property. (84)

However, as we can see if we are willing to extend Butler's careful arguments into the realms of race and culture, such entities are not stable, are in fact, sedimented over time through reiterative practice. This, for Coombe, is a good thing. For cultures to be both alive and contemporary, in fact, they must not have "objective oneness over time." Such conceptions of culture, for Coombe, are deeply Orientalist :

> The notion that only pristine objects untouched by the forces of modernization bespeak cultural identities has long been discounted as a form of imperialist nostalgia. The capacity of peoples to live in history, and to creatively interpret and expressively engage historical circumstances using their cultural traditions to do so, is now recognized as the very life and being of culture, rather than evidence of its death or decline. (85)

Romantic notions of the individual and its property clearly do not serve racialized subjects; Orientalist notions of cultural property as adhering to dead and static cultures are not much better. I would argue here, however, that when Indigenous people and people of colour talk about property, they do not embrace an Orientalist view of marginalized cultures. When Lenore Keeshig-Tobias talks about cultural appropriation as theft, she is quite clear that she sees this form of theft as the most recent form in a continuum of forms that began with European colonial appropriation of Indigenous land. Indeed, more recently, Marie Battiste and James (Sa'ke'j) Youngblood Henderson have argued that the act of colonization is itself dependent on the idea of appropriation and control through (Romantic) individual agency (148). The appropriation of Indigenous knowledge and heritage is a continuation of other forms of colonization, so it is no coincidence that modern intellectual property laws do not protect Indigenous knowledge (148).

Coombe argues that while some Indigenous people may feel compelled to articulate their claims in the language of power, using the metaphors of analytic philosophy, the substance of their claims contests the logic of possessive individualism (91). Loretta Todd calls for a recognition of Indigenous conceptions of property, which I think is also what Keeshig-Tobias is getting at when she talks about stories as power. Todd writes:

> Without the sense of private property that ascended with European culture, we evolved concepts of property that recognized the interdependence of communities, families and nations and favoured the guardianship of the earth as opposed to its conquest. There was a sense of ownership, but not one that pre-empted the rights and privileges of others or the rights of the earth and life it sustained.... Ownership was bound up with history.... Communities, families, individuals, and nations created songs, dances, rituals, objects and stories that were considered to be property, but not property as understood by Europeans. Material wealth was re-distributed, but history and stories belonged to the originator and could be given or shared with others as a way of preserving, extending and witnessing history and expressing one's worldview. (68)

Indeed, if Leslie Marmon Silko's witch story in *Ceremony*, in which all the violence of colonialism is articulated as the spell of an Indigenous storytelling witch, is any indication, stories mobilize the movements of history, and the power and place of the speaker is of tantamount importance. By making colonialism an Indigenous story, Silko at once places responsibility for it in Indigenous hands. In so doing, she also gives Indigenous people a great power to tell and so make the world differently. Keeshig-Tobias, further, has a response to charges that Indigenous people are unaware of their use of Western forms of essentialism. Critiquing Robert Fulford's disparagements of curator Deborah Doxtator's *Fluffs 'n Feathers* exhibit, in which Indigenous artists make a critical spectacle of nativist kitsch, Keeshig-Tobias writes:

> Back on the rez, I was listening to CBC radio. Robert Fulford was talking to the interviewer about burying the noble savage. Interesting. Good Show. Very informative. I was indignant (not really). I thought, well finally ... but it's too late. It's too late because we, Aboriginal peoples, have embraced the noble stereotype, adopted him, and he is now one of us, and has been for a very long time. So, back off. I cast Robert into the role of the great Indian agent whose whole reason for living was to make decisions for and about the Indians. Sorry, Robert, I'm just having a little bit of fun here (thanks for all the inspiration). Now if anyone is going to bury the wild Indian ... it is going to be me, I said to my kitchen. Thus I began my "Dear John" letter, waiting for this day, nyah. (xvi)

Her humour here disarms her reader. It is deeply political, without waving the spectre of the law and its punishments. Here, Keeshig-Tobias recognizes the contemporaneity of Indigenous people, and their right to reappropriate tropes of "Indianness" as they have been inherited from Europeans.

The appropriation debates unfolded largely in the context of Native/White relations in the 1980s and 1990s, though other racialized writers, artists, and critics certainly participated passionately and unflinchingly. It may seem that I have employed a great deal of space in thinking through an issue that was not marked "Asian Canadian" in the first instance. But I would argue that the appropriation debates are of tremendous importance to Asian Canadian literature and that Asian Canadian literature owes a great debt to Indigenous literatures and cultures precisely because so many Indigenous critics and writers did front-line work on this issue. More generally, Asian Canadian literature shares a decolonization imperative with First Nations literature and, further, owes a debt to it because Asian Canadian liberation within a national frame is built on the disenfranchisement of Indigenous peoples. And more, as Iyko Day has noted (51), Asian Canadian literature itself rises beside the powerful work that Indigenous activists, writers, and critics have done to produce a literature of their own. Claims to community are not arbitrary, but they are profoundly coalitional, not necessarily in an even way, and often not on the same time frames, but nonetheless, the relational nature of these literary productions should be foregrounded and not forgotten.

Might we understand the *Gold Mountain Blues* case to be the first, belated case of appropriation in an Asian Canadian context?[12] The protracted birth of Asian Canadian appropriation? The emphasis from the 1970s through the 1990s appears, for Asian Canadian writers understood as such, to have focused primarily on breaking the silence and coming to voice. Certainly, from racist anti-Asian comic strips of the fin-de-siècle to the figure of Suzie Wong, Asians have been subjected to gross misrepresentation, but the actual appropriation of voice seems to appear for the first time now, in the early 2000s. But neither Zhang's nor Choy's articulations of their positions would read the same way without the long and painful appropriation debates of the 1980s and 1990s already existing on the public record. The embodied form that the *Gold Mountain Blues* conflict takes, however, is new. Whereas prior to the turn of the millennium, forms of non-white difference tended to be lumped together as consistent with one another—if we think about, for instance, the conflation of Chinese Canadian students with foreign students in the *W5* case, or the invisibilization of the organizing committee for Writing Thru Race—the "Too Asian" scandal makes a distinction between Asians and Asian Canadians, for an instant at least, before it conflates them, and the *Gold Mountain Blues* case forces a distinction between different kinds of Chineseness. That Ling Zhang works in Chinese, while Lee, Choy, and Yee work in English is no small matter. Further, Lee, Choy, and Yee all have their roots in a much earlier wave of Chinese immigration to Canada, from the Pearl River Delta, associated with railway building, laundries, restaurants, and corner stores. In one sense, the repressed Chinese language writing that was considered for *Many-Mouthed Birds*, then dropped, has come home to roost. But in another sense, a new form of global power—that of the newly powerful PRC—has come to Canadian shores to subsume the voices of its native sons and daughters, signalling a rupture in Asian Canadian culture, and a sign of the transformation of the nation itself from its old Eurocentric but also liberal democratic form, to its international, neoliberal form, in which the power of international capital tops the power of the liberal democratic state and its little hypocrisies.

The *Gold Mountain Blues* scandal is thus an instance illustrating that there has been a major shift in global power since the turn of the millennium and the rise of neoliberalism, such that the power of states is no longer what it was. Set in motion at the time of NAFTA, or, some might say, at the other 9/11, in which the democratically elected Salvador Allende was murdered in Chile and replaced by Augusto Pinochet, and coming to a head with the fall of the Berlin Wall in Germany and the rise of Deng Xiaoping in China, it turned again at (the second) 9/11 to produce state power as military power in the service of international capital. In this complicated new world order, Lee, Choy, and Yee are produced on the one hand as the wronged sons and daughters of Asian Canadian literature, but on the other hand as neo-nationalist English-speaking literary elites[13] accusing and abusing the more deeply racialized, ESL speaker Ling Zhang. And on the flipside, Ling Zhang emerges as both the racialized newcomer victimized by these English-speaking literary elites and, alternately, the frightening, moneyed, international stranger, come to steal the intellectual property of oppressed Chinese Canadians. Both sets of Orientalist tropes are hard at work here. And it is these that must be disentangled now. The 1980s and 1990s, empowering as they were, were a time in which racialized subjects in coalition, including Asian Canadians, fought for equal rights and cultural belonging within the bounds of the old democratic nation-state. Such a state is still available to us, beneath the surface of the neoliberal state. But canny cultural activists would do better to attend to the palimpsest of states that still occupy us—neoliberal, liberal democratic, multicultural, bicultural, vertical mosaic, and white settler—and the interactions among them. Through honest (still) analyses of the interactions among these, and the possibilities for more democratic ruptures not yet imagined, we might find new coalitions and new forms of empowerment to make a surprisingly, if not progressively, better world.

ASIAN CANADIAN RUPTURES

The palimpsest of states we inhabit is a large subject—too broad for a single book. What this book does, then is take up a few small ruptures in the constant emergence of a category—Asian Canadian—to investigate what is produced at different moments. I contend that "Asian Canadian literature" is not a consistent category, nor one that develops in a generally progressive manner, but rather one that does different kinds of social, political, and literary labour depending on context and historical moment.

The first chapter, on the work of Wayson Choy and Evelyn Lau, addresses the problem of breaking the silence. I argue that while silence breaking is a necessary first step in the public presencing of Asian Canadians, there is always an element of subjectivity that must be left to silence. "Breaking the silence," as a strategy, is freeing in that it brings to public voice stories and language that were repressed in the production of the white settler state. However, it also may have the effect of retrospectively incorporating the marginalized subject into a narrative of national belonging while encrypting undigested the histories of exclusion it was supposed to have rectified.

The second chapter addresses special issues of literary journals as points of entry into public presencing for Asian Canadian writers. I argue that special issues do supplementary labour in a Derridean sense. They are both exalted and debased; exalted in their specialness but debased in the sense that as interruptions to the regular stream of journal publishing they never constitute the regular stream, but must exist in excess of it. I read two issues closely: the 1990 *Awakening Thunder* special issue of *Fireweed* and the 1994 *Colour. An Issue* special issue of *West Coast Line*. I argue that, in attempting to lay out a history of Asian Canadian women's writing and to give Asian Canadian women's community positive content, *Awakening Thunder* produces a history of the present oriented toward a utopic future. *Colour. An Issue*, framed around the idea of race more broadly, is adamant about the historical contingency of racial formation, and so the future it lays the ground for emphasizes open-endedness rather than happy arrival. Nonetheless, these are not rival texts, but kinship texts and should be read as such.

My third chapter locates Asian Canadian and related anthology production in the neoliberal moment—that moment in which the old liberal democratic state is morphing into the neoliberal economic state. Anthologies can solidify cultural unities, both in a community-producing sense and in a commodification sense. Their most desirable productivity arises, I argue, in the way they produce relation across racialized communities. The relationship between the anthology and institutionalization is a fraught one in the sense that the anthology can provide a basis for institutionalization, but in so doing, runs the danger of undermining the negative capability that drives the most imaginative and democratic possibilities of the concept "Asian Canadian." Those with an interest in the institutionalization of "Asian Canadian" literature as a discipline must be attentive to the dangers of commodification. The affective and affiliative stances taken within the body of specific anthologies matter. Those stances that conspire with desires for marketable commodities, like, for instance, the secrets of Chinatown, are dangerous to empowered communities. On the other hand, those that actively refuse consumption, through, for instance, the invocation of disgust, stand a chance of leaving the field open for further practice and the work of the imagination.

The final three chapters of the book investigate specific strategies of individual subject construction taken on by single authors. In Chapter 4, I read Hiromi Goto's *Chorus of Mushrooms* and *The Kappa Child* as emerging from the complicated interaction of activist and cultural gatherings in the 1980s and 1990s. Goto's work is important to the nonlinear, fractured temporalities of Asian Canadian literature because it is committed to the multiplicity of stories rather than to the singular truth of history. Her work queries the act of representation while using representational strategies to write Japanese Canadian women out of the racist and patriarchal history that would otherwise contain them, and into vividly imagined histories of their own. In so doing, she commits herself to non-realist modes, and a kind of radical carnival that does not ever return to what Mikhail Bakhtin calls "the daylight world." Instead, her stories transform the geographies into which they are propelled.

In Chapter 5, I read the work of Rita Wong and jam ismail as producing creative excesses that include and push past racist name. If "Asian Canadian" is a linguistic category that cannot fully describe the multiplicity of Asian Canadian ontologies, then a poetics that can address material excess is necessary to keep the term "Asian Canadian" from becoming a conservativizing, containing one. Wong and ismail, invested in both the political possibilities of the term and in its breakage, write to show its instability and polyvocality.

My final chapter articulates Margaret Atwood's *Oryx and Crake* and Dionne Brand's *What We All Long For* as producing extra-human subjects in a time of global capital. Atwood's Oryx and Brand's Quy are constructed in excess of the liberal human subject, and as such both are deeply abject and radically free of the constraints of Enlightenment subjectivity. Though Atwood's text is a cynical one that returns power tongue-in-cheek to white patriarchy, Brand offers us a glimmer of hope by constructing the citizen-subject-reader in a profound historical, bodily, and blood kinship with those whom the state, through the logic of exception, seeks to exclude. Hers is a call for an ethics of relation that crosses borders. It depends on intergenerational memory, desire, and artmaking to counter the violence of globalization. A happy outcome is not assured, but the possibility is there.

In the conclusion, I revisit the 1994 conference Writing Thru Race, which marked a turning point in the practice and reading of cultural race politics. I argue that the rise of globalized neoliberalism coincided with a collapse of anti-racist community resulting from the slow leak of the original dialectical conundrum—the problem of reclaiming the racist name that is always tied to whiteness. Anti-racist action and literary production signify and circulate differently in the new global world order, necessitating new models of both individual subjectivity and collectivity. Critics and cultural producers are more necessary than ever to help us imagine how citizens and species can both do and be.

CHAPTER 1

STRATEGIZING THE BODY OF HISTORY
Anxious Writing, Absent Subjects, and Marketing the Nation

WRITING PARTIAL SELVES

Writing the self, in autobiographies and memoirs, is often seen as a way to "break the silence," especially for marginalized subjects and those people who have been rendered invisible through racist exclusion from Canadian cultural life. I want to argue in this chapter, however, that self-writing, autobiography in particular, can produce ambivalent results. In some cases, writing the self can deepen oppression, not just by reiterating it, but by driving deeper underground aspects of marginalized subjectivity that do not fit into conventions of autobiography. This is not to deny autobiography its liberatory power, but only to show that because of generic conventions combined with racist stereotypes, and because of the problem of articulation itself, there is a contradiction; in other words, the liberatory power of autobiography is not pure. There is a tension between generic trope and experience. Important silences can be broken, but others can also be more deeply encrypted. Further, the circulation of the text in the aftermath of "breaking the silence" does work that is partially, but not fully, liberatory and may have the unfortunate effect of retrospectively folding the marginalized subject back into a discourse of national belonging, while actually covering over the violent history of exclusion it was supposed to have expiated.

I want to be very clear that I am not advocating the uselessness or apolitical nature of autobiography. What I do want to do is push the question of how the marginalized subject might productively write herself into presence—personal, social, cultural, national, and political. I recognize the writing of self as important, but not as a complete liberation or a complete presencing. This chapter offers that critique.

BREAKING THE SILENCE

The anti-racist movements of the late 1980s and early 1990s were largely predicated on the notion of "breaking the silence," that is, making space for the articulation of histories that until that point had been kept from the

official record. Working in an oppositional mode, self-identified anti-racist thinkers and activists noted that official histories tended to privilege
the already privileged, that is, the white, male, heterosexual ruling class.
Anti-oppression cultural workers sought the articulation of marginalized
histories as a first step in liberating subjects excluded from official histories.
Under the aegis of "the universal," the histories of racialized peoples had
not only been silenced but also made invisible. Collective texts in particular,
such as the groundbreaking lesbian of colour anthology *Piece of My Heart*,
mark an important turning point in the materialization of marginalized
histories—to frame it in psychoanalytic terms, the "bringing to light" of
"that which ought to remain hidden" (Freud 224). A considerable number
of Asian Canadian texts employed the strategy of breaking the silence as a
mode of empowerment. Examples include Wayson Choy's *The Jade Peony*,
Denise Chong's *The Concubine's Children*, and Evelyn Lau's *Runaway*.

A second, very significant recognition of that moment was the importance of the question "Who speaks?" as Himani Bannerji has articulated
in *Thinking Through* (55). Emerging, at least in the academic world, from
Foucault's recognition of regimes of power, the notion that the marginalized
body articulates her or his own history differently from the way a privileged
expert, however liberal and open-minded, might articulate it may not have
been a new idea, but the extent to which it circulated and was put into action
in the late 1980s was extremely important. Bannerji writes:

> A text which is coherent with my experience as a non-white woman, for
> example, when inserted into the tentacles of an alienating interpretive
> device, loses its original reference points and meaning, and becomes inert
> and inverted. Thus, *The Wretched of the Earth* in the light of O. Mannoni's
> *Prospero and Caliban* becomes an example of Oedipal counterphobia of
> the colonized, or Angela Davis' *Women, Race and Class* an example of
> "black feminism," no more than just a "different" perspective in femi-
> nism. (*Thinking Through* 64)

Bannerji is critical of psychoanalysis and feminism in this context because
she recognizes them as oppressive impositions on the experiences of women
of colour. A politic focused on the body insists that "we the marginalized"
must speak for ourselves in our own voices. It also refuses to make nomen-
clatural equivalences of speaking voices, such that, as Bannerji describes
above, one voice becomes substitutable for another, like in valence, and different only in style. It matters who speaks. What is said, moreover, must be
heard differently depending on the body speaking and on that body's history.
To recognize the radical incommensurability of marginalized difference in

relation to hegemonic power opened liberatory possibilities that were enormously productive but also potentially stultifying in terms of the pressure they put on marginalized writers to speak and (accurately and comprehensively) represent.[1]

THE EXCESSIVE INTERIOR

A feminism focused on the body became, in the 1980s and 1990s, a productive strategy for the writing of a very particular kind of liberatory text. Bannerji writes:

> Feminism ideally rests on a transformative cognitive approach which validates subjectivity and direct agency. It is disinterested in "expertise," which reduces women to outsiders and operators of the machinery of the status quo knowledge. Thus beginning from ourselves, with a project of self and social transformation (encoded in the slogan "the personal is political") does not require an apology but, on the contrary, becomes a basic imperative. (65)

While Bannerji adamantly refuses "apology," the articulation of such a notion in this otherwise determinedly "right on" stance recognizes the potential for backlash. The reactionary reading is held off by the call for social transformation. There is already the expectation that one will not be heard, which, in some measure, produces an unhearing audience (in addition, of course, to audiences that do hear). I would suggest that Bannerji recognizes the problem of identity formation in reaction to hegemonic naming, that is, that it is always both a refusal and a reiteration. Later, Bannerji does indeed say, "[K]nowledge cannot be produced in the context of ruling but only in conscious resistance to it" (82). Furthermore:

> It must retain the integrity of our concrete subject positions within its very project and its present-day method of investigation, in so far as it searches the history of social relations to trace the reasons for and the forms of our oppression. (82)

By recognizing the historical situatedness of this body-based strategy, Bannerji recognizes its contingency, though perhaps not as adamantly here as she does later. Her recognition of contingency is more forcefully expressed, however, precisely in her articulation of the political use of speech:

> "You can't speak my reality" has been a strong demand of ours. But in real political terms, are these the only options that face us—those of mutually exclusive agencies? Or must we begin to use my previously suggested

integrative and reflexive analysis to work out a political position which allows anyone to speak for/from the experiences of individuals and groups, while leaving room to speak "socially" from other locations, along the lines of the relations that (in)form our/my own experience? (84)

In my mind, these are the crisis questions of the political historical moment of the 1980s and 1990s. To phrase it in Marxist terms, this is the turning point of the dialectic. Roy Miki deepens the problem by posing it as an ontological one with serious implications for the subjectivity of the marginalized other:

> A one-dimensional oppositional positioning is hardly an adequate basis for new cultural forms which can represent the localized subjectivities of writers of colour. While such contests of will and confrontation may be a pragmatic strategy for certain instances requiring immediate inter-ventionist action, they do not instigate the internal transformations nec-essary for moving beyond the constraints of racialization to make spaces where difference and diversity are constantly being (re)negotiated. For Canadian writers of colour—and here I speak in (personal) terms of Jap-anese Canadians—the internal "battle" to overcome the powerful effects of racialization may, finally, be the most formidable. (*Broken Entries* 107)[2]

This interior space that Miki describes is so radically under siege that "breaking the silence" cannot articulate it. Noting the pressures that assim-ilationist assumptions exert on the marginalized other, Miki remarks that simple subjectivity is no easy matter:

> Historically and even at present, the strain of a domineering exterior on the interior of those in the state of exclusion created/creates complicated networks of ambiguities, repressions, and compromises that infiltrate the language and geography of their subjectivity. [...] [T]he experience of inner and outer is not merely an instance of decontextualized, abstract binary, but vitally connected to community-based positioning vis à vis—or contained by, or surrounded by—an overriding white majority from which it is estranged either by language, or by sociocultural values, or by the phenomenon of physicality, i.e., the appearance of the semiotic body inscribed with the constructed signs of "race." (109)

He suggests further that the pressure on Japanese Canadians in the aftermath of internment is so extreme that any kind of interiority for the "JC" subject is "erased, rendered speechless, or so devoid of content that the subject does not or cannot even recognize its absence" (110). Instead, "dominant values outside come to censor, repress, or otherwise propagandize the inside" (113).

The political strategy of breaking the silence has necessitated an engagement with an already established tradition of autobiography. Indeed, as Sidonie Smith and Julia Watson have noted, since the 1970s women's autobiography (and that of other marginalized categories, I would suggest) has risen from a status with little respect to a site of privilege for thinking about contemporary issues at the intersection of feminism, postcolonialism, and postmodernism (5). It is thus important to recognize both what it does and does not do, what the possibilities and pitfalls of its writing and circulation are. The drive to "break the silence" layers over autobiographical tradition in interesting and contradictory ways that sometimes foil the intent behind breaking the silence, and sometimes add to the practice of autobiography to make it work differently from how it has historically.

The French structuralist Philippe Lejeune suggests that the true subject of autobiography is the name of author (33). He argues that there exists a pact between reader and writer that promises that the person named as author on the cover of the book is the person whose story the autobiography will tell: "Le pacte autobiographique, c'est l'affirmation dans le texte de cette identité, renvoyant en dernier ressort au nom de l'auteur sur la couverture" (26). However, he also notes that as readers, we tend to find the "truth" of autobiographical texts not in what they tell us directly, but in the moments of rupture, when something more profound and more literary leaks through:

> En face d'un récit d'aspect autobiographique, le lecteur a souvent tendance à se prendre pour un limier, c'est-à-dire à chercher les ruptures du contrat (quel que soit let contrat). C'est de là qu'est né le mythe du roman "plus vrai" que l'autobiographie: on trouve toujours plus vrai et plus profond ce qu'on a cru découvrir à travers le texte, malgré l'auteur.
> (*Le Pacte Autobiographique* 26)

If autobiography is a completely transparent practice that leaves little room for an unconscious of any kind, then there is even less room for an unconscious of the kind Miki describes, an unconscious with indeterminate content, so unformed that it cannot even leak. I suggest that there is a logic of partialness at work here, that the work of autobiography, in spite of its apparent power, does metonymic work. Something of experience is articulated, but the articulation of partial experience drives deeper into repression that which is not, or perhaps cannot be, articulated. Something may be given between the lines, but there is more beneath the lines that does not appear. Further, the appearance of articulation furnishes the autobiographical subject in her or his social context with a kind of solidity, and perhaps even national belonging, that is in fact illusory because of the fundamental absence that does not make it to the light of day.

Miki valorizes writing as a mode of self-knowledge, a way in which the propagandized "inside" can begin to take shape. He does not stipulate whether this shaping might occur transparently or "à travers le texte." But because he emphasizes the act of writing, between the lines or beneath them, the question of knowledge produced in spite of the author is beside the point.

But how to write is no easy question. The silence is complicated. It does not have certain content. Miki theorizes the emergence of the subject as beginning with interchange between inside and outside that is interrupted by doubt:

> [T]he passageway between inside/outside (suddenly) transforms into a place of static, of noise, of perceptual destabilizations. [...] [T]he disturbed subject/writer [is] set adrift in a shifting space of vertiginous pluralities that awaken the desire to speak, to write. But where to begin? (*Broken Entries* 113)

Miki quotes Gail Scott, who frames a similar problem in feminist terms. Scott asks, "What if the surfacing unconscious stream finds void instead of code?" (qtd. in *Broken Entries* 114).

This is a key question in attempting to make sense of writing projects that emerge from the moment of the body politic. As Miki's analysis of Joy Kogawa's *Obasan* suggests, the retrieval of history is not as easy as it might appear on the surface. It is certainly not nearly as simple as an (autobiographical) recounting of "what happened." The content of the silence, if it can ever be materialized, is almost certainly more (and less) than mere reportage. Miki notes that, in the apparently redemptive close of the novel, the speaking voice of the Japanese Canadian subject is absent, papered over by the signatures of three white men (*Broken Entries* 116).

The notion of breaking the silence requires silence to have content. In this historical moment, it seems there are two possibilities for what that content can be—trauma or the void. If it is trauma, the trauma needs to be reconstructed and redeemed. This is indeed what *Obasan* appears to do. But it cannot do so without contradiction. If, as Scott suggests, it is emptiness, what are the consequences of confronting this emptiness? Is this the same emptiness that the deconstructionists would suggest lies at the heart of any attempt at representation? If the play of signifiers is truly endless, does it matter what history is called into play? Or, to frame the problem psychoanalytically, if we can know history only through traumatic repetition and can never know the original event, does it matter what gets repeated? These are problems I shall attempt to explore through two apparently transparent autobiographic texts, specifically those of Evelyn Lau and Wayson Choy.

THE SELF AS ETHNOGRAPHIC SUBJECT

Before I enter into that discussion, however, I want to raise a second problematic, that of the relationship between the writing subject and the ethnographic tradition, particularly for those who have traditionally been the objects rather than the experts of ethnographic research. Through the ideals that emerged from the question "Who speaks?" autobiography became an obvious and important strategy for countering hegemonic white texts that spoke authoritatively and categorically for the other. As a discipline of the other, anthropology in particular underwent massive shifts. Clifford and Marcus's *Writing Culture: The Poetics and Politics of Ethnography* was very important for this reason. A major feature of this shift is the recognition that "literary procedures pervade any work of cultural representation" (4). This recognition takes place, however, at a historical moment when cultural critics are themselves arguing that literature is a transient category (5). The concerns of both disciplines overlap in the sense that they recognize the instability of narrative and narrative meaning. Clifford also notes the rise of the "indigenous ethnographer" as one who is able to study her own culture from "new angles and depths of understanding," (9) though he does note that these are not necessarily better than the depths and angles non-indigenous ethnographers are capable of, only different, and perhaps useful for that reason. It is the repositioning of anthropology with regard to those it studies that Clifford thinks is significant (10). Its authority is no longer automatic. Further, it is not only the object of study who is constructed by the discipline; the ethnographer herself or himself is also constructed through her or his own writing practice (10). Self-reflexivity becomes a necessary injection into the ethnographic method.

Soyini Madison notes a shift from the practice of conventional ethnography to a critical ethnography that "begins with an ethical responsibility to address processes of unfairness or injustice within a particular *lived* domain" (5). Further, she insists on a particular politicized relation to ethnographic practice: "Critical ethnography must further its goals from simply politics to the politics of positionality. The question becomes, How do we begin to discuss our positionality as ethnographers and those who represent Others?" (6).

Further, what happens when the subject and object of ethnographic or literary discourse are identical? Clifford notes that in classical ethnography, while the authorial voice of the ethnographer is clear, there is always a firm separation between the subjectivity of the author and the object of her or his study (13). Of the confident, consistent voice of the ethnographer, Clifford asks: "What desires and confusions was it smoothing over? How was 'objectivity' textually constructed?" (14). The new, self-reflexive ethnography allows discussion of previously unacknowledged concerns including violence, desire, confusion, struggle, and economic transactions with informants (14). I might ask further, if the "ethnographer" and his "object" are identical, are one and the same person, what happens to these fraught power relations? One might think of them as the impossible struggle between inside and outside, ego and superego, that Miki articulates in "Asiancy." One might look to the poststructuralists and the "death of the author" to suggest that the object remains the object, written by a language that allows only a narrow range of discourse, regardless of who speaks it.

In one of the autobiographical interruptions to his theoretical text, Miki recounts a moment as a young student in 1950s Winnipeg, when he had to read aloud from Ann Marriott's Depression-era prairie poem "The Wind Our Enemy." The class reads the poem aloud, one line per student, down the aisles. Coincidence places the line "Japs bomb China" in Miki's mouth. Years later, as a professor, poet, and theorist, he writes: "No one exposed, except for the chuckle chuckle, this moment of linguistic anguish. The match between the word and 'me' struck a chord but the unspoken fluttered out the (open) window. Even 'i' was numbed by the evacuated words" (*Broken Entries* 112).

What if it doesn't matter who the writer is? What if, as postmodern theory suggests, all language is quotation? What I am trying to suggest here is that the coincidence of the marginalized writer with her autobiography can function not unlike the accidental "moment of linguistic anguish" that Miki describes. Without the tools to counter this effect, the subaltern can be left numbed by the emptiness of her own words. Without anyone to expose the anguish, the void that the words were meant to fill is only deepened.

AUTOBIOGRAPHICAL VOID

This might help illuminate, in some measure, what is so discomfiting about certain autobiographical texts of that moment. The most discomfiting of these, in my mind, is *Runaway*, the teenage diary of Evelyn Lau. The coincidence of both text and body with a range of abject signifiers—Asian, woman, child, model daughter, prostitute, drug addict—places both, as objects, within a history and economy of the worst Western stereotypes of the Oriental. As a confessional, lucidly written in a "quality" authorial voice, it verifies for the racist reader (or the racist in every reader) the truth of what that reader always suspected about not these kinds of texts, but certainly these kinds of bodies. I want to be careful here. To blame the text, or its young writer, seems suspiciously like blaming the victim of what was, without a doubt, a miserable and harrowing childhood. What I want to do in the aftermath of not just the writing but also the circulation of the text is to consider the way in which it works, as a small step in beginning to imagine writing strategies that resist such oppressive consumption.

Reading Descartes' *Discourse*, Marc Eli Blanchard suggests that the moment of writing autobiographically is not identical with the moment in which a fiction of the coherent self is delivered to the reader through the autobiography (101). Instead, if I read him correctly, what occurs is a process something like this:

> I doubt myself.
> I write autobiography, attempting to know myself.
> In so doing, I convince others of coherence precisely at the site where I doubt.
> When I see their certainty, I think I know myself, though never completely.
> I doubt myself.
> I write more autobiography, attempting to know myself, etc.

For the marginalized subject, particularly for a child with no reflection of herself to look to in order to know herself, this process can border on the obsessive. Blanchard indeed remarks that autobiography aims to recreate a primal mirror stage (99). I might argue that this is precisely what Lau is doing in *Runaway*. Certainly, she makes no claims to be producing a liberatory text, except in so far as she sees reading as escape:

> By that age [six], I had already become an avid reader—reading was like living in a fantasy world; it had become my form of escape. I thought that by writing I could give that same feeling to other people, that they could open one of my books and disappear for awhile. Even then, it was important for me not to stay rooted in reality. (1)

Interestingly, however, the very next paragraph consists of nothing but truth claims about "reality":

> I was born in Vancouver to Chinese immigrants. I was a shy and introspective child, exceedingly sensitive to the tensions and emotions around me. My parents were strict, overprotective and suspicious of the unknown society around them. By kindergarten, I was already expected to excel in class, as the first step in my pre-planned career as a doctor or lawyer. I wasn't allowed to spend much time with the neighbourhood children; consequently I always had my nose in a book. (1)

What I am suggesting here is that these truth claims are actually the construction of a fantasy about race and childhood.[3] One might argue that, by writing, Lau constructs a kind of escape from reality. And that the problem with her reality is that it is not articulable, that it is, instead, precisely the void that both Scott and Miki point to. By returning, at the paragraph's end, to the book, Lau textually enacts the escape she claims to have anxiously carried out over and over again, when, under her mother's nervous, watchful eye, she was supposed to have been studying:

> They forbade me to write unless I brought home straight A's from school, and right up until I left home at fourteen I was not allowed out of the house except to attend school and take piano lessons—not on weekends, not after school. I went submissively to my bedroom and stayed there descending into months of depression alleviated only by the fact that I would continue to write secretly under my math textbook. My mother would sneak into the room very quietly to check if I were doing my homework; I would hold the textbook tilted upwards with one hand and write with the other, slamming the book down when I heard her footsteps. As a result, I was in a constant panic; a kind of fight or flight reaction to all that went on. (4)

The illusion of reality thus blossoms for a moment only to be pulled down into writing or reading, which Blanchard says for the autobiographer are one and the same. Blanchard suggests that the autobiographer is attracted "by the mirage of his own vision." She wants to see herself looking at the spectacle of herself in order to freeze her own actions in the moment of recollection. She is looking for the feeling of being tangential to herself and the world (105). Blanchard writes:

> By simply looking at *how it was*, or rather *how it might have been*, he may with impunity fulfill his desire and by the sheer magic of memory, substitute for the reality of a time past a scene, a tableau, where implicitly, indefinitely repeatable acts are no longer those of a subject upon an object but rather the scheme of a voyeur constantly reenacting a fragmentary scenario. (106)

For Lau, I argue, writing produces a profound state of non-being, a state of obliteration. In many ways it functions in the same way drugs function, as Lau's psychiatrist Dr. Hightower, in fact, observes.

> I talked speedily about the deepest, darkest things with Dr. Hightower, but like he said, echoing disappointment through me, "You're just relating them. You're recording these experiences, not feeling them,

not reliving them. The drugs are a protective barrier. You can't start real work until you stop doing them." And God, more than ever I need to resolve what's happened in my childhood or else I can't go on. (250–51)

The substitutability of the word "them" in this passage suggests a substitutability between living and doing drugs, experience and its obliteration. There is also, I would argue, a substitutability between experience and writing. They are one and the same, and yet profoundly separate from one another. The writer inhabits what Kristeva, in *Powers of Horror*, calls the abject—that pre-subjective state in which the psychoanalytic child does not know the difference between itself and the world, or itself and its own excrement.

The horror of this book is that it uses void-producing text to cover over a deeper void for which there is no language. It emerges from a profoundly abject state, in the terms that Kristeva describes as the "non-separation of the subject/object, on which language has no hold but one woven of fright and repulsion" (58).

In Lau's family bathroom, the mirror does not provide her the moment of recognition that Lacan tells us it ought (1286). Instead, it provides only another image of her own obliteration where even writing, which perhaps holds the possibility for differentiation, for entry into subjecthood, is not possible: "It was all falling apart. Those visits with my parents, me in their bathroom watching a reflection in the mirror gulping pills, the writing meaning nothing, not wanting to ever write again, the drugs that were my world and my death" (251–52).

In *The Threshold of the Visible World*, Kaja Silverman has noted that the non-identical mirror may produce a fantasy that can be a tremendous relief for those whose subjectivity is too difficult to uphold. She calls this the fantasy of the body in bits and pieces. For Silverman, however, this is a fantasy she associates with the masculine subject, which tends to be overdetermined as whole, perfect, and unitary in a way that is highly constructed and requires great effort on the part of the masculine subject. For Lau, no such socially sanctioned subjectivity is offered. However, if one is to take her at her word, the pressure that her parents exert upon her to perform the "model daughter" is excessive, and certainly more than she can bear. The Lau of this text is both more and less than a full subject. Held together on the one hand by unrealistic parental expectation, torn apart on the other by the most destructive of Althusserian hailings—"junkie whore"—she oscillates between the sublime and the abject: "Not at all short of but always with and through perception and words, the sublime is a *something added* that expands us, overstrains us, and causes us to be both *here*, as dejects, and there, as others and sparkling" (Kristeva 12).

But which is which? Lau states repeatedly that she would rather be living drugged out on the streets than return to the stifling entrapment of her parents' home. She is caught in that abject space of non-differentiation, the inability to distinguish between self and society, inside and outside, in spite of the constant, narcissistic assertion of the "I." It appears that no subjectivity is produced here, but only a deepening of the void. What is produced for public consumption is a doubly virulent stereotype of the Asian woman as innocent and childlike on the one hand and excessive and sexually deviant on the other, given new lease and new power by its packaging as a diary, as an autobiography. To deepen this study, one might examine Lau's poetic and fictional works, particularly *Other Women* and *You Are Not Who You Claim*, to question who the "other" of the former might refer to. Her 2002 memoir, *Inside Out*, might also bear out my claims. If, as I have argued, the writing persona of these texts has not emerged as a fully formed subject, but rather inhabits that unformed, fear-ridden site of the abject, then it appears doomed to repetition, circling around the formation of the "I" until it is able to separate itself from the fear-laden not-yet-objects that swirl around it. I argue that in the case of *Runaway*, the incommensurable gap between inside and outside that Miki discusses is widened rather than narrowed, and it is made all the less articulate because of the appearance of articulation. Autobiography, as a truth regime, has become a kind of camouflage papering over an ever-deepening, ever more desperate void.

The obvious question to ask at this juncture is whether this problem belongs to autobiography in general, or whether there is something particular about *Runaway* that produces these effects. Writing about Doukhobor autobiography, Julie Rak (citing Sidonie Smith and Judith Butler) considers interiority to be a performative effect of autobiography rather than its "originating centre":

> [P]erformativity … can still operate as an effect of language, but one which does not have to work within an economy of interiority and exteriority. This version of performativity can work within an economy of exteriority and event, as a communication of identity issues which does not tell the self to the self, or heal the split between the lonely points of enunciation and utterance, so much as recover the fractured memories of a community, or operate as a means of telling the community story to itself and to other communities. The place of witness narrative here is that it suggests how subjectivity can be constructed to recount a traumatic event so that the community can work through it. Instead of a dependency on temporary identifications which can be unfixed, the event itself stands for interiority and performs the work of identification for those who do not have an individuated subjectivity to unfix. (232)

Two problems emerge from this critique. First of all, if the work of auto-biography is primarily "exterior," in other words social, then the ideological labour of the text matters. As Rita Wong has noted, the way in which Lau's work is marketed functions to reproduce stereotypes. Regardless, unfortunately, of Lau's own agency, desire, or action, it is difficult for her work to escape culturally overdetermined readings. Wong writes:

> Sometimes I have the disturbing feeling that, if Lau had not come along, the machine would have found someone else because it needs to have a bit of "colour" (but not too much) mirroring or serving the symbolic order so that it can disavow its historical and systemic racist tendencies. Luckily for those in the book business who have benefitted from her labour, Lau's literary fixation with Old White Daddies seems to fit the bill. This narrative, only one of many possible narratives, is not to minimize Lau's talent as a writer but to remind us of the many ways in which social relations can influence reader reception. ("Market Forces" 122)

Though Wong is writing about the social labour of Lau's fiction, I would like to recognize here that the work of autobiography is also social. As indeed Robert Stepto, writing of the politics of slave narrative in the American South, tells us, autobiography and its circulation is highly subject to "race ritual," in which certain elements must be offered in order for the text to be received as "real." In the case of the slave narrative, the onus is upon the freed slave to prove not the truth of escape and freedom, but in fact, his literacy (6). Further, a white guarantor is required (8), as well as the whole marketing and circulation machinery of the white publishing establishment. Stepto notes further that the social labour of the text affects its reception:

> Slave narratives were often most successful when they were subtly pro-abolition and they were overtly anti-slavery—a condition which could only have exacerbated the former slave's already sizeable problems with telling his tale in such a way that he, and not his editors or guar-antors, controlled it. (15)

The important thing to be aware of here is the extent to which the partial truth of autobiography reinforces already-received social and political knowledge functioning in the service of the status quo. I would suggest that this knowledge is a complicated mix of both apprehension and misapprehension. Even, for instance, Elly Danica's agonizing *Don't: A Woman's Word*, in spite of the productive feminist work it does, repeats violence against women in its accounting of that very violence. This is the contradiction of reclaiming the name of the other, that Hegel discovered long ago, and that

Frantz Fanon so eloquently elaborates in *Black Skins, White Masks*. In readerly terms, it seems to be important, then, to read autobiography as critically as one reads any other kind of text.

This is not to deny its power as witness for both self and community, as Rak notes. The second, perhaps deeper question that emerges from Rak's observations about performance is the extent to which one considers selves and communities as pure effects of enacted language. If the autobiographical work, as Rak suggests, "stands in for interiority" and "performs the work of identification," then there is no access to language (232). Butler herself is less certain about this. Reading *Discipline and Punish*, she imagines the work of language to produce "the soul" as a kind of exterior, one which obliterates the (interior) body in order to bring the subject into existence. She writes:

> Here it is precisely at the expense of the body that the subject appears, an appearance which is conditioned in an inverse relation to the disappearance of the body, and appearance of a subject which not only effectively takes the place of the body, but acts as the very soul which frames and forms the body in captivity.... The bodily remainder, I would suggest, survives such a subject in the mode of already, if not always, having been destroyed, a kind of constitutive loss. ("Subjection, Resistance, Resignification" 236)

First of all, it seems important to ask if there are other ways to produce the subject that are less violent. Butler has in mind the subject production of "the prisoner" as Foucault imagines him, named, contained, and made by the law. In an Althusserian sense, she acknowledges, we can respond to our hailing, or resist it. Butler places liberatory possibility there. In the act of autobiographical writing, in which one is essentially self-hailing, surely there must be some kind of room for give. When the writer actively works to maintain the body against such a "constitutive loss," I would argue, surely there is the possibility for some kind of interiority. If the writer chooses not to do this, then the loss or obliteration of the interior (however one might choose to name it) remains a melancholy possibility.

In a bleakly optimistic way (in the sense that it still allows much possibility for Bannerji's formulation), it might be worth remarking that Lau's intention is not to "break the silence" in the sense that Bannerji seems to mean. In her thorough critique of *Runaway*, Lien Chao remarks: "Lau's 'I' speaks the voice of a strong ego wanting to be one of the top writers in Canada instead of just a third prize or youth competition winner" (*Beyond Silence* 159). At least temporarily, Lau obliterates herself in the passage Chao quotes:

Evelyn isn't alive at all, it's always her writing, her writing.... She's floundering in some kind of murky half-life, some kind of swamp where she still spins fantasies about seeing her books on shelves and people actually reading them, books that would make people think and feel. (Lau 156)

Here again, the text empties the writer. Lau produces absence for herself, in precisely the same move as she produces powerful self-representation for her readers' consumption. I suggest that Lau fills a Malinche-like position for both white and racialized Canadian society, both debased and empowered by exoticized, heterosexual femininity. As such, she, or rather, her representation of self, is unacceptable in polite Chinese Canadian society. And yet the mirage she offers holds great fascination for uncritical white or white-identified Canadian readers for whom her self-representation confirms all the most virulent stereotypes of the Oriental woman. The position is a deeply archetypical one that does unsettling political work. While I find there is something admirable about Lau's refusal of banal propriety, I find the political labour of her work hard to support, however much compassion I might feel for the evacuated subject who produces it.

In a troubling but compelling article questioning the validity of False Memory Syndrome, Janice Haaken asks why we tend to assume that the recovery of trauma is necessarily the path to healing in women's autobiographical narrative.

The trauma/dissociation model has been important in bridging feminist clinical and political practice and in holding onto a conception of women both as rational agents and as damaged victims. At the same time, this model reinforces traditional constructions of feminine experience that can be debilitating. One problem involves the centering of female disturbances on trauma memories, and of recovery on the retrieval of those memories. The therapeutic preoccupation with the recovery of trauma memory engages women, paradoxically, in a quest that reaffirms their fragility and position of non-recognition. Both therapist and patient assume that women's untold stories are more important than the remembered ones, and that the unrevealed drama provides the key to the kingdom. (359)

She suggests that repressed trauma has been a very useful "container" into which we can project the many unsettling, unresolvable aspects of women's experience, and further suggests that in fact childhood neglect might be just as significant a factor as trauma in the formation of the female subject, but that it gets overlooked because it is more difficult to theorize (357). These ideas echo what I have suggested with regard to *Runaway*.

If autobiographical writing, rather than elucidating a trauma, can, in fact cover over or even produce a fundamental void, to what extent is it a liberatory practice? It has the power to reproduce stereotypes and the status quo, but does it have to? I think I would argue here that there are times when self-narrativizing does in fact "work through" and resolve repression (to speak in psychoanalytic terms) but that this is not a guarantee, and that it is possible for it, in fact, to compound violence in the form of "traumatic repetition." Or, to complicate matters further, it might do a bit of both. As in the reappropriation of the racist name, the subject in question is both freed and reinjured in a single move.

"EVERYTHING THAT OUGHT TO HAVE REMAINED HIDDEN"

Homi Bhabha's work on the uncanny has been productive as a tool for thinking through the ways in which histories of the marginalized can be retrieved. Freud originally formulates the uncanny as "everything that ought to have remained hidden but has suddenly come to light" (224). For him the uncanny emerges when we recognize the familiar in the unfamiliar, which he conceives as a return of the repressed, the expression of something forgotten that presses unexpectedly on consciousness and makes the skin crawl. In his conception of "the beyond," Bhabha reformulates Freud's uncanny as a model of history for the marginalized—those whose histories are broken and fragmented through war, dislocation, slavery, or the loss of language. The uncanny becomes a useful model of memory for those living at the interstices of society, in doubled time/spaces that can be imagined in various ways. He provides examples from the work of contemporary artists of colour—stairwells, radio waves, borderlands of any kind. These sites call up a history different from the linear patriarchal monolithic histories of nation-states:

> For the demography of the new internationalism is the history of post-colonial migration, the narratives of cultural and political diaspora, the major social displacements of peasant and aboriginal communities, the poetics of exile, the grim prose of political and economic refugees. It is in this sense that the boundary becomes the place from which *something begins its presencing* in a movement not dissimilar to ambulant, ambivalent articulation of the beyond that I have drawn out: "Always and ever differently the bridge escorts the lingering and hastening ways of men to and fro, so that they may get to other banks. [...] The bridge *gathers* as a passage that crosses." (5)

While both Haaken and Bhabha theorize a "something" beneath consciousness that may or may not be useful in understanding the psychic life of the marginalized subject, Haaken's is a stable core, where Bhabha's is a more mobile thing—always moving "to and fro," here and there and back again—as he says, ambulant, and ambivalent.

In her relentless drive toward a specified trauma, in the iterations of misery, Lau misses something that may be fundamentally inarticulable. In attempting to write the core that Haaken is so suspicious of, she comes up repeatedly with void, at precisely the site where she needs matter. It may be that it is not so much the act of writing per se that papers over the void, but only a misstep in the directions the writing probes. Wayson Choy, on the other hand, in his autobiographical text *Paper Shadows*, is aware of his ghosts from the outset. The generic descriptor on the cover of the book indeed points to them: "A haunting memoir from the bestselling author of *The Jade Peony*."

The opening conundrum with which Choy hooks his reader is that of the appearance of his mother eighteen years after her death. An uncanny stranger, someone from his childhood whom he has forgotten, calls to tell him she saw his mother on the street. Although the story turns out not to be true, Choy's receipt of the message is the instigating incident in a series of incidents that result in Choy discovering that he is adopted.

What Choy seems to strive for, which Lau does not, is a kind of doubleness in language—what might simply be called metaphoricity. By giving ground to these uncanny, unstable hauntings, Choy acknowledges the presence of the unknowable. It may or may not be traumatic, but that is not what is important. By making space for that which evades language, paradoxically, he makes space for language to matter. It is a kind of feeding of hungry ghosts, in which the void is given a nod in order that it not infiltrate and traumatize the entire work.

After the introduction of the reanimated mother, Choy presents us with three more hauntings. They present themselves narratively as mysteries. Poetically, they work as linguistic parapraxes. The first haunting takes place when the Choy of the narrative is four years old. He presents us with a sound:

> I woke up, disturbed by the sound of a distant clanging, and lifted my head high above the flannelled embankment that was my mother's back to see if a ghost had entered the room. Mother rolled her head, mouth partially open, sound asleep. I rubbed the sleep from my eyes to survey the near darkness. What I saw, reflected in the oval mirror above the dresser, was the buoyant gloom alive with winking and sparks. A cloud of fireflies. (*Paper Shadows* 7)

There is both a wonder—the fireflies—and a terror—the clanging sound—contained in the moment, with the body of the mother there to cleave the two together. The body of the mother looms large. Her back is a "flannelled embankment." The content of the haunting that Choy describes here is highly feminized, and highly ambivalent, wonder and terror rolled into one, redeemable only through story: "I remembered how fireflies came together to rescue lost children in the caves of Old China" (*Paper Shadows* 6).

The young Choy imagines the bedroom he shares with his mother also as a cave, one which is both safe and fraught with danger:

> My mind conjured a wild, hairy creature, eyes like fire, heaving itself, and the chains it was dragging, towards our bedroom cave. I turned to stone.
> My child's wisdom said that Mah-ma and I had to lie perfectly still, or the monster would veer towards our bed, open its hideous wet mouth and devour us. (*Paper Shadows* 6–7)

The child requires the mother to protect him from feminine horrors—of the cave, and the "hideous wet mouth." But as a thing of the feminine, the mother can never protect him completely. Interestingly, it is the presence of the aural uncanny, in the form of the clanging noise, that keeps the sensation of spine-tingling chill in place.

In the daylight world, the clanging turns out to be the chains of the milkman's horse—yet another figure of wet, feminine openings.[4] On one occasion it snatches a carrot stump from the boy's hands and leaves a smear of saliva there.

At the moment of the second haunting, the clanging sound that became a horse now becomes a hearse, in an interestingly poetic turn. It is a turn that Choy himself does not remember. Rather the association is made for him by his Fifth Aunty:

> Fifth Aunty touched my shoulder with her cane and giggled. Death never scared her. She had seen too much death in Old Chinatown. I told her that, if I won the big lottery, I would see her ride into the sunset in the grandest, and slowest, horse-drawn hearse.
> "Remember that day you little boy and saw your very first one, Sonny?" she said. Aunty always went back to the old days.
> "No, I don't," I said. "I remember big milk wagons."
> "Yes, yes, you remember," she insisted. "We stand on Hastings Street, I hold your hand, and your aunty finally tell you that black thing no fancy milk wagon." Fifth Aunty broke into toothless laughter. "Oh, you looked so surprised that people died, just like your goldfish."
> "What did I say?"
> "You cry out 'Mah-ma won't die!'" (*Paper Shadows* 11)

The feminine becomes a sign of death, specifically the death of the mother, who herself belongs to the deathly realm in the traditional metaphysical order of things. The horse pulls a hearse; the nourishing, life-giving milk wagon becomes a death wagon that will eventually take the mother away. The feminine that is fertile becomes both the feminine that obliterates and the feminine that is obliterated.

Choy illuminates for us at the outset a kind of motile liminal space. The mother is both alive—in the story given by the strange woman Hazel, and dead, in Choy's pragmatic recollection of her death and funeral. And so the Choy of the narrative also becomes a figure of Bhabha's interstitial time/space—both a "natural" son of Chinatown and a strange adoptee, the son of a mysterious opera singer, made legitimate through false papers to a mother who herself has become a legitimate citizen on false papers. His mother, Lilly Choy, is officially known as Nellie Hop Wah. But she is Nellie Hop Wah in name only, or rather, in the second place, after the death of the first Nellie Hop Wah, who in fact was a married woman who died abroad and whose papers were later sold. The doubleness of life and death becomes also a doubleness of national and familial belonging. Choy and his mother exist inside the nation-state and inside the family on false papers with names that are not their own. Choy does not even know what his birth name, if he had one, might have been. Outside the clearly false sanctioning of citizenship, Choy and his mother are "paper shadows" without names or existence. Now his mother turns out not to be his mother, and at least in the suspended moment of the text's opening, turns out to be not dead but alive—a returnee from what Bhabha charmingly calls the "*au dela*" (1). A living woman carries a dead woman's name, finally dies, and then is substituted for another living woman in a bizarre series of oscillations between life and death, being and non-existence.

No wonder, then, that this memoir is haunted. Its characters' lives are doubled images of the home in the world, as Bhabha explains in his artic-ulation of the unhomely beyond:

> The recesses of the domestic space become sites for history's most intricate invasions. In that displacement, the borders between home and world become confused; and uncannily, the private and the public become part of each other, forcing upon us a vision that is as divided as it is disorienting. (9)

I want to ask now whether this unhomely effect comes from the writ-ing of Choy's life or from the experience of life itself. As Joan Scott has described for us, a major tension of the identity politics moment is the tension between experience and writing, often figured as a class tension between those with the education and ability to write and those without. The problem is unresolvable because there is no such thing as unmediated experience.[5] The appearance of haunting in Choy's text can be apprehended only insofar as the text is literary. We need the mysterious clanging noise, the fireflies, the poetic resonance between "horse" and "hearse" in order to arrive at the unhomely effects I have described above. We need them also to recognize the crises of life and death, citizenship and being. These are the things that Evelyn Lau in *Runaway* does not provide. In gesturing toward the void, Choy is able to bring it momentarily to life, to create in that uncanny home, that cave of the bedroom he shared with his mother, a momentary haunting that draws us into history and the churnings of national politics. As Bhabha says, quoting Morrison's *Beloved*:

> When historical visibility has faded, when the present tense of testimony loses its power to arrest, then the displacements of memory and the indirections of art offer us the image of our psychic survival. To live in the unhomely world, to find its ambivalencies and ambiguities enacted in the house of fiction, or its sundering and splitting performed in the work of art, is also to affirm a profound desire for social solidarity: "I am looking for the join [...] I want to join [...] I want to join." (18)

I seem, at this point, to be arguing in favour of metaphoricity, as more liberatory and more productive than texts that presume to artlessly represent experience, if only because the latter cannot, in the end, produce experience for the reader. But George Yudice argues this in the translator's introduction to Néstor Garcia Canclini's *Consumers and Citizens*:

> Literary theory and cultural studies are rife with these assimilations of social problems to philosophical and aesthetic categories: Heidegger's homelessness versus homeless people; Kristeva's abjects vis-à-vis social "deviants"; Freud's uncanny vis-à-vis women's sexuality; and so on. (xiv)

One could, of course, leave the act of writing altogether, in order to engage other strategies of self- and community presencing, as indeed many activist-writers and activist-artists did in the 1980s and 1990s and continue to do in the current moment. Some writers have also consciously theorized their writing as an active and contingent practice. Roy Miki's notion of "asiancy" describes precisely that engagement for racialized cultural workers striving for social justice in writing, organizing, and art practice.

It certainly does seem that Choy is more conscious of his writing practice as a metaphorical act of representation than Lau is. He consciously makes space for the rupture, even in the way he names himself. He is "Wayson Choy" on the cover of the book, but "Choy Way Sun" as the protagonist of the autobiographical narrative. It is yet another slippage in a battery of slippages, as I have described above—the recognition that he is someone other than who he was born and that his mother is also not who her papers say she is—that rupture the epigraph of the text: "At three, at eighty—the same."[6] This is also a conscious and productive disturbance of the autobiographic pact. In a sense, it is a call to the recognition of the genealogy of names, something Lejeune himself addresses in *Signes de Vie*, his follow-up to *Le Pacte Autobiographique* thirty years later, in which he writes:

> On risque toujours de croire que, parce que des éléments se transmettent, ils restent les mêmes, alors qu'ils se déforment en prenant une autre fonction. Là où l'on voit une continuité, il y a eu mutation. C'est difficile à penser pour nous, parce que tout le travail de construction de notre identité va dans l'autre sens, nous cherchons à enraciner notre présent dans des continuités en partie illusoires. (*Signes de Vie* 117–18)

While Choy playfully recognizes the genealogical mutations of his own name, however, the deeper question of the representation of Asian bodies and spaces remains ambivalent in relation to the stereotypes of Oriental mystery and inscrutability. I don't want to overload Choy or Lau with the burden of representation. On the other hand, stereotyped representations, deployed in the apparent service of truth-telling, reconfirm racist understanding in a newly powerful way. I want to ask whether more is possible, whether there are deeper ways of activating language in order to escape the virulent stereotype of Chinese secretiveness and inscrutability.

Much of the anti-racist liberatory work of the late 1980s and early 1990s was predicated on a desire by racialized subjects for entry into Canadian cultural life. The introduction of the Canadian Multiculturalism Act in 1988 and the rise of cultural activity in racially marginalized communities in Canada coincided to the great benefit of artists, writers, and their audiences. The moment was fraught, for reasons Monika Kin Gagnon and Richard Fung have documented in *13 Conversations*. What cultural organizers, artists, writers, and critics might not have recognized as we did that liberatory work was the extent to which we believed in the democratic possibilities of national belonging, in spite of our sometimes quite cutting critique. Or perhaps the critique itself was testament to that faith. While the texts I discuss here are not overtly about entry into a national imagination, I argue that they were published in that context and should be read as such.

The 1991 emergence of the anthology *Many-Mouthed Birds: Contemporary Writing by Chinese Canadians* did much to shape the expectations of what "Chinese Canadian writing" ought to do, positing it both within the national container "Canadian Literature" and outside it at the same time. I register autoethnography not so much in relation to nuances of conventional Western ethnography as with the pressure on Chinese Canadian writers to explain themselves to the white mainstream, and the assumptions which that pressure and its categories produce. To the extent that we "tell the secrets of Chinatown" (to whom?) the work is "autoethnographic" in the self-explaining mode that is so often taken on by racially marginalized subjects in white settler nations, in response to their exclusion from national culture life. In the introduction to *Many-Mouthed Birds*, Bennett Lee takes note of SKY Lee's thoughts on *Disappearing Moon Cafe*:

> Her novel *Disappearing Moon Cafe* is one break in what Kae, the narrator, terms "the great wall of silence and invisibility we have built around us." She goes on: "I have a misgiving that telling our history is forbidden. I have violated a secret code." The secret code was that reviving the troubled past would serve no useful purpose and should be forgotten or, at the very least, kept within the family. These writers [the contributors to the anthology] have indeed violated the code. By unearthing the past, breathing life into the characters who inhabited those troubled times, giving them a voice and investing them with human frailties and passions, they open up a world with its own colour, texture, weight and dreams. (4)

In *Paper Shadows*, Wayson Choy matter-of-factly addresses the telling of secrets: "The voice on the hotel phone chattered on, spilling out details and relationships, talking of Pender *Gai*, Pender Street, and noting how my novel talked of the 'secrets of Chinatown'"(5).

The notion of Chinatown as a place of secrets may well have some basis in reality. This doesn't stop it from reinforcing the trope of Chinese inscrutability. Further, it places the second-generation narrators who disclose the "secrets" in the dubious position of traitor (to their first-generation parents), interpreter, and assimilated-but-marked Canadian subject. The "secrets of Chinatown" are traded for national belonging. Of course, the idea of Chinatown secrets is a problematic formulation. The "secrets of Chinatown" may be no deeper or stranger than the secrets of any other neighbourhood—the problem lies in the coincidence of Chinatown secrets with already existing, racist expectations about Chineseness. And so, if to tell those secrets constitutes a kind of autoethnography, it does so on the shaky ground of pandering to exoticist expectation. The problem is first and foremost a problem of reception. The author is not to be blamed. Some racialized writers, however, do consider it their responsibility to take that predictable reception into consideration.

In such a case, the question for the conscientious racialized writer becomes first of all whether national belonging is desirable, and secondly, if it is, how to go about obtaining it without confirming the Orientalist expectations of the mainstream. I think that, for a long time, many racialized Canadian cultural workers did perceive national belonging as something to be desired and striven for, even if the path was always fraught, contradictory, and problematic. We believed in the possibility of democratic equality within the bounds of the Canadian state. However, for writers with commitments to social justice, the recognition that the Canadian state is a colonial state actively engaged in the disenfranchisement and oppression of Indigenous peoples would be an excellent reason not to want national belonging.

POISONED GIFTS?

Today, as I write this chapter, the stage of the nation has been radically altered from its early-1990s condition by free trade agreements and the rise of militarism, fundamentalism, and war. It is important to understand what the texts did at the moment of their emergence, and what they might do (that is, how they might circulate differently) in the present.

As these texts find their place within the canon of CanLit, it is important to ask whether they retain their liberatory possibility. For there is a danger at present that could not have been perceived in the heady moment of their conception. The danger is that, sanctioned through the legitimizing power of the authentic voice, these texts become a new kind of ethnography rife with stereotypes—some old, some new—made all the more salient precisely because it is the native who speaks. Not enough authority has suddenly become too much, though in neither case does the "native speaker" benefit. It is the text, not the body or the history from which it emerges, that is privileged. But it is privileged only in the sense that it is put into the service of the same capitalist white supremacist hegemony under which we still live.

There seems to be a law of belatedness at work here, in the sense that autobiographical texts are a necessary step in the liberation of marginalized peoples, but no sooner do they come into being than their function, or, at least, one of their functions, becomes a very conservative one indeed. There is a parallel here between the writing of autobiography and what Hardt and Negri have to say about the functions of nationalism: that it is liberatory only insofar as it is oppositional—that the nation-state is the poisoned gift of national liberation movements (134).

Once it has been produced, autobiography can work as a sort of retro-spective folding of the marginalized subject into a kind of national cultural belonging. It seems to vindicate the past, but it actually produces a spectral present in the service of a future that requires the redeployment of mar-ginalized bodies in different terms, but often for the same purposes. I am concerned that at the present moment the stories of past wrongs against Asian Canadians get redeployed as a sign of Canada's benevolence, a sign of liberal/multicultural arrival.

What is particularly interesting about Asian Canadian autobiographical texts is the use of historical photographs on the covers, as a way of pro-ducing nostalgia for a moment that could never, even at its best, have been particularly romantic. Certainly this is the case with the cover of Wayson Choy's "haunting memoir," which features a sepia-toned photograph of the young "Way Sun" standing in a small yard, and what seems to be age-stained paper covered in Chinese calligraphy. Denise Chong's *The Concubine's Chil-dren* is all the more loaded because its cover image is an old photograph of the beautiful concubine, her grandmother May-Ying. The stereotype of the exotic, sexually deviant Asian woman is reproduced and heightened by its archival status.

As Roy Miki deconstructs the cover of the anthology *Many-Mouthed Birds* to illustrate how Chick Rice's playful, ironic photograph of Tommy Wong's face is redeployed through marketing strategy to (re)produce an image of the Asian as "secretive and mysterious" (*Broken Entries* 120), so one might argue that book cover art using archival photos, whatever their "original" significance, produces a similar effect. But there is also the added dimension of a strange kind of nostalgia, as I have said, such that these bodies are belatedly incorporated into the mythos of the nation. The exotic other is retrospectively encrypted into a history that did not want these bodies on the first pass.

Through the logic of the future anterior that Marjorie Garber has described in her discussion of Shakespeare's history plays (311), we are given an uncanny vision of the present as the future of a past that never was, in spite of all the trappings of authenticity. The present is newly deployed as the teleogical end of a past that actually wanted the opposite of the newly narrativized "happy ending." What are the psychic effects of this incorpo-ration for subjects represented by this history?

The French psychoanalysts Abraham and Torok propose a theory of "inclusion," in which the subject undergoes a traumatic experience she or he cannot admit to memory because it is too overwhelming. Through the mechanism of inclusion, the subject incorporates the experience into his psyche whole, in the form of a crypt. It is painful, it is undigested, it is inarticulable:

> Between the idyllic moment and its subsequent forgetting (we have called the latter "preservative repression"), there was the metapsychological traumatism of a loss or, more precisely, the "loss" that resulted from a traumatism. This segment of ever so painfully lived Reality— untellable and therefore inaccessible to the gradual, assimilative work of mourning—causes a genuinely covert shift in the entire psyche. The shift itself is covert, since both the fact that the idyll was real and that it was lost must be disguised and denied. This leads to the establishment of a sealed-off psychic place, a crypt in the ego. Created by a self-governing mechanism we call *inclusion*, the crypt is comparable to the formation of a cocoon around the chrysalis. Inclusion or crypt is a form of anti-intro-jection, a mechanism whereby the assimilation of both the illegitimate idyll and its loss is precluded. (141)

What I want to propose here is that through the writing of autobiography, traumatic memory can be momentarily disinterred from its crypt within the psyche of the marginalized subject. I argue, however, that while it might sometimes heal the marginalized subject, it runs an equal danger of reinterment in the collective psyche of the nation. It might be swallowed whole and left undigested. The only evidence of its existence left in that case is the cover of the book, which maintains the status quo—what Abraham and Torok would call "the original topography"—as the romantic, exotic, Orientalized sign of something churning beneath the surface.

To be thus "included" into the social-psychic space of the nation may be partially liberatory, but as long as this effect occurs, it cannot be fully so. Vigilance is required against the seeming comfort of its seamless surface, which has in fact incorporated so many racial traumas. Multicultural incorporation does not necessarily expiate the trauma. Insofar as Canada presents itself as a market, an exporter, and a favourable site of overseas Asian investment, it is important that its cultural workers continue to attend to both the articulable and the inarticulable that roil beneath.

CHAPTER 2

THE TIME HAS COME

Self and Community Articulations in *Colour. An Issue* and
Awakening Thunder

COLLECTIVE STRATEGIES

If the pressure that autobiography imposes on the production of a coherent "I" poses a problem for the marginalized subject at multiple points in the deployment of that "I"—from the initial assertion of "self" and "experience" all the way to the realm of reception and the production of representation and/or stereotype—then surely there must be other modes of presencing selves and communities that are not so overdetermined. In this chapter, I argue that special issues of journals offered an imperfect but productive way of bringing into presence histories, experience, and subjects who had little articulated place in the Canadian cultural landscape until that point. These collective, community-based forms of publishing made space for multiple voices to be heard. What was and is productive about the special issue as a form is that it includes a notion of the collective in its conception. Like autobiographies by minoritized subjects, special issues serve the function of "breaking the silence," creating a forum for marginalized voices to articulate histories and experiences not previously granted legitimacy or space within mainstream Canadian literature. Special issues require host journals whose regular stream of publication is necessarily interrupted by the production of "special" issues. The special issue becomes a disruption in the linear flow of a periodical's history and continues, paradoxically, to marginalize those voices even as it grants them a forum, as Ashok Mathur discusses in his editorial introduction to *Race Poetry, Eh?*, a special issue of *Prairie Fire* (8). Special issues on racialized writers or racialized writing engage the Hegelian "master/slave" dialectic that Monika Kin Gagnon has so clearly articulated in her book *Other Conundrums* on anti-racist cultural production in the 1980s and 1990s: "My sense of the contemporary dilemma is that naming racism's operations means naming oneself and others within the very terms and operations that have historically enabled racist discourses to proliferate" (22). In order to free oneself from a history of racism, one must name that history, but in so doing the old colonial binary ("white"/"of colour") and its attendant social relations are necessarily re-engaged and re-enacted. I will not go so far as to suggest that special issues on the subject of "race" are the only kind of special issue that necessarily engages this binary. But there is always something of the supplement, in Jacques Derrida's sense, that is called up in relation to the special issue; in other words, it points to that which, as "other" to the regular stream of periodical publication, is always both greater and lesser than the regular stream. Always already secondary, it bolsters the legitimacy of the "regular stream" even as it asserts its content, as Smaro Kamboureli has noted with regard to the social labour of "ethnic antholog[ies]" in relation to canonical anthologies (*Scandalous* 134). The flipside of the special issue's supplementary function, however, is that even while it is "lesser" and debased in relation to the regular stream, it is at the same time "more than" the regular stream—exalted, "special." The dedication of an entire issue to questions of racialization or marginality points to the importance of the "issue" in the moment of publication and serves as a fresh reiteration of a subject that has always been with us, albeit valenced differently, and placed in the service of older power structures. However, through a non-dialectic logic it may at the same time remain continuous with the regular stream. Significantly, these tensions can co-exist.

My objective here is not to offer a statistical survey of the relative absence or presence of racialized voices in the mainstream of Canadian literary magazine publications, though I do take it as a given that marginalization is a historical fact. What I am interested in examining, instead, is exactly what kinds of subjectivities get reproduced[1] through the deployment of the special issue as an anti-racist political tactic.[2]

In this chapter, I closely examine two special issues of the 1990s: *Awakening Thunder: Asian Canadian Women*, a special issue of *Fireweed* produced in 1991, important because it was the first Asian Canadian women's special issue; and *Colour. An Issue*, a special issue of *West Coast Line* that came out in 1994, important because of its focus on the language of race and racialization. I argue that *Awakening Thunder*, as the first Asian Canadian women's special issue, is a groundbreaking text, and further that it functions as a productive eruption of its moment (1990). In its eruptive capacity, it refigures both the past and the present by offering an ideal politics for Asian Canadian women, one that articulates itself as linear, but that actually belongs to a history of the present in a Foucauldian sense. I argue that such a rupture, though not imagined as such, can be more freeing than the linear history that its editors claim. In contrast, *Colour. An Issue* demonstrates a deep awareness of the instability of the subject, and further, a special instability for racialized subjects. This awareness, paradoxically, makes the articulation of a clear politics very difficult. The politics of *Colour. An Issue* is a politics of contingency, and such a politics has a range of pragmatic effects and consequences depending on context. Accessibility is the ideal in *Awakening Thunder*, while the breakdown and reinvention of Eurocentric, patriarchal language is the ideal at work in *Colour. An Issue*. There is a tension between them in terms of both strategy and the model of liberation each implicitly embraces. *Awakening Thunder* is utopic in the sense that it implicitly imagines a moment of arrival when no Asian woman is excluded from voice or representation. Conversely, *Colour. An Issue* implicitly refuses the possibility of arrival. I suggest that for its editors, arrival or closure offers up the danger of new violence and exclusion—not that these are things that the editors of *Awakening Thunder* embrace, but only perhaps that they don't foresee them. For both better and worse, the editors of *Awakening Thunder* do not fear "the end of history" that perhaps looms more heavily over the work of *Colour. An Issue*. The strategies of the two special issues, then, do not oppose one another, though they do different kinds of social labour.

SUBJECTIVITIES IN DOUBLE TIME: *AWAKENING THUNDER*

Fireweed's special issue *Awakening Thunder: Asian Canadian Women* was a groundbreaking text in the 1990s' moment of anti-racist cultural production and one of the earliest special issues to emerge in a decade that saw the publication of *Asian Pacific Authors on the Prairies*, a special issue of *Prairie Fire* (1997); *Prairie Asians*, a special issue of *absinthe* (1998); *Asian Canadian Writing*, a special issue of *Canadian Literature* (1999); as well as, at the beginning of the following decade, a special issue of *West Coast Line* entitled *In-Equations: can asia pacific*. The same year that *Awakening Thunder* was published, SKY Lee published *Disappearing Moon Cafe*, and Paul Wong launched the exhibition *Yellow Peril: Reconsidered*, which featured the work of twenty-five Asian Canadian artists working in contemporary media. To my mind, *Awakening Thunder* represents a (contingently) pure moment in the movement because it is uncompromising in its ideals. It also emerges at the beginning of a new wave of discussions on race and racialization that were very productive in laying the groundwork for the emergence of communities of racialized writers, artists, and activists engaged in what Cornel West called "the new cultural politics of difference" (19). The kinds of qualifications, provisions, and uncertainties (not necessarily unproductive) that mark the editorials of later special issues are absent in this one. *Awakening Thunder* was edited by five strong, intelligent, and hopeful Asian Canadian feminists—Sharon Fernandez, Amita Handa, Mona Oikawa, Milagros Paredes, and May Yee. The playfulness of the editors' biographical notes gives some hint as to the delight and empowerment experienced in the assembling of the special issue. The visual artist Sharon Fernandez, who later became the Cultural Equity Coordinator for the Canada Council for the Arts (1996–2003), is described as "a completely sexy and fascinating visual artist with a wild sense of humour and one incredibly fine tuned and youthful body" (136). Amita Handa, described soberly as "currently studying at the Ontario Institute for Studies in Education (OISE) in the sociology department" (137), subsequently completed her Ph.D. and currently teaches at the University of Toronto's Institute of Communication and Culture. She also hosts a radio show called "Masala Mixx" and DJs for clubs in Toronto. In 2003, Handa published a book called *Of Silk Saris and Mini-Skirts*, about identity construction among second-generation South Asian girls in Toronto. Mona Oikawa's biography says she "hopes to continue to explore her history, back through Toronto and British Columbia to Japan" (137). Oikawa also went on to complete her Ph.D. and is now a professor at York University, currently working on a project called Racial Formations in Settler Society: Japanese Canadians' Relationship to Colonialism. Milagros Paredes, like Amita Handa, was a graduate student at OISE at the time of *Awakening Thunder*'s publication. Her biography says she is "trying to write on her own terms." At the moment of this chapter's writing, I can only assume she has escaped to "hot, sunny, fine sand and deep blue sea beaches," as her biographical note states she wishes to do (137). May Yee taught English in the workplace at the time of *Awakening Thunder*'s publication. Her grandfather was a head-tax payer. Thoughtfully, her biographical note declares, "Her year in China is a journey from which she is still returning" (138). What is important in this context is that the editors for *Awakening Thunder* were not "professionals" at the time of their editorial work. Rather, they were students and cultural workers engaged in the new cultural politics of difference and keenly aware of its possibilities.

The editorial for *Awakening Thunder* articulates a feminist, anti-racist politics in clear, certain terms that, I argue, produce Asian Canadian women's identity in a way that is particular to that historical moment, though not necessarily "new." The editors propose a kind of silence-breaking that is invested in "resisting racist stereotypes of Asian women" (7). Through reading Himani Bannerji's text "Sound Barrier" (included in *Awakening Thunder*), the editors of this special issue recognize the difficulty of representing experience that occurs across a range of cultures and languages, particularly the difficulty of representing that experience in imperial English. They write: "We often break through that sound barrier as part of our struggle against isolation and the racist portrayal of Asian women as passive, submissive, and silent" (7). There are, then, two breakages instigated here: the breakage of a sound barrier that is shattered through the act of speaking and the breakage of a stereotype of Asian women as silent and passive.

The possibility of both breakages depends on an existing but unarticulated reality brought into the light of day through the power of a strong liberatory politics. This unarticulated reality that the editors voice is a Marxist materialist one: "We have never been silent, only ignored. The creative workers in this anthology have drawn from the courage of their foremothers' and forefathers' voices raised to protest the injustices of their lives. Our strength comes from these histories of resistance. Our work articulates this inheritance of struggle" (7). "Histories of resistance" and "inheritance of struggle," then, are the moral and epistemological foundations upon which this special issue builds validity, community belonging, and political knowledge/power. The editors specifically reference the Japanese Canadian internment and the Chinese Head Tax and Exclusion Act as founding traumas. They applaud the (at-the-time) recently achieved internment redress settlement and note the connection between the Chinese Head Tax and Exclusion Act and current unjust immigration laws. They emphasize the intertwining character of racist and sexist oppression from immigration process to domestic violence to military occupation to prostitution, particularly as the contributors to this special issue document their experiences of these oppressions. Further, these experiences are connected to racist and sexist events occurring at the moment of the issue's publication in order to recognize the continuity of the oppressions of the past with the oppressions of *Awakening Thunder*'s present. Specifically, the editors note the 1989 massacre of fourteen women at the École Polytechnique in Montreal that later became known as the Montreal Massacre; the Toronto police shooting of a Black woman called Sophia Cook; the police beating of a Chinese woman called Kay Poon; and the killing of a young Vietnamese man by Toronto skinheads. The editors also note the beginnings of inquiries into residential school abuses of Aboriginal children in Manitoba and Nova Scotia.

Bringing the texts included in this issue together in this manner makes a range of disparate experiences coherent in a way that they formerly were not. A political consciousness of the present makes coherent and legible what was not coherent or legible under earlier historical conditions of silence and invisibilization. *Awakening Thunder* actively builds community in the moments of production and publication by providing a conceptual framework through which Asian Canadian women's experiences can be understood and related to one another.

Awakening Thunder begins with an epigraph, or an invocation, ascribed to one of the editors, Sharon Fernandez:

According to Hindu tradition we are in the age of Kali.... [I]n that
tradition she has "historically" been depicted by masculine-biased com-
mentaries as cruel and horrific, a warrior sprung from the brow of Durga
to fight demonic male power and restore equilibrium. I have imagined
her in my own aspect as a creatress and nurturer: the essence of fiery and
substantial love. I feel a transformation of consciousness occurs when we
create identity through the energizing force within us. It is this creative
engagement with our organic and cultural roots that illuminates the vast
memory and connectedness of the human spirit outside of dominant
repressions. (2)

Through both this invocation and in the title itself, a dual temporality is
called into being. "Awakening" suggests both a birth and a rebirth. The
invocation of Kali calls up a mythic past beyond the reaches of patriarchal
history and, at the same time, through Fernandez's reimagining of Kali as
"creatress and nurturer," produces the present as a break from the immediate
past, even as it is connected to an imagined older (her)story. An alternative
present is called into being through the invocation of a mythic past, which
Fernandez describes as "organic and cultural." This invocation also drives
toward a hopeful future. Between the mythic past and a hopeful future,
Fernandez thus produces a community-based present, an Asian Canadian
women's reality that emerges as a kind of Butlerian "repetition with a difference" at the moment of the special issue's publication. What I am arguing,
in other words, is that the present of *Awakening Thunder*'s production and
publication is both continuous with the histories it references and discontinuous—a breakage—from those histories. There is a difference (from the
prior moment) and a possibility produced in the framing and circulation
of *Awakening Thunder* that the special issue, like the goddess Kali, creates.[3]

In its Hindu specificity, the invocation of Kali poses both a problem and
a possibility. Insofar as such an invocation is culturally specific, it hails only
those women identifying as Hindu. However, because Fernandez's Kali is a
"creatress," a mother figure from whom new kinds of women are born, she
offers the possibility for imagining new kinds of kinship—kinships that
emerge from histories of trauma, kinships based both productively and
problematically on the term "Asian," historically used in the colonial context
to marginalize, silence, and exclude.

As Gagnon has noted in *Other Conundrums*, such a reclamation always
contains a dilemma (22). There is empowerment in voicing the terms
through which one has been oppressed in order to point out that such
oppression has existed and continues to exist, and to demand re-evaluation
and restitution. On the other hand, to repeat the name of race—Asian,
Black, Native—is to reiterate old colonial relationships, to re-inscribe the

white/colour binary and deepen its power. If Kali can offer us a transformation of the name, a mother figure in whose arms cultural-activist women can coalesce, then there is a woman-centric empowerment there. I suggest that the problem of Kali's Hindu specificity is also a boon, in that she is a figure of specific South Asian cultural experience. Her centres are thus Asian and non-Western. However, insofar as her cultural signification is not pan-Asian, it seems to me that there is room for a politics and poetics of relationality, one that is present in the spirit of *Awakening Thunder*, though perhaps not fully explored or articulated. If "Asia" is a colonial cartographer's category, then the relationship among "Asians" needs another name in order to have another, freer being. For the moment of *Awakening Thunder*, that name could be "Kali." There is a brave, slightly idiosyncratic but intensely hopeful act of creation and coalition building that occurs under the name of the creatress Kali and brings at least a momentary cohesion to a range of voices that might otherwise be regarded as disparate. Under this rubric, oppressive silences are broken and Asian women fight back.

By reproducing the mythic past in feminist terms, the *Awakening Thunder* collective produces both a possibility and a reality embodied by the text itself. But what is interesting about this production of history is that it is retrospective. It emerges as much from the "reality" of the present as from the "reality" of the past. And yet, paradoxically, the "reality" of the present is produced only in this invocation of the past—the Japanese Canadian internment; the Chinese Head Tax and Exclusion Act; and all the personal, daily experiences of suffering that have been part of life in Canada for many racialized people since the nation's inception(s).[4]

In *Awakening Thunder*, this mutual production of the past and present emerges through the logic of the future anterior. The past is reconstructed so that it seems to predict and produce the present, but it is precisely the force of the present moment that makes possible such a reconstruction of the past. As Marjorie Garber explains with regard to prophecy in Shakespeare's history plays, to write about the past from the present moment, in such a way as to make the present seem an inevitable consequence of that articulation of the past, gives the text an almost mystical sense of legitimacy (307–08). In Shakespeare's history plays, a national, patriarchal history is validated in this way. I argue that, in the case of *Awakening Thunder*, subaltern histories can also be validated. In both cases, however, the logic of the future anterior is a logic that leaks: it pokes holes in the seamlessness of national histories and opens potentially liberatory (but also potentially violent) gaps for subaltern ones.

Indeed, as Homi Bhabha has taught us, alternative temporalities can produce moments of liberation. The haunted temporalities lived by subjects of trauma are markedly different from official history's linear temporality. Bhabha writes:

> [T]o dwell "in the beyond" is also … to be part of a revisionary time, a return to the present to redescribe our cultural contemporaneity; to reinscribe our human, historic commonality; *to touch the future on its hither side.*…
>
> The borderline work of culture demands an encounter with "newness" that is not part of the continuum of past and present. It creates a sense of the new as an insurgent act of cultural translation. Such art does not merely recall the past as social cause or aesthetic precedent; it renews the past, refiguring it as a contingent "in-between" space, that innovates and interrupts the performance of the present. The "past-present" becomes part of the necessity, not the nostalgia, of living. (*Location* 7)

Awakening Thunder illustrates the cultural productivity of such an encounter with "newness." Its voices are the voices of Bhabha's "past-present," erupting and diminishing through the non-linear logic of the haunted "beyond."

The politics produced in *Awakening Thunder* are thus both pragmatic and programmatic, and quite historically specific. The editors actively set out criteria for selection and decide that the works they include ought to

> reflect the importance of communicating our common experiences as Asian women. We also looked for accessibility of language and image, and pieces that were written from a critical perspective free of sexism, racism, classism and heterosexism. While in their entirety, these selections show our common bonds, we were ultimately drawn to work that clearly conveyed the writer's or artist's presence, her uniqueness, her history. (6)

While emphasis is placed on common experience, the tension between the collective and the individual is highlighted through the notion of the writer's "presence" and "uniqueness." There is a tension in that historical moment between, on the one hand, the Enlightenment and Western democratic ideal of individuality and, on the other, an ideal of social interconnectivity and sisterly solidarity that is rooted in class struggle. Most cannily, there is also a comprehension and a claiming of the multiple possibilities inherent in the term "Asian women." The editors recognize it at once as a naturalized "race" category that continues to have contemporary cultural currency, a racist appellation that has made those marked as "Asian women" the objects of racism, colonialism, and patriarchy, and at the same time as a label that can be reclaimed for the purposes of self-empowerment.

While these different modes of the term's circulation are recognized in the editorial, the temporal zone of this special issue is one in which reclamation is emphasized.[5] The "awakened thunder" signals, then, a breaking of silence in order to recognize a common bond for the purposes of self-empowerment. Tied to a mythic past, this politics emerges specifically, as I have said, from a particular moment in the late 1980s and early 1990s in which the possibility and reality of empowerment are simultaneously produced, making room for the articulation of histories and politics for which there were no words and no forum in the contiguously previous moment. Arguably, however, such eruptions have occurred at other historical moments that may or may not be read as causally related to this one. Without official state histories to bestow the appearance of linearity, these moments of eruption belong to fragmented time. In the language of psychoanalysis, they are returns of the repressed. In performance theory terms, they are repetitions with a difference. For a generation of artists, writers, and activists raised under Trudeau's multiculturalism, the possibilities of articulation and thus self-fashioning mark a clear break from the whitewash of the previous era. Thus, whether or not this moment is "new," it has the appearance and feel of newness for those who engage it. With newness goes an attendant risk, for through the articulation of injustice one might gain entry into the public life of the state but, alternately, or additionally, one might be further marginalized. In the 1990s, racialized artists, writers, and critics recognized the timeliness of their work as being "in fashion." Many worried about what would happen to their work and their newfound place in the public eye when they were no longer the "flavour of the month."

The problem of reclaiming the racist name, then, is not solved by *Awakening Thunder*. *Awakening Thunder* embraces the liberatory power produced in the oppositional aspect of naming. It does not concern itself with the problem of re-inscription. I suggest, in fact, that part of what makes the moment of *Awakening Thunder* both radical and productive is precisely its refusal to address the re-inscribing aspect of the white/of colour dialectic. In the "in-between" time of *Awakening Thunder*, the problem of re-inscription does not exist.

The problem is, of course, that in the outside time of right-wing populist discourse, this re-inscribing aspect is the only aspect that exists. The charge of racism against whites, or "reverse-racism" that was to emerge with such force during the Writing Thru Race conference, had not yet arrived at the fullness of its rhetorical power in the moment of *Awakening Thunder*, though that rhetoric and the storm clouds that accompanied it were certainly gathering in that same (linear) historical moment.

While the tension between liberatory naming and the re-inscription of the racist name, as well as the attendant re-inscription of old colonial relationships, is not engaged in *Awakening Thunder*, what is engaged are smaller movements within the liberatory possibilities of naming difference. Gilles Deleuze offers us another, less dialectic, way of thinking about difference. For him, identity is never selfsame, but always differing within itself. If change does not occur in the grand, synthetic steps but rather in smaller, less predictable ones, through the interplay of small differences within a time of repetition, then the conundrum that Gagnon describes in *Other Conundrums* need not be so determining. John Rajchman, in "Diagram and Diagnosis," suggests:

> A "history of the present" is a history of the portion of the past that we don't see is still with us. Thus it involves a concept of historical time that is not linear and is not completely given to consciousness, memory, commemoration. But Deleuze thought it involved something more—a relation to the future. He would put it this way: "Not to predict, but to be attentive to the unknown that is knocking at the door." It was this relation to the future that made the "present," whose history Foucault proposed, something untimely, creative, experimental. (47)

I read certain special issues, such as *Awakening Thunder*, as "histories of the present" that recuperate, however they can, a marginalized past for the purposes of opening out onto a more hopeful, open-ended future.

EDITORIAL STRATEGY

As the co-editors of *Colour. An Issue* (1994), a special issue of *West Coast Line*, Roy Miki and Fred Wah constituted a very different kind of editorial team from the team that assembled *Awakening Thunder*. At the time of *Colour. An Issue*'s publication, both were professors—Miki at Simon Fraser University, Wah at the University of Calgary. *Colour. An Issue* was published six years after the Japanese Canadian redress agreement, for which Miki and a small group of committed activists had worked incredibly hard. By the time of *Colour. An Issue*'s publication, Miki already had a strong record of publication behind him, including two poetry books (*Random Access File* and *Saving Face*), *Justice in Our Time* (an account of the Japanese Canadian redress movement, co-authored with Cassandra Kobayashi), *Pacific Windows* (an edited collection of the late Roy Kiyooka's poetry), and *Meanwhile: The Critical Writings of bp nichol* (also an edited collection). Similarly, Wah was an impressively accomplished writer at the time of the special issue's publication, with sixteen poetry books to his credit, including the

Governor General's Award–winning volume *Waiting for Saskatchewan*, as well as numerous chapbooks, broadsides, and articles. Interestingly, the contributors' notes for *Colour. An Issue* do not provide information about either of them. If *Awakening Thunder* can be characterized as emerging from a youthful, streetwise quickness, *Colour. An Issue* seems to emerge from an attentive sense of responsibility backed by the wisdom of experience. It is probably overdeterministic to suggest that *Colour. An Issue* takes its cue from *Awakening Thunder*, but I think it is important to note that it was graduate students and unestablished artists and cultural workers who took the early risks in the anti-racist movement of the 1980s and 1990s wave.

Rather than declaring a politics, as *Awakening Thunder* did, *Colour. An Issue* lays its parameters a lot more contingently, without driving toward a synthesis, a liberated "end of history" or "revolution." Rather, its (very short) preface foregrounds the utterance of "race" as a moment of breakage, a moment at which the speech of linear history is radically disrupted, and reduced to meaningless noise:

> "Race"—that four letter word, making a headway on visibility: the zone of the body scanned by surveillance monitors. The squawking of ruffled feathers shakes loose the tiles which spill into the public squares. There is nothing more apparent, and nothing more transparent, than the signs of "race" that circulate in the everyday lives of people of colour. Drop it into most public conversations on writing, culture and representation and the whole mainstream hall shudders, as the shutters come down and all the mechanisms of power fill up the stuttering spaces with the discourse of muzak muzak muzak. (Miki and Wah 5)

As in *Awakening Thunder* the racialized body remains in focus, but it is the body under surveillance, the body already drawn into signification as a site of contention that holds the editors' attention here. "Race" is a dirty word, a swear word, that brings on stuttering and empty mall music in the halls of power. What is repeated in the stutter, or in the mechanical blandification of the music of bygone times? The racialized body, the visible body "of colour" remains in the panoptic eye (of the state or the shopping mall), as a disruption in the flow of unmarked, "colourless" bodies. But articulation of this difference is unacceptable, especially when that articulation emerges from the mouths (or pens) of the wrong bodies.

Through the swear word "race," as much a promise as a curse, the language of the colonial moment returns with a difference and a vengeance. Those against whom it was applied, as I have described in relation to *Awakening Thunder*, have produced a new kind of power in its redeployment. Time is out of joint. The empire is haunted by the ghosts of its own violence. But the ghosts (of colour) have to live out the haunting if we are to be empowered by it. And this living out is no easy task.

Colour. An Issue lacks the optimism of *Awakening Thunder*. But it is also less prescriptive. "Colour," unlike "Asian women" (in the contexts of the respective issues), is not an identity, or a politics. While *Awakening Thunder* emphasizes set criteria—common experience; accessibility of language; critical perspectives; and absence of racism, classism, and heterosexism (6)— *Colour. An Issue* is consciously contingent. "Colour" is deployed as an open-ended term around which thinking, being, and writing coalesce:

> *Colour. An Issue* is not an anthology, a collection of texts that have been selected, arranged and edited into a "whole" that advances the coherence of the collectivity. The methodology adopted proposes an open-ended process that could yield much more provisional patterns of interconnections for the diverse materials included. (5)

One could, of course, argue that the refusal to set criteria is a kind of setting of criteria and that the refusal to select is actually a kind of selection. In the historical moment of this text, as poststructural as it is postcolonial,[6] it is impossible to ignore the ways in which the privileges of class, education, access—all those things that *Awakening Thunder* is so conscious of and determined to undo—still shape any text, "edited" or not. However, the drive toward contingency is very different from the drive toward common experience. While *Awakening Thunder* emphasizes commonality, specifically in the experience of race and gender oppression, *Colour. An Issue* emphasizes diversity and "provisional patterns." Its editors recognize profoundly the incompleteness of conversations about race, indeed the fact that the power of these conversations lies precisely in their incompleteness.

I have been discussing these two texts comparatively not in order to ascertain whether one organizational strategy is "better" than the other but rather to ask how they work, both separately and together, within practices of community separated by (a short) time and (a short) geographical distance, but nonetheless closely related in terms of their political and imaginative projects.

As the historically prior text, *Awakening Thunder* could be said to lay groundwork. The pieces included in this special issue tend to be biographical or autobiographical in nature, and emphasize experiences of oppression based on race, class, gender, and sexuality. Formally, the fiction included in the issue follows realist literary conventions; the poetry tends to be lyric in form; the essay pieces strive for clarity and transparency. The contributions include, for instance, an oral history from the then-in-progress book project

Voices of Chinese Women; "Safer Sex in Santa Cruz," Mona Oikawa's delight-ful account of an Asian lesbian retreat in California; Kaushalya Bannerji's poem, "Remembrance Day: For Anthony Griffin age 19 murdered Novem-ber 11/87 Montreal Canada"; and "English Classes for Immigrant Women: A Feminist Organizing Tool," an extraordinary account by an immigrant academic woman, Pramila Aggarwal, of how she worked with immigrant women at a pizza crust factory to organize for better working conditions. The linguistic transparency of these works is precisely what gives them their impact and their liberatory power.

Indeed, one of the stated criteria for inclusion in the issue is "accessibil-ity." The issue and its editors are not directly critical of formal innovation. However, what is not questioned in the production of this issue are the ways in which literary conventions tend to reproduce existing power structures in language. There is a real tension, then, between the practice of writing and the practice of disrupting white supremacist norms in the world of work and everyday life.

In a poem called "Grief" in *Awakening Thunder*, Kim-Man Chan writes:

Loneliness
A sense of not belonging
A sense of not being at home
A need to talk to somebody
Who would understand me
A need to be appreciated
For what I am, and where I came from.

Neither here nor there,
Not working class, not middle class.
Children of a proprietor
But lived in a storeroom,
Slept under table, worked seven days a week,
Scrambled money for groceries—ten apples, ten oranges ...
Member of the petty bourgeois?
A text-book case of the integrated structures
Of patriarchy and capitalism? (106)

Chan, we are told in the biography section of this special issue, is from Hong Kong. She came as a visa student to Canada and, at the time of publication, worked as an English instructor with immigrant workers. She has not gone on to write books; she is not a known figure in Asian Canadian literature.

(Does this mean she is less commodified or commodifiable?) Whether the writing is "good" or "bad," the "I" asserted here is full of pathos. A silence has been broken. The poem "Grief" fits perfectly the criteria laid out in the editorial—it is accessible, it is free of racism, sexism, classism, and heterosexism. It expresses a unique history and at the same time recognizes common experience. As such, it works in support of the social/political stance taken by the editors. In a sense, its publication, if not its writing, becomes an inscription as much of the editors' agency as of the author's own.

As Kamboureli notes in her discussion of ethnic anthologies, however, writing that foregrounds immigrant experience without full attention to language and form raises the question of how we are to understand such work in literary terms (*Scandalous* 150). Kamboureli suggests such work, in fact, fulfils the expectations and funding criteria of government officials by presenting the voices of racialized subjects in the form they expect—that is, in mimicry of accepted colonial form and with content that confirms what the colonizer already expects of the colonized (151). As such, poems like Chan's serve to reinforce the stereotypes of the mainstream and, in so doing, undermine the liberatory project they appear, at the first pass, to support. Kamboureli suggests that such work raises the question of whose aesthetic values are reproduced in such instances. Her argument echoes the point I make in Chapter 1 in which I consider this problem in relation to autobiography by racialized writers. There, I conclude that the articulation of experience is an important step in the marginalized subject's entry into subjecthood and citizenship, but that the texts produced invariably function to fold the subject in question rapidly back into the containing norms of the state. Such texts, especially when actively marketed as objects of white atonement, give the state and its mainstream citizenry the appearance of having made up for the violence of the past, even as such violence continues, unremarked upon, in the present.

The remaining eight stanzas of Chan's poem go on to document the tortured emotional state of a young immigrant woman whose family struggles for pride as much as for connection among its members. Good or bad, these stanzas are wrenching. However, as much as the poem's speaker is a "textbook case" of immigrant misery, the poem's structure is a "textbook case" of lyric mimicry, complete with capitalized letters to begin each line and a culturally non-specific, mimetically universal "I" who outpours her grief:

> A hand on my hair, long long time ago.
> Tears streaming wildly down my face as I write this,
> At twenty-three supposedly a grown woman. (107)

For me, in cold critical mode, the poignancy of Chan's expression is undermined by the knowledge of the state-preserving service to which this poem and others like it are routinely put, as in fact are the subjects who produce these heart-rending, confessional texts. The cultural bind of the text is as painful as the text itself. But the textual moment, like the critical moment, matters. I recognize here that the cathartic and community building power of such texts can sometimes outweigh the cold critic's concern or even the inevitable return to state containment that regularly occurs with regard to such texts.

While *Awakening Thunder* occurs at a specific moment in history—1990—I would argue that its temporality can erupt unexpectedly at any time and produce important and necessary catharsis and community for individuals deeply in need of it. I am conscious of my politically liberal use of the word "individual" here; confessional lyric poems like Chan's are about the production of Western liberal subjectivity—but always with a supplemental difference that, as I argued in the last chapter in relation to the poetry of Evelyn Lau, necessarily produces the need to write more, since the racialized subject writing from a lyric location can never have the originary citizenship bestowed on the nation's founding races.

The "I" of Mark Nakada's "marginalia" in *Colour. An Issue* expresses similar dislocations to Kim-Man Chan's, but these are explicitly integrated into the formal structure of the poem.

```
cant feel how this sand   place (a beach   is an area where   if not for
greed                                                              lust
                                                                   land
only                                                               power
nine                                                          dominance
i pick                                                          c. 1609
up a                                                           a chance
handfull                                                       movement
of sand                           e                              escape
these                             g                              denial
okinawans                          a                          forgetting
(relatives to      here eh            u                         i might
what                              g                                have
speak to                          n                                been
me                    l                    a                     margin
in my                 u                    l                        the
```

```
own lost          f                              language
tongue            e                              almost
i slowly          s                              mine
spill my          u                              can
grains                                           never
back into                     e                  really be
the foreign                 r                    but a
beach                     o                       canadian
they                    m                         nonsense
wait
for me to answer   but i cant    perhaps my unintelligible okinawan
words                                             are a (29)
```

Nakada's consciousness of the formal rules that conventionally govern a page of poetry allows him to deliberately place his words in the margins. He offers breakages in the seamlessness of the lyric "I." The poem's structure reproduces, for the reader, its speaker's struggle with Okinawan language and the frustration of not being able to communicate with his Okinawan relatives. The text, then, is conscious of the histories of colonialism and displacement that lead to the way English rolls off Nakada's tongue.

It may be that Nakada means to deride texts like Chan's with his empty pointer "more useful language" running backwards up the centre of the page, unsettling further the reader's capacity to register sense in his text. It takes slow and careful puzzling to work out the fact that the apparently random letters in the centre of the page say "more useful language." In this way, the reader is confounded by Nakada's language in ways that parallel the poet's unsettling experience of being confounded by speakers of his mother tongue.

Like Chan, Nakada recognizes his own marginalization. But the structure of his poem also recognizes a kind of training that Chan may have also encountered, although in all likelihood has not. So she places her lyric language in the centre of the page, following lyric convention. Nakada's poem is more "successful" than Chan's in the sense that it disrupts the linearity of official English and presses its reader into a reading experience that parallels the speaker's experience and deployment of his two fraught tongues—Okinawan and English. The temporality of its social usefulness is thus different. If Chan's text is an early disruptive rumble of thunder (and here I mean "early" not just in the sense of linear time but in the sense of the temporality of engagement with "race" issues in a racist society), Nakada's belongs to a moment of contemplating "colour" as "an issue." It resists the reincorporation into state understanding that Chan's falls easily prey to.

Formally, one might read Nakada's and Chan's texts as oppositional to one another. But in the sense of "common bonds" (6) that the editors of *Awakening Thunder* value, these are ally texts. It would be interesting to pursue a politics of coalition building between or among these writing practices in order to understand what their relationship can be to one another. They might speak differently to one another than they do to the centres that they address. It would also be worth asking what might happen to those centres if marginal texts ceased to address them but addressed one another instead.

Formal innovation does not make Nakada's text any less lyric than Chan's. In its desire for an "I," Nakada's poem might be thought of as a lyric/anti-lyric in the sense that Douglas Barbour describes—"lyric straining against itself" (19), blasting out of tradition even as it repeats it. What is interesting about both poems is the production of an excess to identity, that element that identity cannot name—the "evacuated subject" Miki describes in *Broken Entries*.[7] The "more useful language" of Nakada's poem or the "neither here nor there" of Chan's might just as easily be a language that articulates the inarticulable void Miki describes. "More useful language" and "neither here nor there," in other words, point to an impossible text, a magical text that frees the marginalized subject from the name of her or his oppression, a text that Chow might posit as existing at the moment of the racist name's disappearance. Contemplating the problem and the possibility of reclaiming the racist name, which both frees the racialized subject from silence and re-inscribes the dialectic relationship between "colour" and whiteness, Chow concludes in "Ethics After Idealism" that the "void," that is, the site of inarticulation that exists in excess of the possibilities of articulation, is a place of hope and possibility (54). In the present imperfect, in which we are always inheritors of colonial history, we cling to the name of race as our only out—even as it produces and reproduces melancholy subjects like the speaker in Chan's "Grief." The magic time that I envision here is a moment when we escape the bonds of racist history and thus no longer need the name of race. This is, of course, the moment that mainstream Canada imagines we already occupy, not understanding or not wanting to acknowledge how the traumatic past roils beneath the surface. It is thus an impossible time that can never arrive in the linear order of national history, and yet a time that those of us who still cling to some utopic impulse still long for because resignation and cynicism are even less appealing options. If the mimetic humanist feeling in "Grief" is also a Marxist feminist grief, then I claim a moment of strategic individualism in the early time of *Awakening Thunder*.

In *The Cultural Politics of Emotion*, Sarah Ahmed makes a useful distinction between the fetishization of the wound that leads so easily to its commoditization, on the one hand, and the need for testimony in order to

"break the seal of the past" (33) and mobilize pain into political action, on
the other. It seems to me that both "Grief" and "marginalia" do this work. In
more complex ways, so do the special issues that they appear in.

What if Nakada's "more useful language" were not the language of
oppression at all but a liberatory language belonging to an alternative temporality—language from the future for which one can leave only a blank
space, a space that waits? The unknown knocks at the door. The phrase "here,
eh" indicates at once a circumscribed national and a much more open-ended
site of possibility. As a distinctly "Canadian" interjection, "eh" locates "here"
as a tightly delineated (white) national space. But "eh" is also an interjection
of uncertainty, a sort of verbal question mark. "Here" is thrown into contest.
It is open-ended. It could mean anything and contain anyone, even someone
with such a hybrid body and experience as Nakada—or Chan. Nakada does
not specify whether "here" is also "now." The phrase "more useful language"
ironizes the position of the master tongue, but it does not close that discourse off as the only possible discourse that might fill in the blank. I want
to suggest here that the ontology of the future does not include "I": rather,
it conceives of "I" as a much more open container than an Enlightenment
humanist ideology might allow.

As co-editors, Miki and Wah are more interested in "you" and "we," but
these are pronouns that oscillate, that jump from body to body depending
on the moment:

> Or "Colour" with a "you." How "we" has to figure it out. How some of
> us can't make a move without thinking it. How some of you never think
> it, don't have to, don't even bother because it is no bother to you. How
> some have to double-think it, hyphenate it, dilute it, disappear into it.
> Yellow on the inside, white on the outside. Invisible. Except for a name,
> a history, a dream, a resonance, a trace taste that becomes a hunger, a
> deep need, to spit it out. (*Colour. An Issue* 5)

Because it includes the letter "u," the Canadian spelling of "colour" can be
read as more open to relation than the U.S. spelling of "color." "U" sounds
like "you"—the "Other." But the "u" whom the co-editors refer to is a hostile
"u," a "u" with a colonial history and continuing white privilege that prevent
it from seeing the marginalized histories and bodies that hold it up. Not that
the United States is without its colonial or its neo-imperial masters. But to
embed the master into "race" ("colour") is to recognize the deep intertwining
of the two concepts. Thus "we" has no natural being; it is a subject position
to be occupied rhetorically in order to work out power differences that are
nonetheless highly material. "You" is embedded in colour but never thinks of

it; it is the normalized white universal. But "you" is other to the speaker. This is a turn from its habitual usage in the (neo-)colonial sense that it is usually the white speaker addressing the brown "Other." Subjectivity and power bounce through the pronouns "I," "you," and "we" in a way that destabilizes all three. In the movement of pronouns through a range of bodies, those that are racialized and those that go unmarked, the social relationships of those bodies are reorganized. The "you" of privilege is drawn out of blindness, is made to recognize its own privilege, is suddenly held responsible. "You" is used to point out the ways in which positions of power are not recognized as such but allowed to pass as normal. Through this usage, power relations are made manifest. By destabilizing the assumed gender, race, and class of the speaker, co-editors Miki and Wah call a different kind of "I" or "i" into being, or rather into becoming, in ways that are hopeful and productively incomplete.

STRATEGY'S TIMING

The cultural moment of *Awakening Thunder*'s publication was one that emphasized the historical as a mode of legitimation and empowerment. Indeed, the notion of the historical is something that is repeatedly recognized in the editorial itself: "Many of the stories and articles in this issue of *Fireweed* show how the histories of Asian women and men are also part of the history of colonialism" (8). And later, referring to eruptions of violence against women and people of colour near the time of publication, the editors write: "Although these events are being portrayed as 'isolated incidents' by those in power, we know they are all interconnected as part of the long history of racism in this country" (8). The liberatory model proposed is one that recuperates history for the purposes of empowerment. In naming the violence that has been directed against racialized subjects, the editorial sees that liberatory power lies in testimony. To the extent that testimony can rapidly be fetishized and consumed, *Awakening Thunder* requires, indeed demands, an audience able to inhabit the uncomfortable but potentially liberatory time/space of Fernandez's Kali.

The future of *Colour. An Issue* is not liberation or revolution but rather possibility: "[T]his 'issue' is a transitional zone that functions, in this instance not as a showcase but as a catalytic kindling of marginalized discourse, imagined possibilities in language and thought—the intent of a dialogue, a forum of diversity, finally, shared" (5). By including "issue" in the title itself, *Colour. An Issue* foregrounds its own situation in fleeting time, in the sense of being just one issue in the flow of *West Coast Line*. By locating itself within the genre of special issues, it declares its solidarity with other special issues.

like *Awakening Thunder* and the concomitant politics of contingency that recognizes the issue's "special status." But further, "issue" implies an orientation toward the future, as in "to issue forth." It also offers "issue" in the sense of "offspring": a kind of child, full of hope, the intellectual and creative issue of communities cross-fertilizing. And of course, "issue" invites controversy. "Colour," unlike "Asian," is not an identity, in spite of that moment's preferred terminology for the racialized—"person of colour." It is a conundrum, a problematic, and, as Wah and Miki write, a kind of kindling to fuel the flame of that moment's already burning politics.

These two issues, then, emerge from different moments within the anti-racist movement, which might account for some of the differences in their orientation toward politics and the future. Further, while *Fireweed* is a Toronto-based feminist magazine with Marxist feminist underpinnings, *West Coast Line*, with its roots in the critical journal *West Coast Review* and the experimental-poetics journal *Line*, tends toward embracing open-ended experimentation. If there is tension between the two special issues, it is marked by their classed, gendered, and geographic differences. Here are a few productive questions: To what extent does desire for recognition by the centre emerge from the fact of living at the centre of the nation? To what extent does the rush into a more fragmented, fleeting kind of liberation belong to an already established Western dream of the ever-expanding frontier? To what extent is literary experimentation a realm of masculinist/academic discourse? To what extent does the need for the immediacy of accessibility override the long-term uncertainty of time invested in the experimental and the contingent? These are highly ideological questions that I could not possibly begin to answer here, except perhaps by way of saying that a linguistic strategy for speaking into silence depends on the moment in both linear and haunted time, as well as on the intentions of the speaker. That one issue occurs later in the linear historical trajectory than the other, however, is not a coincidence. The contingent and open-ended require a prior certainty and idealism to posit themselves against.

I would like to suggest, in conclusion, that between the time of *Awakening Thunder* and the time of *Colour. An Issue*, the shift in the capacity of the subject to articulate experience parallels a shift on the global stage, in which the power of subaltern discourse to bring about liberatory change becomes incorporated into the power of neoliberal capital to control international markets and the flows of subjectivities and bodies that follow those markets. The steer away from the lyrically mimetic "I" to the shifting "i"-as-container parallels a shift in the capacity for anti-racist work to draw marginalized subjects into the nation as full citizens. To the extent that citizenship in liberal democratic states depends on the coherent ego of the lyric "I" to declare allegiance, mark a ballot, and take on civic duty, the recognition that no real freedom lies there complicates matters, as does the evacuation of the power of citizens by neoliberalism in the same moment. In its "special" status, the special issue both interrupts and continues the regular flow of journal publishing. It hails its audience slightly differently. In so doing, it opens the possibility for journals to take alternative directions. Thunder could (re)awaken at any moment. "Colour" continues to issue possibility in the imperfect present before the disappearance of the name of race.

CHAPTER 3

ROMANCING THE ANTHOLOGY
Supplement, Relation, and Community Production

NEOLIBERALISM AND CULTURAL CAPITAL

A seldom queried historical fact of the 1980s and 1990s is that its forms of anti-racism arise beside the economic project of neoliberalism with its commitments to privatization, "free" trade, and economic deregulation. In an era marked by the penetration of capital more deeply than ever before into what theorists of biopolitics call "life itself," the fraught concept of race becomes weighted and freighted in ways that are profoundly tied to the political and economic conditions of that moment. What Foucault recognized as a category tied to "blood" under the power of the old sovereign has returned as a biopolitical category to be penetrated by the new forms of management under high capital.

Concerned about the reification of race and the inward gaze of racialized communities in the United States and Britain, Paul Gilroy takes up the term "privatization" in the following passage. He is concerned about the rapper Ice Cube's call for a separation between whites and blacks, and a broader call in diasporic African communities for black men to take responsibility in family contexts. Gilroy writes:

> Fatherhood becomes the principal means of community reconstruction. Its primary characteristic is not tenderness, insight, patience, love, sympathy, or care but strength— preferably the same variety that is currently lacking from the actions of those "spineless" black leaders who "took their eyes from the prize in the 70s" and, again according to [Ice] Cube, committed the grave mistake of "trying to make the public schools better instead of building our own schools." This remark reveals the logic of privatization operating here. Racial identity is being privatized in exactly the same way as [Ice Cube thinks] education should be. The motif of withdrawal—civic and interpersonal—governs this new form of segregation being proposed. (Gilroy 216)

What is important for the purposes of this chapter is Gilroy's recognition that anti-racist politics can and do sometimes work through the logic of privatization. Further, though the focus of this book is Asian Canadian literature, its overlaps, debts, and relationships to critical work in Black Atlantic, Black British, or African American contexts is closer than we might first imagine, as Lily Cho articulates in her article "Asian Canadian Futures: Diasporic Passages and the Routes of Indenture."

John Guillory, writing in the context of the canon debates, suggests that the (U.S.) right wing has already won an ideological war if the public is made to understand as normative an equal valencing of cultural communities as though they were market commodities, and not profoundly related to one another and marked by specific power imbalances and specific forms of difference that are not necessarily commensurate with one another. He fears that cultural unities have become cultural units that hide their internal conflicts and are inadvertently packaged by their members as market ready and available for consumption:

> There is no question that cultural unities, especially unities in opposition have political effects, that the concept and experience of "solidarity" is essential to any struggle. But the pedagogic imaginary within which the critique of the canon has been advanced is at once in excess of that solidarity, because it constructs out of its alternative canon/syllabus/ list a culture (of women writers, or Afro-American writers, etc.) more homogenous that it actually is, and in defect of that solidarity, because the image of cultural homogeneity it disseminates is only an image for those who consume it in the university, where it is consumed *as* an image." (Guillory, *Cultural Capital* 37)

Though neither Gilroy nor Guillory focus their arguments on the market as such, their analyses of race and canonicity are useful for this discussion because neoliberalism provides the economic backdrop against which they write.

In a Canadian context, Daniel Coleman and Donald Goellnicht see racial categories—African Canadian, Asian Canadian, and Native Canadian—as already institutionalized (1), productively so in the sense that institutionalization gives younger scholars ground to stand on. But they also recognize institutionalization as a problem in the sense that it reifies categories that are constructed and historically contingent (19).

The master/slave contradiction that I laid out in the Introduction via Hegel, Fanon, and Gagnon manifests historically in the 1980s and 1990s in the sense that the construction of communities around the idea of race creates a material positivity at the site of what we know to be a relational construction. Coleman and Goellnicht cite Gayatri Spivak's famous formulation "strategic essentialism" in which Spivak recognizes that it is sometimes politically expedient to temporarily posit as natural that which we know to be constructed. For me, Judith Butler's notion of identities sedimented through performative iteration and repetition in language helpfully illustrates how constructed identities become experienced and embodied "realities." However, a specific danger arises in the 1980s and 1990s moment because it is a moment in which high finance and the commodity are bitingly salient as both economic and cultural presences. Strategic essentialism, reification, institutionalization, and other kinds of solidification tend towards commodification in ways that they might not otherwise. It seems important to me to ask what kinds of essentialisms really are strategic, and if they are strategic, then to what ends? For indeed, if it is the case that the commodity form is the only positivity that survives under neoliberalism, then it becomes the only form through which to retain and articulate recently unearthed histories. Nonetheless, in copping to the commodity form, scholars, artists, and writers need to be aware of what gets lost.

Coleman and Goellnicht argue the institutions of race—for them, "Native Canadian," "Asian Canadian," and "African Canadian"—function as absolutisms on the surface, absolutisms that cannot hold because as soon as one scratches that surface, internal diversity and intra-community coalition work immediately become evident (22). I agree, but it seems important to recognize that surface absolutisms have a great deal of cultural power in our contemporary moment, and internal diversities and intra-community coalition are not particularly prioritized or visible unless they are made so. John Guillory is concerned that U.S. society is increasingly divided into constituencies that thrive on their own internal culture and build walls that shut out everyone else, to the point that no one constituency can meaningfully communicate with any other (*Cultural Capital* 26). Writing in the context of university culture and the usefulness of the school, Guillory solves the "polity" problem by arguing for a "mildly coercive" "unitary" education for all (52), in which "*everyone* has a right of access to cultural works" (56; emphasis in original). Like a good liberal, he struggles mightily to reconcile a desire for the universal, against an attentive recognition that difference and power imbalance exist and must be attended to: "There is not, and should not be, one national culture, but there is, and there should be, one educational system" (52). What he neither acknowledges nor addresses is the problem that students and professors come to the practice of knowledge from embodied histories, as I discussed in the Introduction, that fundamentally shape the way they engage. Guillory proposes a "distribution of cultural capital" (54) to replace pluralist critique. He uses the term "cultural capital" rather than "canon," presumably because he means something more inclusive than "canon" by it, careful though he is to recognize that texts directly represent neither communities nor values as such. There are times, however, when he equates them: "Individual works are taken up into this system (preserved, disseminated, taught) and confront their receptors first as canonical, as cultural capital" (56). In making this equation, Guillory reveals his faith in institutions, or "schools" as he calls them, to perpetuate if not "the best of all that has been thought and said" (Arnold viii) then at least "a specific *relation* to culture" (*Cultural Capital* 56; emphasis in original). He does not have an answer for how this relation might come about, acknowledging that the literary syllabus's claim to universality has meant in practice that it has taken on the universalization of "every specific system of domination," thus opening it to "every specific force of resistance" (80–81). Writing in a U.S. context, he argues that composition takes on the universalizing function within a postmodern moment in which trained elites guiding their nations toward emancipation are no longer the focus. Instead, those elites have been replaced by management-oriented students studying to acceptably fill pragmatic posts required by capitalist institutions (82). I find Guillory's diagnosis of the "polity" problem to be compelling, though his solution does not fully grasp the structural and embodied restrictions to the universal access he calls for. Further, as Janice Newson has recently recognized in a feminist context:

> [I]mportant to grasp is that corporatization is not only a matter of external agents, such as private-sector businesses, reaching into universities to gain access to their intellectual resources. Rather, corporatization is a *two-way*, outside-in/inside-out process. Universities ... adopt a corporate-like modus operandi, using their human resources, intellectual property and material facilities to compete with one another to increase their market share of research dollars and student tuitions.... Corporatization is best understood in terms of complex realignments, in the *social relations* of academic work. (45; italics in original)

What is important in Newson's mind is the recognition that marginalized groups, even as they struggle for things like equal representation and social justice, may inadvertently find themselves participating in economic processes they would not necessarily agree with if they were to consider them clearly.

My project here, then, is to further and articulate what Asian Canadian literature is and can be in a neoliberal, institutionalizing moment. Specifically, I am interested in retaining the work of social justice, coalition building, difference, and power analysis that has historically occurred under an Asian Canadian umbrella among others. I fear both the commodification and the depoliticization of the term. I am concerned about co-optation of its community-based and anti-institutionalizing work through a politics of incorporation, as Scott Toguri McFarlane recognized early in his essay "The Haunt of Race." So, for instance, it is important to recognize that Jan Brown's outrage at the use of Department of Canadian Heritage monies to fund Writing Thru Race was about the fact that Heritage's funds were public funds and not a judgement of the incorrect perception that the conference "excluded whites" as Robert Fulford so vehemently pronounced in the *Globe and Mail*. (I discuss this more specifically in my Conclusion.) Through the logic of neoliberal backlash, a politics of contingency is a racist politics. But this is only a problem insofar as it is publicly funded; for Brown, implicitly, it would be fine under privately funded circumstances. Thus, under neoliberalism, to understand justice categories as justice categories rather than market demographics is not enough. Newson notes the ways in which universities use even the idea of justice as a marketing tool:

> What to make ... of the fact that university administrations were appropriating the successes of women's activism?... Is it possible ... that the advances made in the 1970s and 1980s to increase the presence and influence of women in academia have become assets to university administrations, as they respond to increasing demands to pursue commercial and entrepreneurial success? (47)

I argue that one of the ways that justice-minded people, both inside and outside the university, can undermine the commodification of justice work is by recognizing their relation to one another. It is important that this happen across constituencies, not triangulated through whiteness, or through any form of hegemonic power masquerading as normative universality. We must not lose the powerful politics of difference inaugurated by Cornel West and others in the 1980s and 1990s. We need to be aware of the problem of polity as Guillory articulates it, but a return to the old (white) normative universality is not a solution precisely because it cops to Eurocentric norms. What is necessary, I argue, is the genealogical production of relation that makes room for multiple histories and seeks overlap and compatibility without erasing real historical difference.

To turn then to the 1980s and 1990s moment, in which the anthology form proliferated, I argue that anthologies, though they appeared to produce identities, were actually profoundly dependent on relation across categories to make meaning and be understood. As Kamboureli argues in relation to ethnic anthologies:

The anthologizing of ethnic writing since 1990 reflects a determination to foreground ethnicity not only as a compensatory knowledge emerging from within the binary paradigm of Us and Them but also, and more significantly, as relational knowledge. In this context, "the word 'multiculturalism' has no essence, it points to a debate" (Shohat and Stam 47). This debate takes the form of a dialogue between [*sic*] various cultural communities. Ethnic voices are no longer segregated within the space of individual ethnic groups; they converge as they speak with each other, but—the most important element here—they do so without being reduced to sameness, as they often speak across each other as well. Thus they do "not preach a pseudo-equality of viewpoints." (Shohat and Stam, in Kamboureli, *Scandalous Bodies* 161)

I'd argue further for a kind of radical relationality that recognizes the necessity of coalition across racialized categories, but one that refuses to be triangulated through whiteness, and so refuses what Shohat and Stam call "pseudo-equality." This is, in other words, a refusal of the false universalism that has been a cover for white norms and white privilege, and is becoming a cover for corporate ones, but rather attempts to recuperate a more honest sense of equality that may shoot a rhizomatic thread toward Enlightenment histories, but shoots others toward the experiential history of racialized people, and yet others toward contemporary analyses of power difference coming from contemporary marginalized communities—racialized, feminist, queer, critically class conscious, and disability. Here, I understand rhizomes in the sense that the Martinician critic Édouard Glissant, reading Deleuze and Guattari, means it: "The notion of the rhizome maintains ... the idea of rootedness but challenges that of a totalitarian root. Rhizomatic thought is the principle behind what I call the Poetics of Relation, in which each and every identity is extended through a relationship with the Other" (11). For me, Glissant's understanding of relation as a poetics rather than as a theoretical totality is particularly helpful because it leaves the practice of relation to productive contingencies and imaginations rather than attempting to nail it down. It helps me see the literary and the poetic at work in Spivak's idea of strategy, and to begin to respond to my own question concerning the directions in which Spivakian strategy ought to point. It also helps to clarify the concern about the reification of minority positions expressed by critics as disparate as Kamboureli and Guillory.

CATEGORIES, SUPPLEMENTS, RELATIONSHIPS

While the special issue and the anthology are formally similar, their history, intent, and impact could not be more antithetical. The special issue, as a momentary interruption in the flow of a journal's publishing stream, is impermanent and, as such, enters pointedly into the historical moment of its production. It makes no claims toward the production of a canon, rather it is invested in its own fleeting moment, and thus embraces contingency. The anthology, on the other hand, with roots extending back to a medieval moment, at least in the history of English language texts, is fully invested in its place in history and has a vested role in canon formation. As much as the special issue is caught up in its own fleetingness as a political strategy, the anthology is invested in permanence. While the intent of both strategies may be presencing, their understandings of these things are, I argue, quite different from one another. The anthology demands a kind of closure. The special issue is more interested in open-ended time—contingent moment upon contingent moment.

Having made this observation, however, I argue that the counter-anthologies of the late 1980s and early 1990s have a lot more in common with the special issue of the same moment than with an earlier anthology tradition in which notions of "quality" and "representativeness" were the characteristics most valued by editors.[1] (See George Woodcock's "Old and New Oxford Books: The Idea of an Anthology.") They may, however, have something in common with anthologies in English of the medieval period which were constructed not around notions of "objective quality," but rather around what Seth Lerer has called "private, individual canons" (1253).

Interestingly, in spite of the fact that the term "Asian Canadian" is on the ascendant in the 1980s and 1990s, there are many special issues, but no literary anthology built around the term. The small, magazine-like collection *Inalienable Rice*, published in 1979, declares itself an anthology. Writing against a discourse of arrival, I would argue that the 1980s and 1990s are a moment that recognizes the instability of the term "Asian Canadian" and so produces it through the fleeting form of the special issue rather than the institutionalizing, reifying form of the anthology. But this does not mean that the idea of Asian Canadianness is absent from anthology production in this period. Rather, it is produced in relation to other terms, which are multiple and proliferating: Black Canadian, Indigenous, queer, Japanese Canadian, South Asian Canadian, feminist, lesbian, gay, Chinese Canadian, trans. Obviously, it overlaps with some of these terms. With others, I suggest, it emerges through a complicated kind of "besideness" that is sometimes friendly in the sense of alliance-building, but sometimes competitive, alienating, and/or outright racist. Regardless of the affective form of relation, the discourse of Asian Canadianness parallels that of other discourses of difference.

The term "Asian Canadian" is troubling in that it tends to foreground Chinese and Japanese Canadian, although ostensibly it includes Korean

Canadian, Filipino Canadian, Vietnamese Canadian, Cambodian Canadian, Indonesian Canadian, Thai Canadian, and more. Its inclusion of South Asian Canadian and Near Asian Canadian as categories is sporadic. The reasons for this—geopolitics, immigration patterns, settlement, modes of categorization, affiliations, demographics, population sizes, wealth, relative access to cultural and political venues—are multiple and complex.

It is neither my intent nor my desire to justify Chinese/Japanese dominance within deployments of the term, though I recognize it as a historical fact. However, I do wish to interrogate the problem briefly. In the catalogue for *Yellow Peril: Reconsidered,* an exhibition of twenty-five Asian Canadian artists working in contemporary media in 1991, Paul Wong writes:

> The exhibition and publication focus on specific works that reflect Asian Canadian sensibilities. I have defined "Asian" by the colour of our skin and the geographic regions it implies. The ways in which we have been depicted, treated and consequently viewed by others in the New World are different from those of other visible minorities: Blacks, Natives and Indo-Canadians. (6)

The essay proceeds to describe the legal and social forms of discrimination that have faced Chinese Canadians and Japanese Canadians—the Chinese Head Tax, the Exclusion Act, the Japanese Canadian internment during World War II, but also social strictures ("try hard not to be noticed") and stereotypes (Susie Wongs and Geisha Girls) (6). The racism at work in this range of instances has been well documented in publications from *Inalienable Rice* to *The Chinese in Canada*, so I will not unpack it here. What I do want to recognize is that these instances are arbitrary in the sense that they don't really delimit the category "Asian Canadian" though they do show the traumatic instances of the term's formation. Further, they illustrate the arbitrary nature of racism itself. To attempt to delimit the category any more "scientifically" would only produce a racist science. We are returned to Fanon's recognition that the "the Black man" (or any other raced position, in this case, "the Asian Canadian") has his ontology only in relation to whiteness. This is why Roy Miki's recognition that it is important to ask what the term can *do* rather than what it *is* really matters.

Ontological questions are profoundly limited, but questions of praxis are endlessly productive. Proliferation, of course, can be its own problem, but, as Derrida recognized, it is only at sites of supplementarity that a kind of abject freedom can be found. In relation to the range of possible inhabitants of the term "Asian Canadian," I would argue for the most inclusive framing possible. What remains to be done is a study of why the framing has not been fully inclusive. This chapter, however, attempts to historicize a few of the most proximate relations through which the idea of "Asian Canadian literature" emerges in the 1980s and 1990s as it was produced historically rather than as it ought to be ideally, in other words, to ask what it has been so far. I am of course very interested in what it might be in the future. I hold up inclusion as an ideal, but I also recognize that concepts, though they may evolve, never fully lose the trace of their prior iterations.

So then, one key problem is that official multiculturalism enacts and makes into law the conundrum that Fanon so presciently demonstrated. The relationships of variously racialized groups are set up in relation to the white and Eurocentric norms of the state. (I unpack this in my discussion of the 1994 conference Writing Thru Race in the conclusion of this book, and so will not elaborate here.) What I would like to observe, however, is that a discourse for interrelation among marginalized positions was largely missing in the 1980s–1990s moment. There was a well-intentioned, politically necessary logic attached to this, one that could not be spoken because a strategic silence was necessary in order for the anti-racist work of that moment to retain its power. The logic goes like this: *I am a racialized person who understands the plight of other racialized people. I don't want to take up space in communities that are more oppressed, or just differently oppressed. (I don't want to take up space needed more by others, as so many egocentric white people do.) So I don't talk about them. I don't even talk about a relationship with them. And yet, those relationships are key to my understanding of myself within the complicated matrices of race and racialization.*

This means that inter-racialized relations is a taboo subject, at least among activists, artists, writers, and thinkers with anti-racist leanings, at the same time that it is massively productive of many ontologies/subject positions. It is also a repressed of that 1980s–1990s moment. Meanwhile, discourses of empowerment, silence-breaking, and subject production were and are happening through multiple communities side by side. Simultaneously, the umbrella term "people of colour" opened plenty of opportunities for interaction along a range of identifications. Anthologies from the 1980s and 1990s moment leave a trace of these ghostly relations.

In so doing, they sit in a productive tension against more canonical forms of the anthology that attempt to capture "the best of what has been thought and said," making all kinds of assumptions about whose cultural norms are central without acknowledging doing so. Counter-canonical anthologies, by contrast, fill another role. Their logic is one of both community and subject production, however fraught. Some of them recognize the instability of the racialized subject, but still contend that there is something worthwhile to be captured in anthology form. Others reify community and identity positions in ways that may make critics cringe, though this doesn't necessarily negate the cultural labour they do. Kamboureli worries that some ethnic anthologies, in reifying subject positions, are inadvertently complicit with official multiculturalism (*Scandalous* 150). And official multiculturalism, for her, is a state strategy of containment that falsely "dehistoricizes the social and political conditions that have discriminated against many Canadians, the same conditions that, through colonial history, contributed to the formation of the Canadian state" (*Scandalous* 101). I absolutely agree. However, thinking through the social labour of the so-called multicultural festival, she recognizes that participants in projects that might seem to be complicit with the containing project of the state may in fact, through interaction with one another, refuse the Althusserian hail and engage with ethnic or racialized markers in ways other than those anticipated and sanctioned by the state (*Scandalous* 104–06). I suggest that a parallel logic might hold for the contributors to racialized, ethnicized, and otherwise marked anthologies. While anthologies as wholes might, at their best, break silences and articulate subjects and communities, and at their worst, name and thus contain their contributors within narrowly defined identity categories, specific contributions might exceed the intent of the editors. Further, the juxtapositions of texts within anthologies does relational work simply by putting in proximity work that might not otherwise be associated, producing unexpected relations and ruptures and making community through difference as much as through sameness.

CANON, COUNTER-CANON, ANTHOLOGY

In his critique of calls to open the canon to racialized voices in the 1980s and 1990s, John Guillory makes an adamant and painstaking distinction between the literary and the social. He wants to be very clear that the absence of racialized voices in the historical Western canon does not emerge from overt acts of exclusion on the part of gatekeepers, but rather that it has its roots in broader exclusions at the level of the social whole (18). For him, this misperception supports another one: that texts transparently represent their writers and their writers' experience: "The typical valorization of the noncanonical author's experience as a marginalized social identity necessarily reasserts the transparency of the text to the experience it represents" (10). The error here, he argues, is mistaking democratic representation for the complex institutional process of valorization presumably attached to reading, rereading, circulation, criticism, and educated judgement. Jibing Barthes in particular and poststructural theory in general, he writes: "The author returns in the critique of the canon, not as the genius, but as the representative of a social identity" (10). Finally, Guillory cautions his reader against equating canons with social values. He argues that canons are neither progressive nor subversive in any absolute way (21), but can shift in terms of how they are perceived from one historical moment to the next (24). One should not value texts on purely moral grounds (24). Following Kant, he says that value is not intrinsic but extrinsic, that is "relative, contingent, subjective, [and] contextual" (25).

There is much to like about Guillory's patient and nuanced critique, especially emerging as it does when temperatures associated with revisions to the canon are running so high. However, in opposing genius to social identity, Guillory closes off the possibility that the two may not be mutually exclusive, and further that the valuation of genius belies its Arnoldian roots and thus a connection to an overtly social, political, and elitist project in the sense that Arnold was highly anxious about the enfranchisement of the (male) British working class. Further, as Gauri Viswanathan has noted, the growth and development of English literature is deeply tied to the British civilizing mission in India and is formed in relation to it (2). She writes:

> The history of education in British India shows that certain humanistic functions traditionally associated with literature—for example, the shaping of character or the development of aesthetic sense or the disciplines of ethical thinking—were considered essential to the processes of sociopolitical control by the guardians of the same tradition. (3)

Thus, the identities that Guillory is so anxious about are in fact complex products of history of subject production that is profoundly tied to English literature as both an aesthetic and a sociopolitical project. Though it is beyond the scope of this chapter, I think it would be possible to tie the marginalization of racialized texts to the work of an aesthetic sensibility that is not value free, but is tied to complex processes of social control, not just in India and Britain, but also in the Americas. Guillory may well be right that there is no set of transparent, one-to-one relationships connecting the terms "canon," "identity," and "values," but these are nonetheless bound up with one another in profoundly ideological ways.

Further, the fiction of transparent, one-to-one relationships among these terms has been acceptable when put into the service of nationalist history. For instance, Leon Surette writes: "Canadian literary criticism has always been an enterprise in which the central purpose was the discovery of the Canadian-ness of the literature written in this country" (17). Similarly, reading the introduction to E. H. Desart's 1864 anthology *Selections from Canadian Poets*, Dermot McCarthy remarks:

> Poetry brings about the unanimity, the spiritual cohesion and coherence,
> of the worlds of matter and spirit, of fact and value, of the useful and
> the beautiful. The poetry anthology seeks to do this in terms of and for
> the "national" entity, the "people." Thus, if "the Poet's work is a lofty and
> sacred work" (*SCP,* xiii), so too is the anthologist's. For the anthology
> aspires to give "permanent form" to this sense of a nation as a coherent
> unity made up of complementary rather than contradictory elements.
> (34)

It is interesting that the critique of the non-coincidence of text and experience arises in the context of raced and feminist critiques of the canon. The anxiety is there only when the nationalism expressed is a minor one.

Kamboureli notes that, in spite of its self-reflexivity about canonical form, the Lecker collection *Canadian Canons* nonetheless reproduces this form, still leaving unspoken and unspeakable the critics of ethnicity who instigated the canon debates. She writes: "[H]is collection illustrates what happens when literary values are questioned while the edifice containing them remains intact" (159). Kamboureli productively posits the 1990 anthology *Telling It,* as an instance of a collection that foregrounds both embodied and critical difference, contesting difference within the margins that the mainstream of Canadian literature was then working so hard to hold at bay (159). I would suggest that in the years that have passed since the publication of *Telling It,* racialized texts and bodies are no longer held at bay in quite the same way. This is not necessarily progress, however. Rather, complex forms of incorporation function in both the publishing world and the academic arena to manage and neutralize difference.

The question remains then what the relationships among value, experience, and the canon ought to be, and what role the anthology ought to play in constructing these relationships. I agree with Kamboureli that *Telling It* is an excellent early example that includes marginalized writers without shying away from questions of power and difference. I think we need to be cautious of Lien Chao's brave but perhaps too easy call for Asian Canadian literature to right wrongs and reclaim heroes in the service of personal identity (36).

More recently, Kamboureli has critiqued Donald Goellnicht's "A Long Labour: The Protracted Birth of Asian Canadian Literature" as a text that sets Asian Canadian literature up as the weaker cousin of Asian American literature by articulating its inadequacies in relation to Asian American norms, and thus setting Asian American up as the hegemonic term. While Goellnicht posits the strength of Asian American literature because of its roots in civil rights protests, its connection to African American activism and literatures, and its entry into the academy in the 1970s through an ethnic studies framework, against a Canadian "languishing in the wilderness," Kamboureli sees the strength of Asian Canadian literature in its negative capability connected to critical work that recognizes the constructed and contingent qualities of the term ("(Reading Closely)" 44). For Goellnicht, the relationship of Asian American studies to activist modes working in opposition to a violently nationalist state gives that discipline teeth that a literature contained by benign if misguided Canadian multiculturalism could not possibly hope for. Kamboureli, however, suggests that the strength of Asian Canadian literature comes precisely from its ambivalent relationship with its "quasi-institutional status" (46). She is also critical of "younger scholars" for taking up the call for a U.S.-style area studies formation of Asian Canadian literature/studies without querying the value of doing so. Though she names Lily Cho, Iyko Day, and myself, her concrete critique is directed at Guy Beauregard and Chris Lee. Her critique is not meant personally, so I won't take it up in that regard, except to note that all five of the critics named have very different approaches to the idea of the institution and don't form a bloc or even necessarily agree with one another. They come from very different histories and different relationships to the practice of Asian Canadian literary criticism. Kamboureli's critique itself is productive, however, in the sense that it recognizes the way certain philosophically inherent instabilities get played out in a particular historical moment. Specifically, she notes Beauregard's recognition of the unstable terrain on which "Asian Canadian studies projects" are built, and his desire for an institutionalized Asian Canadian studies as a "strategic base [] from which to rethink social and cultural formations in Canada" (Beauregard qtd. in Kamboureli 57). Kamboureli writes: "Scholarly projects that operate meta-critically, engage with social history, and trouble established disciplinary constructs (irrespective of how they do this) are granted the capacity to effect change at different planes inside and outside academia, a clear instance of the mimetic fallacy.... As I have argued elsewhere, 'a turn to ethics is not an ethical act by default'" (56).

Though both Goellnicht and Beauregard are aware of the cultural labour that has taken and continues to take place outside the academy, both claim institutionalization as desirable and belated. Institutionalization has obvious benefits for professors and students in the sense that it legitimates their work. It may be less beneficial if it unwittingly reproduces essences or other consumable solidifications at sites already recognized to be unstable. Further, at a material level, it may force into the service of the academy work that was made outside of it for multiple audiences. Given my own trajectory (as a person largely educated in community, activist, and creative contexts), I wonder, for instance, what options institutionalization might open and what options it might close for imaginative and language-oriented young people who, before the institutionalization of Asian Canadian studies and the drying up of arts funding, might have found themselves thinking, writing, learning, and creating in writers' collectives, artist-run centres, or activist communities. While perhaps less theoretically sophisticated than some academic spaces, these were and are sites of a much greater freedom to think, act, and create. Of course, people who care about the full breadth of Asian Canadian possibility can support both institutionalized and community-based modes; the problem under neoliberalism is that the public arena is getting shut down through concrete funding cuts as well as ideological delegitimation. If an institutionalized Asian Canadian studies rises under such circumstances, then in fact a displacement will have taken place. In particular, the positing of methods and canons for Asian Canadian studies might foreclose other ways of working before young people can even begin to imagine them and see their possibilities. In recent drives toward "professionalization" within the academy, methods and canons are becoming requirements, mimetic of more conservative and Eurocentric ways of constructing a discipline, and thus hegemonic forms that within the broader hegemonic form of the university itself run the danger of obliterating other ways of working and thinking. Specifically, both creative and activist modes could get quashed or at least minimized in favour of the critical mode, when actually all three have been necessary for the production of so-called Asian Canadian studies. We need to be very careful not to imagine Asian Canadian studies as the teleological end of previous work.

Further, within the institution the relationship of "Asian Canadian" to governments and corporate world is altered. On one hand, it gains a legitimacy, and so, as Beauregard says, "a platform from which to speak"; but on the other, it loses at least a measure of its oppositional power. Oppositional knowledge, once it becomes curriculum does not have the same live force that it does in non-institutional spaces. Given one of the most important facets of "Asian Canadian," theoretically speaking, is its quality as an oppositional construct, we might ask ourselves what the consequences of willingly stepping toward incorporation (in both the psychoanalytic and capitalist sense) might mean for the activist node, as one among many, from which "Asian Canadian" erupted.

It seems important at this juncture to take up the tension between the idea of the "foundational" on the one hand and the idea of "instability" on the other. If, as I have been suggesting, there is something interesting about the 1980s and 1990s, not as temporal markers of upward progress on the Gregorian calendar, but rather as a haunted but productive "occult instability where people dwell," as Homi Bhabha reading Frantz Fanon puts it (35), then it seems important to interrogate the search now for foundations, when the critique of foundations is already behind us, as it were, and already, paradoxically, a part of what makes Asian Canadian studies/literature/possibility what it is at present. Kamboureli is right to note my affirmation of Goellnicht in the sense that I agree with him that there does lie in "Asian Canadian" a quality of belatedness. But I read this not in relation to Asian American studies but in Bhabha's sense as an ontological instability that gives it also an instability in time. It belongs to what Bhabha calls Third Space:

> The intervention of the Third Space of enunciation, which makes the structure of meaning and reference and ambivalent process, destroys this mirror of representation in which cultural knowledge is customarily revealed as an integrated, open, expanding code. Such an intervention quite properly challenges our sense of the historical identity of culture as a homogenizing, unifying force, authenticated by the originary Past, kept alive in the national tradition of the People. In other words, the disruptive temporality of enunciation displaces the narrative of the Western nation which Benedict Anderson so perceptively describes as being written in homogenous, serial time. (37)

In his new book, *The Semblance of Identity: Aesthetic Mediation in Asian American Literature*, Chris Lee is profoundly aware of the instabilities of the Asian American subject and of referential meaning in an Asian American context: "[N]ot only has it become impossible to speak of Asian America as a coherent entity, but the very critique of identity politics has been widely embraced as valuable and necessary" (5). He clearly articulates his Asian American project as a post-identity one interested in the problem of aesthetic representation and the non-coincidence of the subject with language, and yet at the same time embedded in identitarian assumptions even as it seeks to critique them. It is interesting and somewhat surprising, then, that his essay "Enacting the Asian Canadian," published in the *Asian Canadian Studies* special issue of *Canadian Literature*, he foregrounds origins, beginnings, and foundations. This piece is not just embedded, it actively produces identitarian assumptions. The opening paragraph of the essay locates the historical beginning of Asian Canadian literature with the anthology *Inalienable Rice*. However, in the next sentence, he distinguishes beginnings from origins, locating the latter with the work of Sui Sin Far/ Edith Maude Eaton and her sister Onoto Watanna/Winnifred Eaton and with the writings of Chinese immigrants on detention centre walls in British Columbia (28). Of course Lee understands that Asian Canadian is every bit as unstable a category as Asian American. For Lee, foundation making constitutes action as Hannah Arendt articulates it: "Action, in so far as it engages in founding and preserving political bodies, creates conditions for remembrance, that is, for history" (Arendt 8–9, qtd. in Lee 28). In recognizing *Inalienable Rice* as foundational and identitarian, but not originary, Lee also recognizes the disjunctive temporality of its moment. The question becomes what kinds of conditions for remembrance anthologies set up, and thus what histories are constructed. Further, if the foundational action of *Inalienable Rice* in fact creates the conditions for institutionalization, how are we to understand its non-institutional roots? For indeed, almost all of the anthologies, novels, and poetry that make up what is now being claimed as an Asian Canadian tradition were created under non-institutional, but nonetheless agented and articulate, conditions. This is why Goellnicht is so clear in "The Protracted Birth of Asian Canadian Literature" that he is talking about the entry of Asian Canadian literature into the academy, and not the actual conditions of its production. Though he does address conditions of production, the teleological end of the article is the institution. This is Kamboureli's critique.

What I propose to do in the second half of this chapter is to interrogate the non-institutional conditions under which anthologies generate ideas and practices of Asian Canadian subjects and literatures. In so doing, I illustrate Asian Canadian relations to other formations. For indeed, I think Hannah Arendt would want justice-minded people to query the conditions of their own bureaucratization.

MANY-MOUTHED BIRDS: LITERARY ASPIRATIONS, EXPERIENTIAL HAUNTINGS, AND MINOR AFFECTS

Edited by one of the main founders of the Asian Canadian Writers' Workshop, Jim Wong-Chu and screenwriter/translator Bennett Lee, the Chinese Canadian anthology *Many-Mouthed Birds* was published in 1991. By focusing in the first place on "quality" as its principal criterion, it accepts traditional Eurocentric/academic conceptions of what anthologies should be and do, as laid out, for example, in the George Woodcock article described above. Although the anthology is not broken up into thematic sections, Bennett Lee's introduction lays the anthology's themes out in no uncertain terms. He insists on the literary quality of all the pieces included, perhaps as an antidote to the unspoken anxiety that the text might otherwise be read anthropologically, as the words of a sample group of "native informants" giving the inside dirt on a target culture. The tension between the literary and the experiential, which so worries John Guillory, is present from the introduction's very first words:

The intention of this collection is to bring together a representative sample of work by Chinese-Canadian writers. These are relatively uncharted literary waters, so the boundaries for this anthology were flexible—we cast our nets wide and considered anything with a literary flavour. (1)

It is important to recognize, however, that this striving toward the literary occurs at a time when Asian Canadian critics had no place in literary institutions, English departments least of all. Some whom we currently might understand as Asian Canadianists may have been academics working inside various institutions, but they weren't yet focused on Asian Canadian subjects. "The Protracted Birth of Asian Canadian Literature" was still nine years from publication. Donald Goellnicht was writing about the fate of Romanticism in the wake of poststructuralism. Eleanor Ty was writing about eighteenth-century British women writers. Smaro Kamboureli was writing about the Canadian long poem and Canadian multiculturalism. Roy Miki was just emerging from the success of the Japanese Canadian Redress movement. His first book of poems, *Saving Face*, came out the same year as *Many-Mouthed Birds*. SKY Lee, who is a writer but not an academic, published *Disappearing Moon Cafe* in 1990 and was organizing, powerfully, with feminist writers like Lee Maracle, Jeannette Armstrong, and Daphne Marlatt in community spaces outside the academy. Some of these connections can be traced in the post-conference anthology *Telling It*. Jim Wong-Chu and Bennett Lee, then, were claiming quality and literary strength from a profoundly community based location—Wong-Chu's house in East Vancouver—without access to institutional discourses, resources, or processes. In a way, I understand it as a space of profound desire for entry into social acceptance. Its politics is a politics of heartfelt uplift, but one that cannot foresee how that politics might get taken up twenty years later. The call to quality in *Many-Mouthed Birds* must be understood, I think, as continuous with the call to justice and recuperation in *Inalienable Rice*.

Its orientation toward silence and speaking is similarly not oppositional, but interestingly complicated. In a call close to, but not the same as, the call in the lesbian-of-colour anthology *Piece of My Heart* edited by Makeda Silvera, with its insistence on the liberatory act of "breaking the silence," *Many-Mouthed Birds* purports to tell secrets. Discussing SKY Lee's *Disappearing Moon Cafe*, which is excerpted in *Many-Mouthed Birds* one year after *Disappearing Moon*'s publication by the same press (Douglas and McIntyre), Lee writes:

> *Disappearing Moon Cafe* is one breach of what Kae, the narrator, terms
> "the great wall of silence and invisibility we have built around us." She
> goes on: "I have a misgiving that the telling of our history is forbidden. I
> have violated a secret code." That secret code was that reviving the trou-
> bled past would serve no useful purpose and should be forgotten, or at
> the very least, kept within the family. By unearthing the past, breathing
> life into the characters who have inhabited those troubled times, giving
> them a voice and investing them with human frailties and passions, they
> open up a world with its own colour, texture, weight and drama. (4)

The prohibition against "breaking the silence," in Lee's view, comes from
"within" the community, rather than being forced upon the subaltern from
the outside, already giving us a clue that something there is something
shameful in the telling of community secrets. Sylvan Tomkins writes:
"[S]hame is an experience of the self by the self" (136). In the context of
Many-Mouthed Birds there is shame associated with the breaking of silence
that does indeed come from an interior place—interior to both a social
group (Chinese-Canadian community) and the individual. This anxiety, in
fact, lies at the heart of the anthology's title:

> The title *Many-Mouthed Birds* comes from a Chinese expression used
> to describe someone who talks too much. If you are a "many-mouthed
> bird," it means you do not know how to hold your tongue. You have a
> big mouth. You speak up when you are supposed to be quiet. There may
> be nothing wrong with what you say; it may all be true. The point is, you
> are being indiscreet because you are saying things that you should keep
> to yourself, that not everyone wants to hear, that may get you in trouble.
> The writers in this anthology are "many-mouthed birds" because they
> are breaking a long and often self-imposed silence. (7–8)

Audre Lorde's much-quoted slogan, "Your silence will not protect you,"
comes to mean something much more complicated in this context. In his
closing words, Bennett Lee attempts to synthesize two ways of looking at
the breaking of silence: "We should not be surprised to find that what they
[the writers in the anthology] have to offer is not shameful at all, but only
a few songs straight from heart" (8).

What is offered here is an association of keeping quiet with a stoic, heroic
loyalty to community, against an individualistic, selfish need to speak out
"straight from the heart." The Western Enlightenment individual is valued
over the traditional, Chinese/Confucian stoic, even though these stances
toward silence and speaking, individuality and community are not openly
named.

Lee describes the contents of the text as "not shameful at all" precisely because anxiety about shame permeates the project. I would argue, however, that a new kind of community is produced in this "shameful speaking," community that is no longer located with traditional Chinese, Confucian group ethics, but rather a hybrid one that clings to that ethic on the one hand, but also embraces a Western individualist ethic on the other. The problem is that the two do not mesh well, and that shame seems to be the mitigating affective stance that binds the two together. Pride and shame are located differently in the Chinese and Western ideals of the honourable subject. The problem of identification is compounded by the fact that shame as an affect is bound up with questions of identity: "[Shame] ... is the not at all ... the place where identity is most securely attached to essences, but rather ... it is the place where the *question* of identity arises most originally and most relationally" (Sedgewick, "Shame, Theatricality and Queer Performativity" 51). As such, it is an uncomfortable and distinctly unheroic place for the writers in this anthology, these silence-breakers, to occupy. Lien Chao's desire for heroes and justice is uncomfortably undermined here. One could read Confucian ethics on the one hand and Enlightenment ones on the other as dialectic poles producing a hybrid identity that shamefully incorporates both.

In Garrett Engkent's "Why My Mother Can't Speak English," the first piece in the anthology, the pull between these two incommensurate poles is what drives the story. The Chinese-speaking mother is at once a victim of Confucian misogyny and an upholder of traditional Chinese values. She cannot speak English because her husband did not allow her to work in the dining room of the family restaurant, but rather kept her at work in the kitchen, insisting: "All you need is to understand the orders from the waitresses. Anyway, if you need to know something, the men will translate for you" (12). But later, when he dies, she mourns his death deeply: "When my father died five years ago, she cried and cried. 'Don't leave me in this world. Let me die with you'" (14). Further, when her son, the speaker in the story, takes her to Citizenship Court, two things happen that the son finds deeply embarrassing. First, the liaison officer who takes up the mother's case gives the son quite a grilling on why his mother can't speak English:

> "Your mother has been living in Canada for the past thirty years and she still can't speak English?"
>
> "It happens," I tell the officer.
>
> "I find it hard to believe that—not one word?"
>
> "Well, she understands some restaurant English," I tell her. "You know, French fries, pork chops, soup and so on. And she can say a few words."

"But will she be able to understand the judge's questions? The inter-view with the judge, as you know, is an important part of the citizen-ship procedure. Can she read the booklet? What does she know about Canada?"

"So you don't think my mother has a chance?"

"The requirements are that the candidate must be able to speak either French or English, the two official languages of Canada. The candidate must be able to pass an oral interview with the citizenship judge, and then he or she must be able to recite the oath of allegiance—"

"My mother needs to speak English," I conclude for her.

"Look, I don't mean to be rude, but why didn't your mother learn English when she first came over?" (10–11)

Without saying a word, the mother is the focus of shame in this scene. It is, in fact, precisely her silence that is shameful. But it is also her silence that is non-compliant, that runs against the repressive apparatus of the state that demands that she speak English. Her silence does not protect her, but nei-ther is it exactly about being a docile subject. On the other hand, it is not a rebelliously heroic silence either. It is silence that comes from another kind of oppression—Chinese, Confucian patriarchal oppression which dictates that good women remain uneducated and don't attempt to enter the mas-culine world of engagement with foreigners and entry into Canadian citi-zenship. Caught between two patriarchal systems, two words of the father, her very being is a slap in the face to both. But that doesn't necessarily mean it is good for her. She is also oppressed by both systems, even as she is an unruly subject of both.

An interesting aspect of this scene is the son's relation to the two patri-archies. In response to the liaison officer's first query about the mother's inability to speak English, the son says, "It happens." He does not blame his father. But in response to the officer's evasive speech about the useful-ness of speaking English, it is the son who articulates the law of the state: "My mother needs to speak English." In a sense, he chooses the law of the Canadian state as the one he will abide by, even as he does not exactly betray his Chinese roots, his Chinese father. His mother, on the other hand, has no such choice because she has no such power.

In the second shameful moment, the mother acts, or at least attempts to. Unable to understand the conversation about her not speaking English, her inability to understand, the mother thinks that the liaison officer wants money:

I have not been translating this conversation, and Mother, annoyed and agitated, asks me what is going on. I tell her there is a slight problem.

"What problem?" Mother opens her purse, and I see her taking a small red envelope—*lai-shi*—I quickly cover her hand.

"What's going on?" the liaison officer demands.

"Nothing," I say hurriedly. "Just a cultural misunderstanding, I assure you."

My mother rattles off some indignant words, and I snap back in Chinese: "Put that away! The woman won't understand, and we'll be in a lot of trouble."

The officer looks confused, and I realize that an explanation is needed.

"My mother was about to give you a money gift as a token of appreciation for what you are doing for us. I was afraid you might misconstrue it as a bribe. We have no intention of doing that."

"I'm relieved to hear it." (11)

The language of money, in this instance, is clearly not universal! In the gap between "a token of appreciation" and "a bribe," the son finds shame and discomfort, while the mother finds annoyance and agitation. This situation, of course, is constructed to illustrate "cultural difference." With the traditional Confucian mother on one end and the liaison officer on the other, it is the son who occupies the synthetic space—both artificial and healing. But, as I have said, there is a lot of shame and embarrassment in this mobile site of the "in-between." It is shame and embarrassment that occasionally swings into a deeper site of inarticulate pain, and site of excess where no words, Chinese or English, will go:

Perhaps I am not Chinese enough any more to understand why my mother would want to take in the sorrow, the pain, and the anguish, and then to recount them every so often.

Once, I was presumptuous enough to ask her why she would want to remember in such detail. She said that the memories didn't hurt any more. I did not tell her that her reminiscences cut me to the quick. Her only solace now is to be listened to. (13)

I would like to suggest that the reason the mother's stories don't hurt her any more is precisely because she passes the pain on to the son. His relationship to the pain is different from hers because he has not experienced it. As unexperienced, undigested pain, it is endlessly repeatable, as Freud has shown us in *Beyond the Pleasure Principle*. Abraham and Torok in *The Shell and the Kernel* have theorized this kind of pain as located in a crypt. Encrypted pain can be passed on undigested from one subject to the next, so that the one who has not experienced it must endlessly act it out precisely because he cannot quite get to the root of it. Though Abraham and Torok theorize the construction of the crypt through examples about lost objects of romantic love, it seems worth registering that such crypts might also get built through the mechanisms of what Marianne Hirsch calls "post-memory," in which unresolved traumatic contents are passed on from one generation to the next (106). In the case of the son in Engkent's story, this phenomenon produces doubled moments when the "hybrid" subject is forced to choose one law or the other, one father or the other. At such moments a small part of the cryptic contents rushes to the surface, causing shame and embarrassment.

Jim Wong-Chu[2] in the poem "How Feel I Do?", addressed to a new speaker of English as a second language, writes:

> to tell the truth
> I feel very much at home
> in your embarrassment (17)

Embarrassment, in this poem, occupies a doubled space in which the "you" is at home neither in Chinese nor in English, while the "I" has found a home in the discomfort itself. It is not a synthesis of any kind—there is no completion, no revolution here. Instead there is minor emotion, what Sianne Ngai would call an "ugly feeling":

> [T]he feelings I examine here are explicitly amoral and noncathartic, offering no satisfactions of virtue, however oblique, nor any therapeutic or purifying release. In fact, most of these feelings tend to interfere with the outpouring of other emotions. (6–7)

Shame, irritation, and anxiety are in fact affects that arise regularly in the fictions of *Many-Mouthed Birds*. In Engkent's story, the mother is irritated at not being able to understand the conversation between her son and the liaison officer, and both irritated and anxious at the prospect of having to learn a new language at such a late moment in life. The son is irritated by having to help his mother through the citizenship ritual his father "should" have taken care of years ago (as a good Canadian subject, though not necessarily as a good Chinese one). If such affect is not oppositional, it is not compliant either. For the mother there is no delight at being brought into the fold of the state. There is relief, perhaps, at not losing her old age pension.

Writing about the affect of apology among white Australians, Sarah Ahmed suggests that the individuation of shame turns the self both toward and away from herself, and thus that shame experiences are intercorporeal and social (104–05). Further, shame intensifies the relation of the self to the self—as the self appears to the Other. Shame requires a witness. Ahmed says: "In shame, I am the object as well as the subject of feeling." Shame requires identification with a desired Other who, in witnessing shame, returns the subject to itself (Ahmed 106).

But for the second generation subject, the Other is double—of China-town on the one hand, and of whiteness on the other. If to be visible, rather than invisible, is at the same time to be shamed, then there is no heroic agency for the second-generation subject. In Kristeva's terms, such a subject is abject—fixated on more than one object, and thus unable to access the ego ideal or enter into a fully coherent subjectivity.

Ahmed suggests that shame "burns on the skin" as a consequence of being *seen* in the shameful act. Shame is thus tied up with what Eleanor Ty has called "the politics of the visible" in her work on Asian North Ameri-can fiction, a politics which is, as Foucault has taught us, produced in the simultaneity of vision and representation, the coincidence of seeing with always-already-cultural modes of classifying and containing. It seems to me that in the case of *Many-Mouthed Birds*, however, there is an interest-ing excess produced between the politics of the visible and the politics of the aural. Bryan Adams notwithstanding, to be seen *singing* "straight from the heart" is to allow the sensation of burning skin to pass. And to write "straight from the heart," supplementally, still opens up the haunted and flickering "Third Space" that Bhabha offers as open to marginalized subjects engaged in the practice of memory.

Ngai remarks that of all the minor emotions she discusses, the only one that holds the possibility for action is disgust, the others tending more toward encouraging the subject to speak. She quotes Bertrand Noel: "Revolt acts; indignation seeks to speak." But if disgust is an actionable emotion, it is also a morally suspect one (Ngai 340), in the sense that it is inextricably linked to its dialectic opposite, desire. And desire, of course, is overtly sus-pect because it is the primary emotion through which capital keeps consum-ers fixated and therefore docile. What I would like to ask here is whether there is liberatory possibility in minor emotions that are not dialectic, and if so, how that liberation might work.

Discussing Bruce Andrews's *Shut Up*, Ngai suggests that one way to aggressively occupy the position of the disgusting is to refuse consump-tion. In Anne Jew's *Everyone Talked Loudly in Chinatown*, a young Chinese Canadian girl is attempting to balance her shameful desire for a white boy against a feeling of responsibility toward her dying grandmother, whom she has to feed, and whose sick, frail body disgusts her:

> We start with the soup. The spoon makes a clanging noise as it knocks against her teeth, sending a shiver through me. She still has all of them. She doesn't chew the food very much though. It stays in her mouth a

while, and then she makes a great effort to swallow. I try to show her
how to chew by making exaggerated movements with my mouth, but she
just ignores me. She finishes the soup, and we start on the rice in water.
Some of it dribbles out of her mouth, so I have to scrape it off her chin
and spoon it back in like I'm feeding a baby. I feel disgusted and guilty
and I don't know why. I also feel guilty for not spending more time with
her. Todd would die if he knew I had to do this. (24)

The woman who can barely consume her food herself resists consumption
because she is an object of horror. Confronted with her utterly foreign body,
the protagonist (and the reader) are moved to disgust, guilt, and shame.

What is interesting about this story, however, is that the white boyfriend
elicits from the protagonist a similar kind of disgust. The black felt drawing
of the Led Zeppelin logo on the back of his jean jacket "bothers" her (22)
in the same way the role reversal with her grandmother, in terms of who
takes care of whom, "bothers" her (24). Further, the experience of kissing
him is oddly gooey, visceral, and disgusting perhaps to a lesser to degree,
but nonetheless in the same palpable way that feeding her grandmother is:

Halfway through *The Great Santini* and after we've finished the popcorn,
Todd offers me a Certs. Then after a while he turns to me and kisses me
on the lips. He opens his mouth on mine, and not knowing what to do,
I open my mouth. I feel his tongue moving around in my mouth, so I
move my tongue around in his. He still tastes faintly of popcorn under
the flavour of the Certs. Just as I'm becoming used to the new sensation,
he stops and kisses me on lips and turns back to the movie. I can feel
saliva clinging to the edges of my mouth, and not wanting to wipe it
away with my hand, I press my face into his shoulder, hoping his shirt
will absorb the moisture. It works. (26)

Cognizant as she is of her ambivalent feelings for this boy, as evidenced in
the gooeyness of the kiss, and her dislike for his favourite band, the protagonist's desire for the boy is undaunted: "As we leave the theatre, Todd takes
hold of my hand. I am quickly beginning to fall in love" (26).

This love, I argue, is inextricable from the disgust she feels for both Todd
and the grandmother, and the attendant guilt and shame that are attached
to both. When the shame she feels is made public and external through her
mother's inadvertent discovery of her and Todd kissing, it is to the dying,
disgusting grandmother whom the speaker runs for comfort:

She is so still in the moonlight. I go to her and touch her face. It is soft,
but cool. The shadows make it look almost ghostly. I take her hand, bony

and fragile, and find she has no pulse. I drop it instantly and stand back to look at her. She is dead, I think. I take her hand again, kneel beside the bed, and rest my head against her. Soon I am asleep. (27)

Although no causal link is overtly expressed, the coincidence of her first kiss with the death of the grandmother implies some kind of connection. Desire, disgust, guilt, and shame are thus connected to mortality and loss and a kind of cultural betrayal that is the closest thing to heroism the story offers. In not offering a tidy heroics, the story resists consumption. While the narrator's upholding and preservation of a heterosexual desire that is also a desire for whiteness, might function in the service of assimilation and individualist, Enlightenment values, through the action of disgust, the story resists consumption. Though the narrative of the white boyfriend has become a little worn with use and is easily thematized, there is something still interesting and productive at work in the entanglements of shame, disgust, and desire here.

What is productive about this anthology is perhaps the fact that its affects are ambivalent and complicated. If extreme affects, as Ngai suggests, are morally suspect, it is because they have tended to work in the service of naïve ideology; they are manufactured in order to drum up loyalties to single causes and thus are fundamentally fascist by nature. In the move away from the heroics of *Inalienable Rice*, and in its embrace of what Ngai calls "minor affects," *Many-Mouthed Birds* makes room for paradox and complication, perhaps in spite of the collection's introduction.

The question of thematization remains to be asked in relation to this anthology. Bennett Lee gives us figures, stock types, who recur through the stories: the sojourner, the family figure who is a conduit to the past, the misanthropic woman writer, the dying grandmother, the white boyfriend. He also gives us tropic situations: the telling of secrets, the eating of bitterness, the criticizing of tradition, the changing of attitudes. Kamboureli is concerned that thematization in ethnic anthologies falls into the trap of complicity with the "sedative politics" of official multiculturalism. Lee insists that he and Wong-Chu did not curate the anthology with these themes in mind, but rather that they emerged in the aftermath of the selection: "We were curious as to whether or not the results would reflect a sensibility which was identifiably 'Chinese Canadian,' but imposed no such conditions on the subject matter" (1). Lee and Wong-Chu's insistence on "literary quality" means that they don't include the kinds of pieces that Kamboureli critiques as "artless" (*Scandalous* 150) and that some anthology editors admit as "primarily of historical or sociological value" (Balan and Klynovy qtd. in Kamboureli 150). That said, however, the tension between the sociological and the literary remains in Lee's decision to recognize themes. Of course, it is the job of a good editor to offer framing. In addition, as Lee himself recognizes, *Many-Mouthed Birds* is an early anthology. He expects "better things to come" (7). Interestingly, he is not plagued by anxieties about belatedness that haunt so many critics. He is not worried either by the concern that the dead author of poststructuralism returns as a representative of social identity (Guillory 10). For Lee, there is no contradiction here. Though he and Wong-Chu refuse texts that constitute only "compelling sociology" (3), he has no problem with the idea that a writer can be both literary (if not Guillory's "genius") and Asian Canadian. What is troubling and remains open for presencing and discussion is that fact that Lee and Wong-Chu, after careful consideration, decided not to include Chinese language texts because in their minds these texts did not translate well; they are what constitute the sociological. The privileging of the English language, which troubled Lien Chao in her analysis of *Inalienable Rice*, remains a problem for *Many-Mouthed Birds*. The border between the sociological and the literary also remains porous here.

I think it is important to remember that in the latter half of the twentieth century, both sociology and anthropology are changing rapidly as disciplines. Given that these are the disciplinary formations through which the idea of the Chinese Canadian was being produced prior to the rise of "the literary," it is no wonder that Chinese Canadian anthologists are anxious about them. Helpfully, Paul Lai writing in Eleanor Ty and Christl Verduyn's collection *Asian Canadian Writing: Beyond Autoethnography* pushes critics to recognize that the reason we are so worried about autoethnographic writing is that the autoethnographer is a recent replacement for the disenfranchised "native informant" of traditional anthropology (56). He writes:

> For literary studies at large, autoethnographic fiction carries a veneer of the unsophisticated. It is the underdeveloped cousin of serious literary fiction or experimental writing; it is fiction that mimetically produces the cultural experience of the author's ethnic group (usually in non-white or off-white understandings of "ethnic"), writing that strives for unquestioning verisimilitude. (56)

Reading Kandice Chuh, he proposes the idea of "autoethnography otherwise," which shifts the burden of the autoethnographic reading onto the critic (57), pushing critics to consider how we take up variously racialized writers and texts within institutional contexts. While many critics, including myself, have been suspicious of texts and writers that fall too easily into the managing tentacles of official multiculturalism, Paul Lai's critique is

compelling in the sense that it allows more room for both the broad historical and the personal/historical location of the writer and her own relationship to language, poetics, and narrative. It allows also for eruptions of the
unpredictable and/or that which counters or exceeds the expected form. Lai
notes further that ethnography itself has become a self-reflexive and creative
discipline, a far cry from the old ethnography that aimed to "document
objectively some static foreign culture." Rather, the new (auto)ethnographers
often have community-activist commitments (59). Lai writes:

> Rather than give up on autoethnography, ... these approaches to
> "autoethnography otherwise" challenge the bleak perspective that the
> cultural critic Rey Chow brings to the study of ethnicity when she argues
> that all ethnic cultural production in inescapably bound up in a "coercive
> mimeticism," the incessant and necessary performing of an ethnic self
> for a mainstream audience as well as one's own ethnic group that only
> serves to circumscribe any revolutionary potential of such productions.
> (60)

What I take from Paul Lai's incisive critique is the possibility that racialized
critics and writers, and again, I include myself, have been over-anxious about
falling into the ethnographic or the sociological for fear of being judged by
white critics as insufficiently literary. In so doing, we actually buy into an
Arnoldian ethics that says that in order to rise from the mud of our racialized origins, we must aim to produce "quality" writing to prove ourselves
worthy of the white man's approval.[3] If we accept Lai's critique, then the
blurring between the ethnographic/sociological and the literary in Bennett
Lee's introduction to *Many-Mouthed Birds* is less of a problem, and in fact,
makes a good measure of sense.[4] There is something freeing in not having
to worry about it.

What remains to be addressed with regard to *Many-Mouthed Birds* is the
editors' decision to frame it in national terms—Chinese Canadian rather
than Asian Canadian. In the aftermath of *Inalienable Rice*, why the return to
a Chinese Canadian frame? In documenting the politicized use of the term
"Asian Canadian," Xiaoping Li notes that the Asian American activist and
professor Ron Tanaka introduced Asian American activism in 1970 to his
Chinese Canadian and Japanese Canadian students (18). She tells us it was
introduced as a politicized and coalitional term. While the implication that
Ron Tanaka is the sole source of the term "Asian Canadian" is a problem,
what is interesting and useful about Li's articulation of his contribution is
the recognition that both Asian American and Asian Canadian are politicized, coalitional terms. Li, in fact, faults Lien Chao for not recognizing this

in Chao's articulation of the term "Chinese Canadian": "Chao fails to take
into account that fact that Chinese Canadian writing emerged and devel-
oped as an integral part of the Asian Canadian movement" (3). And what
is important here is not so much the denigration of Chao as the recognition
of the coalitional roots of the term "Chinese Canadian," particularly in its
artistic and activist modes. Of course, I am not suggesting that any of these
terms must be true to its history, nor, in fact, that they cannot have more
than one history. Miki's recognition of its multiple valences remains important here. Still, what is productive about Li's articulation of its development
is that it illustrates the ways in which Chinese Canadian and Japanese
Canadian students, activists, writers, and thinkers were politicized together
by doing social justice and art making together. Thus, they enter together
into a politicized and practised subjectivity understood as Asian Canadian.
Li explains further that, under Tanaka's direction, students formed a Japanese Canadian group—Wakayama—and a Chinese Canadian group—Gah
Hing (18). Thus, the broad coalitional banner—Asian Canadian—retains
the national separations through which Chinese Canadians and Japanese
Canadians have always been managed by the Canadian state, in addition to
reclaiming them for complicated cultural and national(ist) identifications
and for social justice purposes. In the form of Asian Canadian activism that
unfolded prior to the essentialism debates, Tanaka advocated for a political practice that profoundly involved the cultural: "[T]he end of all art
should be to bring about an understanding of the community's being in the
world" (Tanaka qtd. in Li 20). Without the uncertainties of a poststructural
approach, productive as they have been in more recent years, Tanaka could
call for a kind of passionate commitment that seems less accessible in this
early twenty-first-century, institutionalizing moment:

> There is one thing only that gives the Sansei artist a voice and that is his
> commitment to the best interests of the community and his willingness
> to suffer for that commitment. And why does he do this? Because he sees
> his own spiritual survival and that of his people are one and inseparable.
> (Tanaka qtd. in Li 20)

That Asian Canadian artists, writers, and activists did so much important
work on the basis of such calls illustrates the false dichotomy implicitly at
work in Guillory's mourning for the displacement of the artistic "genius" by
the "representative of social identity." If these two terms are not opposed,
then Paul Lai's assertion that cultural critics and producers need not be so
anxious about the sociological or the autoethnographic is further bolstered.

What cultural critics and producers do need to be concerned about, I
would argue, remains the politics of incorporation, institutionalizing or

otherwise. The framing of *Many-Mouthed Birds* matters for this reason. It is hard to be clear why Bennett Lee and Jim Wong-Chu decided to work with a Chinese Canadian frame instead of an Asian Canadian one, since they leave the Chinese Canadian framing of the anthology as self-evident. Did they do this because they felt that the Chinese Canadian writing community had reached a critical mass, and so did not need other Asian Canadian writers any more? Are there nationalist feelings that linger, perhaps connected to feelings of resentment against Japanese imperialism on the Asian continent, in spite of the fact that both Chinese Canadians and Japanese Canadians have suffered at the hands of the Canadian government here? Or is there a more complicated problem at work in the fact that Korean Canadians, Filipino Canadians, and South Asian Canadians also belong within the designation "Asian Canadian"—a designation that has always been problematic for placing Chinese Canadians and Japanese Canadians at the centre? These are problems that Lee and Wong-Chu, in spite of Chinese Canadian critical mass, might not have been equipped to address. The messiness of coalitional identification does not package well. It does not mainstream, sell, or institutionalize easily. In the commitment to "literary flavour" and a thematizing introduction, I would read this anthology as a push toward the mainstreaming of Chinese Canadian writing, particularly in the moments when Lee calls for a recognition of the universal in the (culturally) particular: "If the writing is true, it strikes a common chord in all of us, and we gain a deeper satisfaction because it stimulates our imagination and challenges our moral judgement. Otherwise, it will not endure, and no amount of novelty or exotic ornament can preserve it" (7). In this quote, the dichotomy between the white universal and the racialized otherness is preserved.

That said, in the title, *Many-Mouthed Birds*, activist roots still show. This is the case, as I have shown, in spite of the problem of silence-breaking in a Chinese Canadian context. In taking up the problem of silence-breaking, *Many-Mouthed Birds* already shows its connection to other racialized movements for which silence-breaking is a central practice. There remains beneath the surface, however, a lot of complication that affects relationships in the present moment. I am really just scratching the surface here. The recognition of a Chinese Canadian debt to Asian Canadian coalition building is, however, a good start.

While it is important to recognize coalitional terms because they build relationship across difference, it is also important to recognize the ways in which they become umbrella terms for easy packaging and easy management, as the term "people of colour," read from a mainstream media point of view, did during the scandal around Writing Thru Race. The danger of national terms like "Chinese Canadian," however, is that they give rise to the condition Rey Chow has so cogently called "the fascist longings in our midst." By the same token, both kinds of terminology are necessary under ongoing conditions of racial oppression. How they are deployed absolutely matters, and those who do justice work need to be very clear about their deployments. Here, because it has not been done sufficiently in an Asian Canadian context, I am trying to highlight that term's coalitional connections in order to hold its fascist dangers at bay.

QUEER AFFILIATIONS: "WE HAVE ALWAYS BEEN HERE"

I turn now to think through one instance of Asian Canadian literature's queer relations as they leave their trace in the important lesbian-of-colour anthology *Piece of My Heart*. The editor of *Piece of My Heart*, Makeda Silvera, explains in the introduction to the anthology how hard she struggled for critical mass. The problems that affected *Many-Mouthed Birds*, of timing, momentum, and enough writing to comprise an anthology, is compounded by the fact that lesbians of colour must deal not only with racism and sexism, but also homophobia (xiii). This homophobia comes as much from intimate locations—family, friends and community—as it is does from the broader society (xiv–xv). Audre Lorde's dictum "Your silence will not protect you" (qtd. in Silvera xiv) is of tantamount importance. Within the ethical frame of this book, coming out is a desirable and necessary action. Silvera doesn't articulate shame as a problem in so many words, but she does recognize coming out as a danger for lesbians of colour because it could very well bring about the loss of family and community, which provide necessary comforts within a racist society. The intersectional compounding of oppressions means that lesbians of colour are caught between a rock and a hard place when they decide to come out. To break the silence is thus, implicitly, to enter into an economy of shame—a different one from the one that is produced in "telling the secrets of Chinatown" but one that is no less safe, and one that is a great hindrance to publication. Interestingly, however, Silvera does not address shame as a hindering affect; rather, for her, it is fear that operates most strongly in stopping lesbians of colour from coming out and from putting their voices into print. Indeed, as Sarah Ahmed notes, thinking about racialized subjects in general and Frantz Fanon in particular, "it is the black subject, the one who fears the white child's fear, who is crushed by that fear, by being sealed into a body that tightens up, and takes up less space" (69). The parallel to lesbian-of-colour subjects here should be obvious. To break through not only one's own fear, but the fear of privileged others then, does constitute a heroics. In that sense, *Piece of My Heart* is a romantic text, but one that is necessarily so. Silvera is aware of this and makes no room for shame in her introduction. Instead, she theorizes the emergence of the voices included in *Piece of My Heart* as predicated on a kind of empowered "readiness" for a brave act, that she locates with the writers themselves (xiii). She is fully aware of the material consequences of coming out, in print, for many of the women included:

> It is a serious and brave act each time one of us comes out, because for some of us the danger is real. There is always that threat of physical violence depending on the community that we live in, and depending on our socio-economic condition. (xv)

I would like to argue, however, that while this "readiness," within a Western individualist culture that values agency, may be one way of explaining the moment of this explosion of voices, that there is another kind of timeliness at work, one that is oriented as much toward the future as toward the past. By this I mean that for those of us who do not place our faith in eternal and unchanging ontologies, we might still recognize productive acts of self-fashioning in the brave acts of coming out that Silvera describes. Subjects with histories grounded in experience are made present as subject through these acts, through performative iteration as Judith Butler has described it: "[T]he norm of sex takes hold to the extent that it is 'cited' as such a norm, but it also derives its power through the citations that it compels" (*Bodies That Matter* 13).

For Silvera, the question of "the literary" is a ridiculous question, when one writes under such circumstances:

> [S]omething must be said about those stilted voices, those voices that would not come out many years ago. In times like these, I like to go back to the personal, to turn the question around, "what about you? Would you have readily answered the call to such a book if you were not the initiator?" I have to honestly answer no. I would have hungrily bought the book, to read about others like me, to find strength and comfort in their words, but I might not have readily contributed without some coaxing. Why? The very thing Audre Lorde so eloquently speaks about, that fear, that silencing of our voices, of our lives as lesbians. (xiv)

Piece of My Heart is, then, a text that does not concern itself with the separation between the sociological/ethnographic and the literary. Its purpose is presencing and community building in the first instance. As such, though published in the same year as *Many-Mouthed Birds*, 1991, it is more like *Inalienable Rice*, in its initiatory impulse, and in its refusal of mainstream conceptions of "the literary."

Further, in order for this anthology to do its empowering work, it cannot afford a notion of social constructedness. It depends on the concept of naturalness. In retrospect, however, I think I would argue that this moment of the natural was one that was necessary, but also one that could not be sustained. The liberatory power of this politic lies in the movement of ideas, but it is a movement that cannot keep still. It is interesting that in this moment, identity is crystallized through a recourse to history, a notion of eternal time that is itself not eternal at all, but fully contingent.[5] *Piece of My Heart* is counter-canonical in its active production of history, what the Martinician critic Édouard Glissant calls *outilization* or utilization—drawing on the past according to the needs of the present in order to produce the future differently for its marginalized subjects (xvii).

Another kind of anthology tradition—that carried out through such established institutions as Norton, or Oxford University Press, anthologies that are assembled with the high-minded and often xenophobic practice of defining a tradition in the sense of "the best contemporary consensus of critical opinion," as George Woodcock in an essay entitled "Old and New Oxford Books: The Idea of an Anthology" attempts to outline for his readership (121). Woodcock spends the bulk of his essay explaining the relative merits of an "objective" anthology such as Dame Helen Gardner's *The New Oxford Book of English Verse, 1250–1950,* which he holds up as infinitely superior to, for instance, W. B. Yeats's *Oxford Book of Modern Verse.* Yeats's text he considers flawed because of Yeats's "strong convictions about the purpose of poetry or to equally strong loyalties towards his own past and friends" (121), the latter of which are suspect because they are, of course, Irish.

Silvera does not acknowledge these anthologies because they do not constitute a centre for her. The point of an anthology like *Piece of My Heart* is that it emerges from radical, liberatory histories, not conservative canon-building ones. The question here becomes how to think of such texts which have some relation to their institutionalized, canon-forming cousins, but a relation that is not linear or lineal, a relation that is not sanctioned, intended or desired by either party.

Both types of anthologies have a stake in the power of definition, though the "Oxford book" type is interested in a notion of tradition, while *Piece of My Heart* is more concerned with community construction. As such, it belongs more properly to the history of such texts as *This Bridge Called My Back,* edited by Cherríe Moraga and Gloria Anzaldúa in 1984.

The history of the community-based anthology is a relatively short one. While it relies on a kind of recourse to history for its solidifying power, its real power lies in its orientation toward the future, as John Rajchman describes in his essay "Diagram and Diagnosis":

> Nevertheless, the question often arises in relation to problems that come from population or demography. It comes from circumstances that place people in situations where, in relation to themselves and one another, they are no longer able to tell straight narratives about their "origins." Then they become "originals" without origins; their narratives become "out of joint," constructed through superposition or juxtaposition rather than through development or progress, in the manner of the "third worlds" which Deleuze thinks came to interrupt the political assumptions of more progressive narratives in cinema. It is this other kind of "synthesis of time," complicating our sense of "time," that shows a minority to be a "future people," a "virtual people," a "people to come." (50–51)

Through the production of identity in the present, one that calls to lost or unwritten histories, anthologies like *Piece of My Heart* complicate our sense of linear time and official history, while at the same time producing a hopeful future peopled by a new kind of subject that is not the liberal individual subject, but rather his politicized cousin (who emerges from a different relation to the same history, with something added that has yet to be named or written, that belongs to the irretrievable past), named for her particularity and her oppression but also her desire for a better, more self-affirming way of being and writing, and for her hope that there is an outside to the master/slave dialectic. She writes to embody this hope. It is on occasions like this that I see a progress narrative as still valuable and viable, though not in any totalizing kind of way. It is a kind of progress and a kind of hope, rather, that is profoundly haunted and paradoxically nonlinear. The access to history that is available for the writers in *Piece of My Heart* is the access Homi Bhabha has famously described in the introduction to *The Location of Culture*, in which he writes of subaltern histories as "not part of the continuum of past and present" (7) but still accessible to us through nightmarish returns of the repressed, that is through the uncanny, which Bhabha characterizes as "the beyond":

> The beyond is neither a new horizon, nor a leaving behind of the past ... Beginnings and endings may be the sustaining myths of the middle years; but in the *fin de siècle*, we find ourselves in the moment of transit where space and time cross to produce complex figures of difference and identity, past and present, inside and outside, inclusion and exclusion. For there is a sense of disorientation, a disturbance in direction, in the

"beyond": an exploratory, restless movement caught so well in the French rendition of the words *au-delà*—here and there, on all sides, *fort-da*, hither and thither, back and forth. (1)

The "we" of Silvera's "We have always been here" is marked by precisely this quality. Here is also "there." It is a "we" constituted in the present moment to refer to a set of historical practices that are highly embodied. The movement between identity and practice is ambulant and ungraspable. The self that is affirmed is under construction, affirmed differently each time, and yet highly necessary to a politics of empowerment that was so essential to the moment of *Piece of My Heart*.

With these considerations in mind, then, it is interesting that the projects I have been calling counter-anthologies, for the most part, emerge from outside the academy. Silvera, in fact, does not address the institution or the question of canon formation at all. She is interested in the production of history and community. While the conventional anthology struggles with a problem of too much (to administrate and contain) the counter-anthology struggles with a problem of not enough (due to systemic exclusions from access to reading, writing, and knowledge).

Insofar as the anthology, conventional or counter-, is itself an institution, however, it seems necessary to ask what exactly is produced in its construction. The act of self-naming, as I discussed in my Introduction, is of tantamount importance. That this is necessarily a reaction to master narratives about the Other remains a problem. I suggested earlier that marginalized voices emerge from a different relation to the same history as sanctioned, canonized voices, and further that multiple subject positions and histories cross through one another in complicated and interesting ways that show the barely hidden relations of marginalized people to one another if we are willing to see them.

For instance, the first poem in *Piece of My Heart*, "Coming Out at the Sushi Bar" by Mona Oikawa, is simultaneously productive of both Asian Canadian and lesbian subject positions from the very first line:

> The *maguro* is the colour of dawn
> The day I tell you
> "I am a lesbian." (*Piece of My Heart* 2)

In this dawning of Asian lesbian identity, this moment of fishy (maguro) birth, the speaker produces herself in a single speech act. It is a speech act that belongs to the present moment, the opening of both the poem and the anthology—not the death, but the birth of the author, as both talented and specifically located. Further, her locations are multiple: woman, lesbian, Japanese Canadian. In this opening moment the present is held up and sustained, but only for these three lines, before it falls again into the past:

> We had taken our places
> at our regular table
> nestled in the privacy
> of white *shoji*
> far from the men
> at the sushi bar … (2)

Later, the straight friend or relative addressed in the poem falls into the need to "analyze and rationalize," in other words, to historicize:

> "I knew after you had been away—
> Was it 1977?—
> that you came back different.
> I figured something horrible
> had happened to you.
> You had changed so much." (3)

The Asian lesbian speaker in the poem responds also through recourse to history:

> "It was actually after
> I'd gone away in 1980 that
> I decided I was a lesbian,"
> I reply. (3)

The attempt to historicize the birth of the subject in the first three lines becomes complicated, temporally uncertain. Clarity is lost because the dates referred to—1977 or 1980—are not moments of articulation, not moments when the subject is spoken into being, but moments of silent knowing not yet brought into language. The assertion "I am" is further complicated by the recognition that identities cannot be reified, an acknowledgement, in a sense, of the inadequacy of dialectic ("I" am a lesbian only because "you" are straight):

A familiar frost
is forming in my mouth
down through my chest,
reducing rich words of
lesbian complexity to
these elementary explanations
of why and how. (3)

The naming is a beginning but it is also a middle. The lesbian subject is produced in the middle of being, in the middle of the complexity of living. For
those on the privileged side of any binary it doesn't make sense, because they
do not have to account for themselves through recourse to identity. Living in
the middle of being is taken for granted. To be identified is to be an object
that must be explained and understood. The privileged and the marginalized
may emerge from the same history, but, as I have said, their relation to it is
very different. The something added to the marginalized position may well
be the something added that Kristeva discusses in *The Powers of Horror*:

> Not at all short of but always with and through perception and words,
> the sublime is *something added* that expands us, overstrains us, and causes
> us to be both *here* as dejects, and *there* as others and sparkling. A diver-
> gence, an impossible bounding. Everything missed, joy—fascination.
> (12)

For indeed, what the speaker in the poem tells her dining companion and
what she wants to say are related through both delight and loss, though it
is only a meagre kind of delight that she is able to express:

For what I really want
to tell you is that
my relationship with
my lover is turning,
may be ending.

I want someone who has
known me all my life
to see this pain,
to see how my insides
are being ripped away
leaving me hollow.

> But all I say is,
> "For me it is not
> something negative
> to be a lesbian." (4)

The "loss" perceived by the straight friend or relative, that of the speaker's heterosexuality, papers over a deeper, more complicated loss, that of the speaker's lover. The "negative" is thus misplaced, it is elsewhere and at the same time supplemental to the what the dining companion thinks. This "something added" is both sublime and abject—it belongs to a delight in being beyond the possibilities of normative heterosexuality, and at the same time is marked by losses greater than those possible in straightness—losses, further, that can't be articulated because the listener has no context through which to understand them. In this misrecognition of what was lost, something has been added beyond the mere production of identity, something in excess of the subject herself, pain in the movement of emotion between lesbian subjects. A politics of identity cannot account for this excess. And interestingly, this is acknowledged in the anthology's first poem—one that is first and foremost about the production of identity: "I am a lesbian."

Oikawa opens up the possibility that in the future, this sublime excess can be articulated:

> May be next time
> I will tell you
> how loving women
> did change my life—
> then describe to you how
> a woman's touch is soft,
> and how only a woman's touch
> can send me beyond
> the grief of this world—
>
> But not tonight— (4–5)

What is interesting about this future, this later location of "a people to come" (pardon the pun) is that it is based in action—"loving women"—rather than ontology—"being lesbian." A different kind of movement is at work in this possible future, one based on movement rather than stasis, action rather than being.

At the close of the poem, the two women return home. The straight friend returns to her family in the suburbs. The Asian lesbian speaker returns to a much less stable place, but a place no less beautiful for its constant movement:

> And I will return
> to my home,
> moving in the wind
> of women's voices,
> lesbian voices,
> honouring our passionate
> comings and goings
> through these life-long
> journeys of coming out. (5)

Oikawa acknowledges that for the marginalized subject, the return—to home? to history?—does not have the luxury of apparent stability that the straight woman's home does (though of course, were one to do a post-structuralist analysis of heterosexual suburban home life, one might easily illustrate the constructed, ideological underpinnings of the ideals it is based on). The speaker's home moves "in the wind/of women's voices." It is contingent and ephemeral, even as the poem establishes a sort of home place for lesbians of colour within the covers of the anthology. This poem, which at its beginning was about being a lesbian, concludes that this "being" is never done, but is rather a "life-long journey ... of coming out." Leading into the rest of the anthology, this poem, in a sense, offers the rest of the anthology as part of that "life-long journey."

For Silvera, the U.S./Canada border is not an issue. She notes in the introduction that the first call for submissions, issued in 1985, was distributed in Canada only, but that it went out in the United States later. She does not single the Canada/U.S. border out for analysis; there are so many differences at work in this text that the Canada/U.S. border is just one of many. Importantly, however, she includes Audre Lorde's "I Am Your Sister: Black Women Organizing Across Sexualities." The Caribbean-American civil rights activist and writer Audre Lorde is important because her writing, teaching, and activism formed the basis of later work by lesbian-of-colour writers and activists across Europe and North America. Her work is not particularly connected to ethnic studies programs in the United States or elsewhere, though they no doubt take it up. But her reach is infinitely broader than this. In the context of *Piece of My Heart*, it grounds this text, which includes lesbians of colour from both the United States and Canada without distinguishing national boundaries. What I would like to take up here is the tension between doing and being that arises in "I Am Your Sister" because it tells us something about the way lesbians-of-colour subjects both come into being and have always been here. Its original importance, however, is in the way that it pushes African American activists to recognize the lesbians among them, and to recognize sexuality as an African American issue.

To think about identity as motile space of becoming is not always better than thinking about it in terms of a blunt simplicity of being. In "I Am Your Sister: Black Women Organizing Across Sexualities," the famous essay that in many ways grounds the anthology, Audre Lorde reminds us:

> When Yoli and I cooked curried chicken and beans and rice and took our extra blankets and pillows up the hill to the striking students occupying buildings at City College in 1969, demanding open admissions and the right to an education, I was a Black Lesbian. When I walked through the midnight hallways of Lehman College that same year, carrying Midol and Kotex pads for the young Black radical women taking part in that action, and we tried to persuade them that their place in the revolution was not ten paces behind Black men, that spreading their legs to the guys on the tables in the cafeteria was not a revolutionary act no matter what the brothers said, I was a Black Lesbian. When I picketed for Welfare Mothers' Rights, and against the enforced sterilization of young Black girls, when I fought institutionalized racism in New York City schools, I was a Black Lesbian.
>
> But you did not know it because we did not identify ourselves, so now you can say that Black Lesbians and Gay men have nothing to do with the struggles of the Black Nation.
>
> And I am not alone. (*Piece of My Heart* 97)

While the past political actions of the speaker in this text are clearly important, the point of each rhetorical turn is identity, not action. And it is in this identity that the political power of the subaltern resides. The perpetual present of Black Lesbian being lies as a constant beneath activist contributions that fall continuously into the past. It has power *in this moment* because this is the moment at which it emerges into the light of day. This is the moment between invisibility and appearance, and thus the moment of maximum rhetorical power. It is a location that Homi Bhabha has described as the in-between, the middle passage. As such, it is a moment of becoming, in spite of its apparent stasis.

What is interesting about this moment of becoming is that it is not dialectic. It does not emerge in opposition to the political actions Lorde describes, nor in opposition to other identities named—straight Black men and straight Black women. Rather it is a movement to declare solidarity in difference: "I am your sister." It is a speaking with, or a speaking alongside, without erasing power imbalance, without letting the privileged other off the hook.

Deleuze's anti-Hegelianism may be useful here to think through non-di-alectical productions of difference. Deleuze argues that Hegel's notion of the dialectic cannot work because it depends on polarized, essentialized positions for its thesis and antithesis. These positions are last instances that no one ever occupies. Further, they deny the progression of positions between poles, and the whole range of difference that occurs through that progression. In a way, he posits a kind of false consciousness with Hegel's dialectic—which ought to have massive repercussions for our readings of Marx later on! If "the proletariat" or "Black Lesbians" are not essential identities rooted in class consciousness, but rather identities continuously produced through an Althusserian kind of hailing, or a Butlerian performance, this means something quite different in terms of the movement of difference between "the proletariat" and "the bourgeoisie," or between "Black Lesbians" and "straight Black women" or "straight Black men." In pragmatic terms, it changes the necessity of class war into something much more complicated and subtle.

Janet Jakobsen writes:

> A feminist politics addressed only to oppositional gender is part and parcel of a political configuration which isolates binary pairs from each other so that gender, race, class, and sexuality are all constituted as separate areas of analysis and of political action. In this configuration, analyses of race focus on a black/white opposition, class analyses concentrate on the bourgeoisie/proletariat split, the study of sexuality focuses on the hetero/homo binary, while gender analyses become the study of men and women as opposites. This type of knowledge production and its concomitant politics does not ultimately challenge the binary pairs on which it depends. (9)

She is arguing, in other words, against dialectic difference as a liberatory mode of analysis, but rather proposes that it, in fact, solidifies binary positions. She does not seem to place faith in the moment of synthesis, when thesis and antithesis are resolved.

The production of difference at a micro scale may well be more import-ant than the production of large-scale dialectic difference. Certainly, if the right-wing deployment of the term "politically correct" to shut down pro-gressive discourse of any kind by the late nineties is any indication, dialectic difference has proven to be far less useful than it first seemed. What is interesting about "I Am Your Sister" is that it produces both difference and sameness between action and identity: when I did this, I was that. Doing and being cleave together, as both the same, and different, in a single move. This kind of difference works to produce an actionable solidarity, not one that denies dialectic difference, but one that includes it as only one kind of difference, and not necessarily the most useful. These small, non-dialectic movements of becoming have been largely undertheorized, especially in marginalized communities.

Reading Deleuze's *Difference and Repetition*, Manuel De Landa notes:

> [T]hat which is beyond what is given to us in experience is not a being, but a becoming, a difference-driven process by which the given is given.... [M]any phenomena ... emerge spontaneously from the interplay of intensity differences. (31)

Incompleteness and motion, the play of difference, tells us more about ourselves than static being:

> [M]ost of the important philosophical insights can be grasped only during the process of morphogenesis, that is, before the final form is actualized, before the difference disappears. (32)

This emphasis on "becoming" is important because it does not require the truth of any essence in order to be productive. Deleuze, of course, is highly critical of essence of any sort. This is why he eschews Hegelian dialectic altogether. He doesn't accept the truth of its endpoints—its theses and antitheses. But if these things cease to be important, if instead, what leads to an open-ended future is the flow between intensities, then liberation resides not in any synthesis, not in any revolution or any institution, but in the imperfect moment of flow, in the unruly present. What becomes necessary for this kind of liberation is not a polemic, but rather a catalyst:

> [A] catalyst intervenes in reality, recognizes specific targets, triggers effects, causes encounters that would not have taken place without it, and yet is not consumed or permanently changed in these interactions, so that it can go on triggering effects elsewhere. (37)

What I would like to suggest here is that the so-called identity-based texts of the late 1980s and early 1990s, that have fallen so out of favour of late, were doing, and continue to do that catalytic work. In spite of the fact that they can be read as polemical, as over-simplistic or too essentialist, perhaps those readings are, if not beside the point, exactly, but less useful at present than they were at an earlier moment. What is useful now is to think of these so-called identity-based texts as catalysts for an open-ended future that place their writers and readers into an open flow that moves from intensity to intensity. In other words, it is not their "truth" that is important, it is their catalytic power. The question we need to constantly ask then, is what the intensities of the moment are. This way of thinking differs from a Butlerian approach that sees identities as being crystallized through repetitive speech acts: "I take you to be my wife" or "I am a Black lesbian." The identities themselves become less important than the action taken to produce them. To emphasize the temporal instability of identity is to refuse identity as an object or as a category that can be written over for the purposes of marketing, institutionalization, or any other solidifying force.

In "A Lesbian Love Letter," Joanna Kadi opens with a single, italicized sentence, which gets repeated five times over the course of the letter: "*This is the letter I wish someone had written for me when I was a young woman*" (*Piece of My Heart* 100). In a sense, she writes the letter to herself as a young woman, in retrospect. This letter becomes the future of a past that never was, but that could have been. In the logic of what Derrida has called "the future anterior," it produces the subject of that lost future in the present, through its present articulation. Like the anthology itself, this piece is a kind of self-birthing, or rather a self-rebirthing, in which the writer calls to the past in order to reproduce the present in a less monolithic, more hopeful, open-ended form.

What I am suggesting here are two things. First of all, that the truth claims about identity made by radical anti-racist politics in the late 1980s and early 1990s were productive not because they were "true" but because they were "intense" in the Deleuzian sense. Thus, reactionary arguments against them ("reverse racism," "politically correct," and so forth) are beside the point because they fail to recognize or actively refuse the intense productivity of that language for subjects historically marginalized by racist discourse and practice. Further, this way of thinking opens the way for alliance building between (white) left-leaning intellectuals of that moment (mourning the death of the author, the absence of the transcendental signified at the root of any signifier and so on) and anti-racist activists of colour, lesbians of colour, working-class people of colour in ways that did not seem possible in that moment. While certain thinkers recognized the temporal fluidity of so-called identity politics, through such terms as "contingent," "strategic," or, more cynically, "flavour of the month," what is important here, I think, is to recognize the democratic usefulness of that temporal fluidity, in the sense that something is freed up that was bound before. It opens the possibility that other contingent stances can be useful in the (hopeful) future.

The second thing I want to recognize is that a creative call to history in the present can be deeply productive of intense if contingent ontologies. So when Joanna Kadi writes that "[l]esbians of colour have always existed, and we will always exist," she is right, regardless of the recentness of the notion of "lesbian" as an identity. To regard the perpetual present as a valid and productive site of political production is to regard many futures as possible, even as one keeps a steady eye on the past so as not to become completely unmoored from the material and dialectic ways in which it has produced us. This, I think, is the contradiction our present moment needs to work with, not necessarily to resolve, but to move through in small, non-dialectic turns.

REMEMBERING THE FUTURE: ASIAN AMERICAN HAUNTINGS

To that end, I would like to close this chapter by discussing an anthology that is aware of what the conventional anthology form does, and attempts to do something else. On the dust jacket of Walter Lew's *Premonitions*, Stephen Sumida remarks:

> Up to recently, Asian American literary anthologies have served to canonize authors, works, tastes, and ideas. *Premonitions* is different. From conception to layout, it explodes impulses to map centers and margins of Asian American poetry. Instead *Premonitions* gives us a brilliant variety of poetry and poets who together show: we are all this and more.

Sumida does not claim that *Premonitions* works against the more conventional type of anthology like *Many-Mouthed Birds*. Rather it adds to it, and in doing so produces a more open-ended kind of subjectivity for poets marked "Asian American."[6] It seems important to note, however, that the supplemental quality of this anthology is only possible because conventional anthologies have preceded it.[7] Without them, its innovation, however extraordinary, would not be legible.

The two anthologies I have discussed prior to this both take recourse to history in order to produce a very particular kind of present, one that produces a new kind of subject from the spectres and disjunctures of the past, in much the way that Homi Bhabha describes in the introduction to *The Location of Culture*. There is an ambulant motion to and fro between past and present, in order to make the liberatory subject anew, in the present, a subject fundamentally different from the subject of official, linear, national histories. I wonder what kind of social labour this subject does, once drawn into the folds of the nation-state, that is once it has received a Canada Council grant, been read by the mainstream press, or for that matter, been anthologized. However productive the motion back and forth between

disappearance and appearance, between marginalization and self-articulation, the minute marked subject gets the acknowledgement it seeks, it loses
its subaltern power.

What is generative about the subjects of *Premonitions* is that they don't
look to the broken past for reflections of themselves with which to cobble
themselves together in the present. Rather, they look to the future: "The
premonitions in this book remember the future, augur the past, play the
present apart from itself—especially where 'history' is too much agreed
upon" (Lew 583).

Its project is very different from that of *Many-Mouthed Birds*. Instead of
attempting to fix a history with themes and a cast of characters, a history
articulated by "authentic" subjects of that history, it takes on the term "Asian
North American" in all its troubled forms—racist, anti-racist, anthropological, authentic, self-identifying—and allows its subjects to draw from
the future to ensure that the present is never entirely graspable, but rather
caught in an endless play of *différance* in which the subject cannot be fixed,
cannot be read the same way twice, and therefore cannot be commodified.

There is something about seeking a reflection of oneself in the past, however uncannily produced, that remains an exercise of legitimation, that is,
asking for entry into the nation-state. It is this future orientation toward the
subject that makes the project of *Premonitions* different from that of earlier
progressive community-building projects. I would like to consider Homi
Bhabha's introduction to *The Location of Culture*, as a piece that clearly eluci-
dates a prior progressive project. While it productively locates the history of
racially marginalized people in an uncanny past that appears and disappears
through the logic of fort/da, which Bhabha borrows from Freud's theory of
the *unheimlich*, it still seeks the production of subjectivity in the past, that is,
in history. Further, it still looks to the master for recognition. Bhabha quotes
Fanon: "As soon as I desire, I am asking to be considered" (8). The desire to
belong is the desire to remain inside the master/slave dialectic.

In looking to the future, *Premonitions* produces a more open-ended present. The people to come revel in their futurity; they do not need the legitimation of history. This is what makes Lew's move a bold one.

The recognition that Bhabha comes to, that to do the work of the uncanny
is still to "pressure power along its borders from the inside" emerges, I argue,
from the desire to be considered, the desire to belong to the patriarchy, the
state, and other institutions, however ambivalently. And indeed, as long as
one remains on the margins of these institutions, that project is a liberatory
one. But I would like to question what happens to a liberatory politics from
the margins once a few bodies and a few texts have been admitted.[8]

Were one to embrace the minor emotions Sianne Ngai discusses, or to build one's subjectivity by remembering the future, as Lew proposes, it may be possible to produce an outside, perhaps one that is abject and unstable, but nonetheless one that is full of possibility and therefore hopeful.

What makes *Premonitions* interesting is that its "desire to be considered" is a secondary concern. This is a firmly rebellious text (albeit non-dialectically rebellious!), with no intention of appeasing or explaining. Lew is much more concerned with bringing into view those poetic practices that expressly do not fulfil expectations of what an Asian North American anthology should be or do. He looks to those works that have been routinely excluded from other anthologies. In his afterword, he writes:

> The work in this anthology is not confined to conventional models of verse and encompasses many ways in which language is drastically reshaped into fresh articulations, ranging from video collage and highly compressed prose poems to cyberpunk critiques of ethnic mimicry. Previous anthologies have been either too small or conservative to convey the astonishing diversity and eloquence of new poetries spread out among numerous networks and poetics—both esoteric and activist, imagist and deconstructive, pidgin and purist, diasporic and Americanist, high literary and pop cultural. (595)

Rather than revealing secrets or answering (implicit) questions from a white mainstream outside, *Premonitions* launches into the being of writing. Indeed, the strategy of providing an afterword rather than a foreword, allows the reader to directly experience the text first, without the authoritative, translational explanation that most anthologies posit as necessary. Its stance toward the texts between its covers is deeply respectful. It allows them to speak for themselves. In so doing, it also places faith in the reader in a way that anthologies with introductions or prefaces do not. It respects; it holds no one's hand. In that sense it also demands. It does not ask to be considered. It insists its presence.

Oddly, however, Lew's first move in the anthology is a commemorative gesture to the past. The anthology is dedicated to three deceased Asian North American writers: Theresa Hak Kyung Cha, Roy Kiyooka, and Frances Chung.

The epigraph following the names and dates of the dead writers (which also marks the anthology's first "zone") reads:

                                                    sculpted

        in a vertiginous light

The commemorative gesture is interesting in the sense that, while honouring the deceased writers, it also produces them in a heroic idiom that none of them experienced in life. Theresa Hak Kyung Cha, at the time of her murder in New York City in 1982, had just published *Dictée*, her first and only book, and was just beginning to garner a reputation as a filmmaker, artist, and writer. Roy Kiyooka, though currently enjoying some fame/notoriety among a small circle of Asian Canadian and/or avant-garde writers and artists, was largely marginalized as both a writer and artist during his lifetime. And even more than the previous two, whose works have enjoyed some resurgence of late, Frances Chung is hardly a heralded poet in North American letters, though Lew has recently edited and published a volume of her poetry. To "sculpt" them, then, is an act of recuperation as much as an act of commemoration. But they are not sculpted in marble, stone, clay, or any other kind of traditionally commemorative material. Rather, they are sculpted in a dizzying light from on high—light, perhaps, from the future, in which their outlines appear quite differently from the racist light of the past, which passes right through them, barely registering them at all.

By calling to the practice of sculpting in this opening epigraph, Lew also gestures to an outside to writing practice. And indeed all three of these writers have practices outside writing, which Lew highlights through his editorial selection of their work. The first piece in the book, a fragment from Theresa Cha's *Commentaire*, is highly visual in its intent and construction. The first page, interestingly, is pure black. The second facing page is a grainy, black and white film still, which we learn at the end of the piece comes from Carl Theodor Dreyer's 1931 film *Vampyr*. The still, in fact, comes from a moment in the film when Allan Gray, the protagonist, has become one of the undead and is looking out from a window in his coffin at the face of his former host, who collaborates with vampires. The shot is from Gray's point of view.

As an editorial choice for the anthology's first page of poetry, this is an odd and interesting one, first of all because it is not "poetry" in the conventional sense, but rather an image. Further, it is contained within a series of quotation marks. Cha quotes Dreyer; Lew quotes Cha. It is as though Cha has had a premonition of her own murder, and her own return from the dead, as something of a "cult figure" for Asian North American writers, artists, and activists. She looks out at us and sees traitors who have collaborated with vampires (!), or at least those who would consume us. Lew's act of commemoration is thus simultaneously Cha's act of augury, and both are frozen in the perpetual present of the anthology.

Page by page, or screen by screen, Cha plays anagrammatic games with the word "commentaire": "comme," "comment," "comment taire," "tear." Or:

"like," "how," "how to shut up," "tear." She is playing with the question of point of view. Though she doesn't refer to either gender or race, the problem of subjectivity is important here because the piece seems to be about precisely the problem of where to speak from. Posthumously, questions of race and gender are supplemented by questions of mortality. How can she speak to or about this strangely xenophobic film—as a woman, as a Korean American, from the dead? How to shut up when one is speaking to a film that hangs halfway between silent and speaking, dead and undead? For indeed, the film is odd in this way. It follows many of the formal conventions of silent film. There is much textual narration between photographic segments. The film depends on textual narration for its sense. But it does have a soundtrack. This consists largely of melodramatic music of the type conventionally played live in the silent era, to accompany silent films. But on this soundtrack, we can hear the speakers speaking, though indistinctly. The indistinction is compounded by the fact that most of the speech is in German, while all of the text, in my version at least, is in English. (The film was made in two versions, one German, the other English. It also contains some text in French.) To view it is at once to get caught inside its strange, creepy narrative, but also to be brought further or closer to the text at different moments depending on the form of address.

Cha's text functions in a similar manner. Working in multiple modes of address, it is alternately enigmatic, obfuscating, and then oddly melancholy. At its centre lies an image of a blank but glowing screen in front of an auditorium that looks empty at first glance, until one looks closely. And then it becomes evident that there are prone bodies in the aisles. They could be dead or they could be sleeping. The question of framing is thus paramount. This image is oddly similar to the central image in the Wendy Coburn piece in *Colour. An Issue* (one of the special issues I discussed in Chapter 2) except for the presence of the prone bodies. But while Coburn is at a loss for words in the face of an unresolvable matrix of power, Cha is prone. She sleeps, or lies like one of the undead in front of the empty glowing screen, able to comment only on the expectation of commentary, and the presence of the screen all around us. Obsessively observant, she points repeatedly to the screen: "ecran," then "sur ecran." The screen is everything. We are presented with a photograph of a brick wall, in which the dimensions of the bricks echo the dimensions of the screen, but there are many of them; the screen has multiplied in daily life. The brick wall is an obstacle. We are halted by the screen, its repetitiveness, its omnipresence.

At the close of the piece is an image of Allan Gray, seeing himself in a mirror, after his body has split. A sort of conscious astral projection of the young man wanders the earth, while his undead body lies in a windowed coffin. We see ourselves in windows, or mirrors, from other temporalities, and feel the pressure to comment. We are at a loss for words.

The only text in the piece that might stand as commentary, or content, are two pages, one that reads "WENT PAST MOMENT" and the other that reads "ARILY." We are left asking who or what might have gone past, "airily." The ghost of Cha? Or the images on the screen? And which past moment is important? This is not the return of Morrison's character Beloved, which Bhabha marks in *The Location of Culture*. The memory of a certain trauma—slavery—is absent here. What we do know is that at some point after the making of this piece, Cha will face a trauma of her own—that is, her own murder. The layers of referentiality are different from those of *Beloved*. While Morrison makes a representation to expiate a real history of oppression, Cha stutters, in the end, unable to pass commentary, but only to present a mirror. It is a prescient mirror in the sense that it predicts her own future, but only the editor Lew would know that. Its act of representation is direct, but only in retrospect. In a sense, it is a kind of unintentional autobiography of her own future. Its orientation toward time is thus not *fort/da*, not the cycle of loss and return that Bhabha so eloquently explains, and *Beloved* so beautifully exemplifies in *The Location of Culture* but something more future-oriented, and more open-ended, though not necessarily any less violent.

And indeed, one could say precisely the same thing about *Premonitions* itself. In the final words of the afterword, Lew writes:

> Some of the oldest Buddhist texts describe the pasts, presents, and futures, as each having overlapping pasts, presents and futures, with time flowing backwards through them. Others, to reflect the possibility of enlightenment bursting karmic links at any point, describe the world as destroyed and created at every moment. Premonitional poetry sees clearly the play between all divisions of tense, harmonizes the modal switches where fact and simile still pulse together as the possible, and must believe, like a master fighter or musician, that its throws, strokes, and attentuation, no longer owned by a source, will hit their mark, beyond the tired chords of the known—a "still arc between sight, and more sight" (Yamamoto), one's "hand that close to the unconscious" (Hahn). (584)

If Bhabha has taught us that the past isn't fixed, Lew teaches us that the same is true of the future. As the past can produce new subjectivities in the present, however uncanny, the future can do the same. But these new subjectivities need not be so haunted. The valence of their possibility need not be so grief-stricken, nor so violent, though it certainly can be. Lew produces for us a multi-valenced vision of "the city to come," as John Rajchman, writing on Kant describes:

> In particular, he seems to have in mind the question of what it would mean to introduce into the concept of democracy the as yet unrepresentable "time" of the minority, and so oblige it to experiment with its own concept. What would it mean to introduce this "city to come," which is that of our singularities, our "originalities" without origins, into our idea of what democracy can yet be? (52)

Lew's vision of the future is newly productive in the sense that, loosened (though not divorced) from histories of violence and oppression, it allows for the production of subjectivity that is not overdetermined by the oppressive past. It has not forgotten it. The possibility for a violent future has not been erased. But possibilities for other futures lie alongside it, and are also open for construction, reconstruction, vision, and revision in the present.

CHAPTER 4

FUTURE ORIENTATIONS, NON-DIALECTICAL MONSTERS

Storytelling Queer Utopias in Hiromi Goto's *Chorus of Mushrooms*
and *The Kappa Child*

GENERATION

If, as I discussed in my first chapter, realist modes—including autobiography—run the danger of state incorporation, capitalist consumption, and the repression of racialized trauma, then it becomes necessary to seek other strategies of subject production, other agencies to resist containment. I argue here that the work of Hiromi Goto offers an alternative strategy, one of queer/abject utopianism, which, in taking up and revaluing the waste and excess of the heterosexual, patriarchal, settler state as it is attached to global capital, makes a strange but democratic future to the communities of readers who take it up. Aware of history and of inherited racial trauma and injustice, Goto's narratives assert a critique. She is aware that critique is necessary, and also that it does not produce habitable spaces for living. Goto's work is thus consciously constructive; it engages the imagination as a live force with which to make the world differently. Her storytelling nudges into play what Mikhail Bakhtin calls "the material bodily principle." Goto's work is not, however, carnival in the Bakhtinian sense; it is not a release valve to make the life of the "daylight world" possible. Rather, its materializations have a real political power to build the world and hold that world in place. *Chorus of Mushrooms* and *The Kappa Child* were written at a time of massive social transformation—the 1980s and 1990s. Their narratives are part of a set of narratives that shift the state from its old, racist form to a more hopeful, pluralist one. While her work actively alters the social conditions of queer Asian Canadian lives, it is not able to hold back the cascade of neoliberal economic change.

STORYTELLERS MAKE THE WORLD

Hiromi Goto's novels belong to the anti-foundational moment in the ongoing cycle of Asian Canadian ontologies. For Goto it is stories rather than history that is important. I recognize the movement of racialized ontologies through a cycle of solidification and dispersal, and would like to emphasize dispersal here. If Asian Canadian literature is—sometimes—without an origin, and sometimes belongs to nonlinear moments of rupture, then it is not history but story that keeps it unfolding. As Trinh Minh-ha writes: "In undoing established models and codes, plurality adds up to no total" (*When the Moon Waxes Red* 15). Rather than births or foundations, she emphasizes re-departure:

> Re-departure: the pain and frustration of having to live a difference that has no name and too many names already. Marginality: who names? whose fringes? An elsewhere that does not merely lie outside the centre, but radically striates it.... Identity is a way of re-departing. Rather, the return to a denied heritage allows one to start again with different re-departures, different pauses, different arrivals ... when identity is doubled, tripled, multiplied across time (generations) and space (cultures), when differences keep blooming within despite rejections from without, she dares—by necessity. (*When the Moon Waxes Red* 14)

For Trinh, then, racialized subjects are never born, exactly, but only ever re-depart. Re-departures occur without essence or origin. While it may seem that the idea of the "new" is important for liberation from racialized oppressions, what Trinh teaches us is that the new, because it erupts cyclically, is paradoxically already old and tainted. But this is a boon, not a bane, because it holds what Rey Chow calls "the fascist longings in our midst" at bay. In order to do so, it holds the fully formed subject also at bay. This is something that Roy Miki recognizes in his much quoted "Asiancy" essay: "Historically and even at present, the strain of a domineering exterior on the interior of those in a state of exclusion created/creates complicated networks of ambiguities, repressions and compromises that infiltrate the language and geography of their subjectivity" (*Broken Entries* 108). Further, in his more recent collection *In Flux*, Miki recognizes the profound political and material implications of this recognition for the moment of that text (2011): "Working in the midst of the social and cultural formations that produce indeterminacy and uncertainty in our positioning vis-à-vis a desire to engage in progressive scholarship, the epistemological and social implications of pedagogy have moved directly into the foreground of our work as academics who are also social subjects" (150–51). Here Miki is thinking about the relationship between the institutional and the non-institutional, and in particular the role of racialized professors. What he says is also relevant, however, in relation to writers engaged in both creative practice and the production of community. Trinh is helpful here in recognizing that for racialized subjects, fluctuations through ontological presence and absence make room for the rupture of story, and collectivity in story. For her, the answer to the question "Who speaks?" is "the story itself": "it-speaks-itself-through me" (*When the Moon Waxes Red* 12). The tale is anterior to the teller (12). She emphasizes the fact that the relation between narration and "reality" is mutually productive. Story is returned to people, however—not one person or one teller, but many:

> The story depends upon every one of us to come into being. It needs us all, needs our remembering, understanding and creating what we have heard together to keep coming into being. The story of a people. Of us, peoples. Story, history, literature (or religion, philosophy, natural science, ethics)—all in one. (*Woman, Native, Other* 119)

In emphasizing story, rather than history, Trinh emphasizes collectivity and community rather than hierarchy and the concentration of power.

The recognition of collectivity is of tantamount importance in the 1980s and 1990s. The forms it takes are often oppositional, but they are also profoundly coalitional. As much as anthologies and special issues nurtured writers, so too did a vast array of events and gatherings across a range of disciplinary boundaries, and also between institutions and other organizational structures—often temporary and with fluctuating memberships. Certainly, the 1994 conference Writing Thru Race was important. But so were organizations not directly focused on writing practice or criticism as such, including Chinese Canadian Cultural Projects, Asian Lesbians of Vancouver (and later Monsoon), Asian Lesbians of Toronto, Desh Pardesh (a South Asian Canadian cultural festival based in Toronto), the Minquon Panchayat (an organization of artists and organizers of colour associated with artist-run centres), the Japanese Canadian Citizens Association (which emerged from the Japanese Canadian internment redress movement), and the Powell Street Festival. Exhibitions also supported creative production and critical discussion. Some of these include *Yellow Peril: Reconsidered, Self Not Whole*, and *Racy Sexy*.[1] While the work of many of these groups may have begun from a site of opposition, they rapidly became much more complicated and interesting than that. I have attempted, in the previous three chapters, to address a few of these complications.

Hiromi Goto is a writer who emerges from the histories of community work, including anthology and special issue production, and was also involved in a number of the events described above. In reading Goto's work, I want to problematize the notion of generations, as a structure of succession. In keeping with the nonlinear/out-of-joint temporality I proposed in the Introduction, and emphasizing it because the moment of this book's emergence is one newly fixated on hierarchy and linearity, I want to recognize the simultaneous or near simultaneous emergence of texts that often get understood as separated by a generation (in its conventional sense). Texts that are commonly understood as early were not so very early. Evelyn Lau's *Runaway* came out in 1989; SKY Lee's *Disappearing Moon Cafe* came out in 1990; Wayson Choy's *The Jade Peony* came out in 1995. Hiromi Goto's *Chorus of Mushrooms* came out in 1994. Only Joy Kogawa's *Obasan* (1981) might be read as substantially earlier than the other texts and it still belongs to the 1980s. What marks Goto's work is not so much the linear/Gregorian moment of its emergence as its embrace of an anti-realist stance. In actively querying the coincidence of narrative with the writing self, Goto embraces a self-reflexive relationship to the text and the speaking subject. In so doing, it sits in a different relationship to community, politics, and the idea of "the literary."

Cognizant of the pitfalls of straight autobiography, and also the necessity to address history in order not to fall into denial, liberalism, and whitewash, Goto's narrative practice consciously eschews realist generic conventions. Her first novel, *Chorus of Mushrooms*, is a multi-vocal exploration of other worlds and other modes of storytelling that ask questions about truth, audience, desire, and history. She does not attempt to "set the record straight," but rather is consciously invested in the playing out of new subjectivities that do not deny historical oppression, but at the same time, refuse to be stuck in it, or defined by it.

Much has been written about the oppositional strategies at work in *Chorus of Mushrooms*. But what is important about this text, as Eleanor Ty has pointed out, is the way in which it queries the act of representation itself, as always contingent and differently legible depending on who speaks:

> The various inserted discourses about stories, the truth, and the past reveal Goto's concern not so much with accuracy, but with representation and the power of representation. Whose version of the truth gets told is more important than the question of what is truth. (158)

Himani Bannerji's question "Who speaks?" has deepened. In the moment of Bannerji's query, the material issue on the ground was that of white "experts" speaking for the marginalized in ways that appropriated their/our stories and relegated them/us to the role of anthropological object in their/our own histories. Through the appropriation debates, through critical work done in anthropology, and importantly here, through work done by writer/activists embedded in racialized communities, the question of the speaking subject was asked and experimented with through the 1980s and 1990s. Goto's *Chorus of Mushrooms* is one of the key texts that asks and plays out these questions in an Asian Canadian context.

As the voices of politically savvy writers of colour like Goto come to a place where they can be heard, the question "Who speaks?" becomes more complicated. Spivak, explaining the problem as it was raised by the Subaltern Studies Group, writes:

> Because of ... [the] bestowal of a historical specificity to consciousness in the narrow sense, even as it implicitly operates as a metaphysical methodological pre-supposition in the general sense, there is always a counterpointing suggestion in the work of the group that subaltern consciousness is subject to the cathexis of the élite, that is never fully recoverable, that is always askew from its received signifiers, indeed that it is effaced even as it is disclosed, that is irreducibly discursive. (*In Other Worlds* 203)

There is something at work in the metaphysics of hegemonic language that makes the recovery of racialized consciousness inaccessible, even when it finds speech:

> Yet the language seems also to be straining to acknowledge that the subaltern's view, will, presence, can be no more than a theoretical fiction to entitle the project of reading. It cannot be recovered, "it will probably never be recovered." (*In Other Worlds* 204)

Profoundly aware of this, particularly as it pertains to the character of Grandma Naoe in *Chorus of Mushrooms*, Goto invents a "nearby" language to ventriloquize the speech of Grandma Naoe, while leaving a trace of the impossibility of her speech. In figuring Grandma Naoe as a force of nature—the wind—Goto imbues the impossibility of Naoe's speech with a kind of power that precedes human power. In so doing, she lifts her from the necessity of human metaphysics.

Further, if the irretrievability of subaltern narrative in hegemonic language is compounded by the overdetermination of its connection to trauma, Goto is in need of a new model of story that is not hegemonic, but remembers trauma and subjugation without being solely dependent on the moment of trauma for its vitality. It is here that Deleuze's notion of "a people to come" is productive because it does not look only to moments of past trauma in order to understand "minority," but rather sees the power of the minority as drawn from the future. And this is something that Goto understands. I am thinking in particular of a moment when Murasaki is speaking to her disgruntled lover about her/his concern that their "real life" is too much revealed in the novel:

> "Hey," you say, "you're mixing up the story with what's really happening right now in our lives. I don't know if I like that. I want to be able to separate the stories from our real lives. What we're living right now." You wash out the bowls, the rice cooker and hashi. You are anxious and the dishes clatter noisier than when you are content.
> "You can't. The words give the shape to what will happen. What can happen. I'm telling our future before it ever does." I wander into the living room, touch the back of the couch, thumb a row of books, run a finger through the dust on top of the black stereo.
> "But what if I don't like the future you shape for us? What about my say in our future?" You are wiping your hands on a towel and your hair is tousled from frustrated fingers.
> "When I'm finished my story, you can start another if you want. I will listen as politely as you have listened. At least, I'll try to," I amend. (*Chorus* 186)

Goto's metafictional strategy of pointing to the act of reading and writing opens the boundaries between the practice of reading and the daily practices of living, which are as much acts of cultural production as writing is. There is an autobiographical impulse in this book, but one that recognizes the power and the danger of autobiography, and attempts to take responsibility, however imperfectly, for its effects. As such, it might be thought of as a biotext in the sense that Saul describes, emerging as it does in roughly the same period as the biotexts Saul addresses—after Michael Ondaatje's *Running in the Family* and Daphne Marlatt's *Works*, but before Roy Kiyooka's *Mothertalk* and Fred Wah's *Diamond Grill*. George Bowering's conception of the biotext as an extension of the writer rather than a replacement for him or her (qtd. in Saul 4) is helpful to recognize the generic shift away from autobiography as such to a more complex relation between subject and text. And indeed, Goto—or at least Murasaki—actively extends her biotext into consciously fantastical places, in an act of radical biotextual construction.

In scenes such as the one with the disgruntled lover, she speaks directly to the mutual production of life and text, as a way of opening up conventional ways of reading autobiography. By making the reader conscious of the constructedness of the text, and of any truth, she circumvents the certainty about history that autobiography strives for. The knowledge and affirmation of self that, for instance, Evelyn Lau seeks in *Runaway*, is not on offer here. What is offered, rather, is the textuality of truth. And yet oddly, because her language is so material ("I wander into the living room, touch the back of the couch ..."), a solidity is offered in excess of textuality. The trace of autobiography remains, but in the relation between this materialized speech and the more self-conscious text an interactive relationship to the "truth" of daily life enters into being. "Life" and "text" interpenetrate one another, and the practice of autobiography is radically transformed in this intertwining. Steve McCullough, writing of the intimacy between the listening lover and the storyteller Muriel in *Chorus of Mushrooms*, argues that Goto's engagement of what he calls "postmodern contingency" is an act of profound responsibility:

> The trust that engenders textuality in *Chorus of Mushrooms* shows that such postmodern narrative is far from exercising a nihilist freedom to refashion the world: in fact it is all the more contingent because it is grounded on continual risk and a failure of authority that precludes closure. The fact that language is inevitably polysemic thus does not make meaning and intelligibility either impossible or subject to arbitrary whim. Language is a space of mutually constituting negotiability, and Hiromi Goto's postmodern vision of fiction is enabled and sustained by its open-ended vision of contingency as responsibility. (168)

McCullough is helpful here in his recognition of language as contingent and mutually constituting with its subjects, and I am particularly appreciative of his understanding that working with language this way necessitates a kind of responsibility.

The way in which he locates the idea of the "the postmodern" is also helpful, though it requires further working through. McCullough acknowledges Francesco Loriggio and Guy Beauregard's cautions against using Western theory to transparently analyze "ethnic minority authors." He argues that, from her location, Goto challenges the same linguistic assumptions and cognitive structures that Lyotard does in *The Postmodern Condition*, and further that Lyotard has long focused on ethnic others—Jews and Algerians—on whose exclusion the coherence of Western philosophy is constructed (McCullough 150). I suggest that the relative privilege with which Western high theory circulates through institutions and publics still matters as privilege. Further, there is still embodied, historically sedimented difference that readers, thinkers, and writers need to acknowledge in these mappings. These recognitions are particularly important in relation to Goto's work, because Goto is profoundly aware of the politics of being spoken for. Both Wendy Pearson and Roy Miki take up this quote from Goto's "The Body Politic": "I hold my culture in my hands and form it on my own/so that no one else can shape the way/it lies upon my body" (qtd. in Pearson 79). For Pearson, the power of this quote, especially posited by Goto as it is, beside a drawing of a banana from which the yellow skin is being unzipped to reveal a single, cyclops-like eye embedded in the white flesh, lies in its hybridity and monstrosity (79). For Goto, hybridity and monstrosity are locations from which hope and change can erupt, though not without contention. Here, then, is where the relationship of Goto's work to the postmodern as Lyotard conceives it might lie. It is not so much that Lyotard addresses questions of ethnicity in his critique as that Goto is also an active subject in a contemporary milieu in which postmodernity is a condition. Whether or not Lyotard has read Goto or Goto has read Lyotard, their texts are mutually productive of one another in the sense that they are parts of the same conversation, albeit from very different locations. As text and life interpenetrate each other, so does fiction and theory. What remains to be worked out is the relative privileging of the dominant term in each instance. That this is profoundly political is the point of Goto's work.

Goto creates the possibility for a multivalent future that is always open for revision and re-imagination. Goto's consciousness of the storytelling that has gone on before her, and of the political power of representation, means that her storytelling includes a drive toward an unknown future, not of justice or retribution in the sense of righting past wrongs, but rather a future that opens possibility for anything, including magic. When Murasaki/Muriel offers the lover a chance to tell his/her story, she opens up a relationship to the future that is not singular, that allows for the recurrence of the same time in a different form. It is more than Butler's repetition with a difference in the sense that it allows the continuity of the same (Muriel's story) with a difference (the lover's story under erasure) layered under it. The relationship of story to teller and the problem of the speaking self are precisely what is at stake in this novel. Trinh's idea that it is the story itself that speaks is helpful here. But the speaking self never quite disappears, in spite of the multiplicity of voices. The ontological questions that both plague and produce Asian Canadian literature are, in a sense, thematized in this text.

OBACHAN NAOE'S DOUBLE CARNIVAL

In *Chorus of Mushrooms*, ontological continuity is most obviously played out in the name "Murasaki" or "Purple," as Steve McCullough notes: "The multilingual multiplication of names profoundly challenges the coherence of the narrating voices and identities.... [T]he self (or selves) to which these names refer is (or are) ambiguous at best, and collapsing them into a single character is a profoundly anxious strategy" (159). For indeed, as McCullough recognizes, the name Murasaki has many referents. In the first instance, it is the narrator Muriel's Japanese name—but a Japanese name in a linguistic universe in which Japanese language is sometimes transcribed without translation and sometimes presented as strangely poetic/magical English speech, heard diegetically by the characters as Japanese, but read extra-di-egetically by the English-speaking reader as English text. It is also the name of the woman author of the *Tale of Genji*, an eleventh-century text and argu-ably the world's first novel. It is also the name that Grandma Naoe takes on when she finally escapes the constrained boredom of her rocking chair to enter the adventurous world of the Alberta prairie in the second half of the novel. McCullough astutely notes that this is the moment when, within the realist frame of the novel, Grandma Naoe goes missing. The "realness" of her disappearance is conveyed to us in a short newspaper article with the head-line: "Local Elderly Woman Disappears: Search Continues" (88). However, Goto has already shown us how newspapers cannot be relied upon for any transparent "truth" because they are already racially biased; therefore, they are particularly unreliable when it comes to telling the truth about racialized people. Truth and fiction are extra-fluid categories for those whose racialized truths can only ever be misrepresented by the dominant culture. The liberty that Goto takes with this structural feature of Western epistemology is to produce Grandma Naoe's life after her disappearance as madly excessive and fantastical. Her "real"/newspaper absence magically erupts as a kind of hyperpresence—one in which she becomes a strangely hybrid/monstrous/collective being—both herself and her granddaughter Muriel. Of the name "Murasaki," McCullough says: "It is both an unmistakeable sign of identity and a guarantor of anonymity" (160). I would argue further that it is a sign of collectivity, specifically what Mikhail Bakhtin has called the collective bodily principle.

Goto sets out from the beginning of the novel to unsettle conventional expectations about who and what Grandma Naoe might be. Firstly, Goto's representation of her flies in the face of traditional uses of the grandmother figure as a direct channel to mysterious truths about the past. (Fifth Aun-tie, in *Paper Shadows*, for instance, replicates this trope.) Goto consciously moves away from the grandmother as a representative of lost history, partic-ularly of histories of trauma, if one thinks, for instance, of Kogawa's *Obasan*. Eleanor Ty notes Goto's refusal of this trope:

> There is more of a postmodern play of story and form as fragments, as pieces to be constructed into a whole by the reader. At one point in the novel, Murasaki asks Obachan Naoe to tell her a story: "You're supposed to be the one telling stories to me. You know, the grandmother telling stories of the past to the avidly listening grandchild and all that." But Obachan refuses to claim the authority of the Old World storyteller, and instead says, "And don't you think stories are shared. That there is a partnership in the telling and listening, that it is of equal importance?" (Ty 156)

In the partnership between telling and listening, collectivity erupts. Further, the multiple voices in the novel deepen the sense that Trinh describes of the story telling itself through a people as the people come into being through story.[2]

Guy Beauregard notes a number of ways in which Goto's narrative actively counters the melancholy call for justice in Joy Kogawa's *Obasan*, not because Goto is against justice but because she recognizes justice's obsession with trauma and is looking for a way out. Goto recognizes the necessity of the call for justice. Not to make it would be to deny history. It would be to accept the liberal whitewash that asserts "We are all the same" while perpetuating white norms as universal ones and white privilege as natural, deserved, and not to be questioned. Goto's task is to escape the master/slave binary without resorting to her own invisibilization. Violence and the desire for its rectification must be reconfigured. One way of doing this is to re-invest already established associations with new meanings that trouble and complicate the original. Beauregard writes:

> The very title of *Chorus of Mushrooms* could be read as an attempt to politicize female sexuality by taking the mushroom cloud of atomic destruction that haunts Kogawa's narrative and reconfiguring it as an orgasm.[3] ("Hiromi Goto's *Chorus of Mushrooms*" 52)

Goto is working out the relationship between the inescapability of representation and the violence of history. She looks in toward the body, particularly bodily pleasure as the site of liberation. But this pleasure is haunted by the grief it attempts to counter. The mushrooms of her title can be read as both destructive and orgasmic. What is interesting about the conflation of these two kinds of explosions is that they belong to the realm of the feminine. If one wants to think, for instance, of the pop cultural use of guns or cannons to metaphorize masculine pleasure and violence, one might consider Goto's mushroom metaphor in parallel feminine terms.

But it is exactly in the drawing together of things that don't sit well side by side that Goto pulls us into an alternative temporality in which the associations of privileged culture do not apply. Racist assumptions are thrown up for grabs. So are science and logic. The grandmother, Obachan Naoe, is the most striking embodiment of this alternative temporality. She is the one who enters fully another way of being in time in which she can have a Japanese-speaking cowboy lover and ride bulls in the Calgary Stampede under the moniker "The Purple Mask." But more strange is the way in which the grandmother is produced linguistically in the text. She speaks Japanese in "real" life, but in order to make the text legible to English speakers, and indeed, in order to write a grandmother figure at all, since Goto is an English-language writer, Goto needs to imagine a way of writing "Japanese" in "English." She needs to produce a linguistically transparent environment. It is an impossible task—one perhaps of the fairy-tale kind, like slaying a dragon or separating different kinds of grain from a mountain of mixed grain overnight. In producing this language for the grandmother at the very outset, Goto asks us to suspend our disbelief. She draws us into an alternative present that is strangely autobiographical but at the same time decidedly textual, not unlike the temporality of Angela Carter's Fevvers in *Nights at the Circus*, in which the reader is never sure whether she should read the speaker as "real" or "textual."

Obachan Naoe begins with a breath: "Ahhhhh this unrelenting, dust-driven, crack your fingers dry wind has withered my wits, I'm certain. Endless as thought as breath—ha!" (3). But is it the text that breathes or the old woman? But because Obachan Naoe cannot speak English, and the text is written in a kind of English—one that is both broken and highly poetic—we are forced from the very outset to contend with the question of textuality and its relation to experience, to breath, and to the material. The breath of Obachan Naoe's sighs and complaints is like the prairie wind. There is a tear not just between text and flesh, but also between flesh and air. We wonder whether Obachan Naoe is present or all, or if her presence is only a ghostly imagining brought on by the blowing of the wind: "Not much breath left in this set of bellows, but this wind. Just blows and blows and blows. Soon be blowing dust over my mummy carcass and beetles won't find the tiniest bit of soft flesh to gnaw on, serves them right" (3). She is so old and so close to death, that one might reasonably wonder which side of the great divide she in fact occupies. And yet, in spite of her airy ghostliness, she has a kind of fertility: "Let the piles of dust grow and mound and I'll plant *daikon* and eggplant seeds. Let something grow from this daily curse" (3). What grows, I argue, is language itself. What grows is story. Many critics, including Beauregard, Mark Libin, and McCullough, have written about Goto's use of the invocation "Mukashi, mukashi, omukashi" (in ancient times, in ancient times, in very ancient times) as one that brings story into being. Since Goto is asking us whether there is any real difference between story and truth, one might read the invocation as bringing truth into being. It is a kind of spell that alters the flow of reality. It is the recognition that language materializes by allowing us to see differently.

What is interesting about "Mukashi, mukashi, omukashi" is that it calls up an alternative temporality, one so long past that its distance from the present cannot be measured. At its first occurrence in the novel, it is Muriel/Murasaki who speaks it, and it is inside the framing of the invocation that

Grandma Naoe speaks her uncanny English. However, the time of Grandma Naoe's English speech is not of an ancient time, but of the present—an alternative present in which such speech is possible. What is ancient and what is present are collapsed together, and we are brought into a sort of perpetual now, in which the ancient voice of the grandmother dispenses some very contemporary wisdom about the relativity of truth and infinite possibilities of story. In this alternative present, the violence of history does not vanish, but neither the internment nor the A-bomb define the identities or desires of the characters. The novel notes racism and inequity, but slides away from the call to justice into a magical realm that strives to imagine a kind of agented freedom that does not require justice from the other, but locates liberatory practice with the marginalized self.

The bull-riding grandmother becomes a kind of carnival figure, liberated from the banal temporality of history with its imposition of trauma as much as its demand for justice. It is a kind of freedom—not the only freedom the subaltern might desire, perhaps not even the best freedom the subaltern might desire, but only a fresh one, and one that is open-ended, allowing for endless new possibilities or revisions.

The open-ended and infinite possible futures are the great hope that this novel offers. As soon as one begins to articulate a particular future, of course, all the problems of articulation arise. As Obachan Naoe travels deeper and deeper into the magical future that comes after she runs away, her existence becomes increasingly carnivalesque, as I have noted above, until it brings us to her marvellous performances as a Calgary Stampede bull rider called "The Purple Mask." Mikhail Bakhtin has taught us, however, that carnival is not a true escape from the daylight world, but only an outlet for the actions that the daylight world represses. In a sense, it supports the patriarchal order of things by making ritualized time for those violent impulses that might otherwise overthrow the system. For Bakhtin, this is not necessarily a bad thing. He emphasizes the renewing capacities of carnival:

> We must stress, however, that carnival is far distant from the negative and formal parody of modern times. Folk humour denies, but it revives and renews at the same time. Bare negation is completely alien to folk culture. (11)

It seems worth asking whether the runaway Obachan Naoe belongs to Bakhtinian carnival, or whether there is something more radically liberatory about her carnival time. And if there is not, does Goto's suggestion "You can always change the story" actually free us? At the moment of the novel's publication it was perhaps a useful response to seemingly fixed histories of injustice, and more brutally fixed stories that whitewashed those injustices. I think the question at this historical juncture becomes whether the open-ended future is a sufficient response to the current excesses of global capital and of contemporary religio-military violence, both of which are highly material. This is not, of course, to denigrate Goto's extraordinary leaps of imagination and her drive toward freedom from the constraints of the moment of writing, but only to ask: What next?

I want to be careful here about extrapolating a description of a European medieval grotesque onto a contemporary Japanese-Canadian novel. Nonetheless, there are aspects of Bakhtin's description of the carnivalesque that are very apt, and, I hope, productive, in terms of thinking about Obachan Naoe. The model cannot be applied uncritically, but there are parts that fit:

> All the symbols of the carnival idiom are filled with this pathos of change and renewal, with the sense of the gay relativity of prevailing truths and authorities. We find here a characteristic logic, the peculiar logic of the "inside out" (à l'envers), of the "turnabout," of a continual shifting from top to bottom, from front to rear, of numerous parodies and travesties, humiliations, profanations, comic crownings and uncrownings. A second life, a second world of folk culture is thus constructed; it is to a certain extent a parody of extracarnival life, a "world inside out." (Bakhtin 11)

In the abandonment of her rocking chair and her decision to travel with the wind, Obachan Naoe, in a sense, enters a time of carnival.

Bakhtin points, in particular, to the juxtaposition of fertility with old age as a quintessential carnival principle, one that signals entry into festive, non-official time:

> In the famous Kerch terracotta collection we find figurines of senile pregnant hags. Moreover, the old hags are laughing. This is typical and very strongly expressed grotesque. It is ambivalent. It is pregnant death, a death that gives birth. There is nothing completed, nothing calm and stable in the bodies of these old hags. They combine a senile, decaying and deformed flesh with the flesh of new life, conceived but as yet unformed. Life is shown in its twofold contradictory process; it is the epitome of incompleteness. And such is precisely the grotesque concept of the body. (26)

In *Chorus of Mushrooms*, the official daylight world, where Grandma Naoe rocks in her chair, grows old, and says nothing, is left behind in favour of a carnivalesque adventure that begins with a beautiful, if unsettling, scene of masturbation in the mushroom barn:

Softly, softly, her hands, her fingers, the moisture, her ache, peat warm as blood, the moisture seeping into hair, skin, parchment softening elastic stretch of muscles gleaming a filament of light. Murmur murmur forming humming earth tipping under body swelling growing resound and the SLAM of breath knocked from lungs, beyond the painful register of human sound, the unheard chorus of mushrooms. (86)

While these lines are serious and lyrical, they hark back to a moment when uptight Kay/Keiko catches Obachan contemplating masturbation. Obachan sees her looking and bursts into ribald laughter:

This muttering, old, lamb-haired Obachan wearing elastic-waisted polyester pants, brown collarless shirt with pink flowers, grey cardigan and heel imprinted slippers. Just pulling out the waistband with one quavering hand and the other just about to slip into cotton briefs, toying with the idea of—

"Obachan! What are you doing?!"

I release the elastic and it snaps back to my wrinkled stomach with a flat smack and Keiko standing in the doorway with her mouth open. I start to mutter an excuse, but Keiko's expression, my elastic pants, my horniness, my age, I start laughing and laughing until the old muscles in my stomach start to ache. Ahhh Keiko, it is funny after all. (39–40)

Here, ribald laughter and the sexuality of an old woman are given to us, to counter the expectation that old women are not sexual. In Bakhtin's terms, this is an exemplary instance signalling entry into carnival time.

If Kay belongs to the official world, with all its racisms and the pressure to assimilate, Obachan Naoe, with all her bodily interests and concerns, lives on the border of the carnivalesque, and, in the second half of the novel, fully enters it at the beckoning of the wind. She enters into a world of her own storytelling, or rather of the hybrid Murasaki's storytelling, which is also highly physical, embued with what Bakhtin would call the "material bodily principle" of carnival, which is at once more solid than the body of the official world and yet separate from the hierarchical "reality" the official daylight world offers.

As the sexual grotesque is one way in which entry into carnival time is signalled, the feast is another. Bakhtin points out that practices that deal with flow between the body and the social world are essentially carnival practices:

The body discloses its essence as a principle of growth which exceeds its own limits only in copulation, pregnancy, childbirth, the throes of death, eating, drinking, or defecation. This is the ever unfinished, ever creating body, the link in the chain of genetic development, or more correctly speaking, two links shown at the point where they enter each other. This especially strikes the eye in archaic grotesque. (26)

In Goto's novel, the grotesque feasting aspect of carnival may be read in the form of Japanese food. It is imbued with a quality that is sensual, transformative, but at the same time oddly repulsive. She plays with her readers' racist anxieties about non-Western bodies and eating habits. She both values Japanese food and recognizes the alien light white mainstream culture sheds on it. Murasaki's reclamation of Japanese food does not repress this sense of the alien, but revalorizes it and imbues it with the power of a kind of magical transformation. So when Obachan Naoe is raiding the fridge for supplies to sustain her through her escape, she takes the Western food Kay stocks, but also scrounges desperately for something Japanese, and comes up with a jar of seaweed paste the father secrets away at the back of the fridge. She takes beer to go along with it—a festive drink, and also a gender-bending one in the sense that it is a drink more associated with rowdy young men than with "lamb-haired" old grandmothers. (So there is a kind of carnival reversal at work here.)[4] Later, the beer becomes part of the magical seduction of Tengu, the Japanese-speaking truck-driving cowboy who picks her up from the side of the highway.

Further, after the grandmother runs away, her psychic connection with her granddaughter Murasaki is deepened. She even tells Tengu her name is Purple—a direct translation of "Murasaki." Murasaki and Purple/Obachan Naoe are able to have full-blown conversations without any kind of proximity to one another. The discrete separation between individual subjects is collapsing.

It is indeed through one of these psychic conversations that Obachan Naoe instructs Murasaki how to cure Keiko, who has sunk into a wordless depression. From her carnivalized location, Obachan Naoe instructs Murasaki to cook a Japanese feast. The main dish is to be tonkatsu—"breaded pork cutlets." Tonkatsu is also the family's surname. While Naoe and Tengu eat lobster at the Ruby Restaurant in Calgary's Chinatown (in a sense, eating with the family even as they are absent—another border collapsed), Murasaki cooks up a midnight feast of tonkatsu for her family. Her mother begins to speak. In other words, the carnivalized ritual has a healing effect. The eating of tonkatsu is thus a kind of carnival cannibalism, but one that cures, that is, one that renews.

Bakhtin writes:

The feast is always essentially related to time, either to the recurrence of an event in the natural (cosmic) cycle, or to biological or historical timeliness. Moreover, through all natural stages of historic development feasts were linked to moments of crisis, of breaking points in the cycle of nature or in the life of society and man. Moments of death and revival, or change and renewal always lead to a festive perception of the world. These moments, expressed in concrete form, created the peculiar character of feasts. (9)

The tonkatsu feast in *Chorus of Mushrooms* produces a renewal of the lost past, the one that Keiko had been repressing through her refusal to cook Japanese food. This meal is a carnival feast at which lost culture is returned, and the body and speech are returned along with it.

The most highly carnivalized moment in the novel is the closing one, in which Obachan Naoe becomes "The Purple Mask," a mysterious bull rider at the Calgary Stampede. Here we have again the material bodily principle in full form. An old woman sexualized through her association with the physicality of the bull, she also bends gender in the sense that most of her observers think she is a man. Further, she is participating in a civic ritual that is itself carnivalized. As a celebration of Calgary's cowboy heritage, the Stampede is an event during which the normal practices of the official world are suspended. People can wear jeans to work and drink on the job. The rodeo and the midway on the Stampede grounds are packed with revellers seeking the thrill of the festive moment, suspended from the expectations of everyday official life. As a carnivalized moment, however, Stampede does not completely fulfil the criteria of universalism that Bakhtin ascribes to medieval carnival. Perhaps it cannot, in this contemporary, hyper-capitalized, globalized moment.[5] The cowboy culture it harks back to, is to a great extent, a fiction, in the sense that Calgary is much more a garrison town, a town with a history of bureaucracy more than rebellion. Further, the Stampede is a highly racialized event, privileging in the first place the master narrative of a white settler society, and, in the second place, its Native other.[6] Those racialized outside these two categories are more or less invisible. In a sense, there is no place in Stampede for a body such as Obachan Naoe's, until it masquerades as something recognizable: straight, white, and male—a cowboy. Stampede may reverse official practices of propriety, but it still privileges the same bodies the daylight world privileges. Hence, perhaps, Obachan Naoe's need for a purple mask. In donning the mask, Obachan Naoe effects a second reversal, one invisible to Calgary in its Stampede mode or its official mode. Hers is, in a sense, carnival enacted inside carnival. It is a celebration that both the oblivious Stampede goers and Grandma Naoe herself enjoy, but not for exactly the same reasons. The attendees enjoy her skill and, thinking that she is one of them, identify with her and experience a kind of civic pride. Grandma Naoe enjoys her skill and the fact that she is deceiving her viewers. She has pulled a carnival reversal they cannot see. There is pleasure in this gender-bending turnaround. It is, in a sense, a classic case of repetition with a difference.

In *The Psychic Life of Power*, Judith Butler indeed notes a possibility for the marginalized subject's agency in precisely such a turn:

> The power that initiates the subject fails to remain continuous with the power that is the subject's agency. A significant and potentially enabling reversal occurs when power shifts from its status as a condition of agency to the subject's "own" agency (constituting an appearance of power in which the subject appears as a condition of its "own" power). (12)

By donning the "Purple Mask," Grandma Naoe takes up the power of carnivalized whiteness, inserting into it, unbeknownst to her audience, her "true identity" as an elderly Japanese Canadian woman. In so doing, she opens up that very identity so that it is no longer a marginalized location, but a subjectivity in the process of becoming, that is, moving into an agented, open-ended future. She appropriates hegemonic power in such a way as to work against that power and all the assumptions and misreadings it habitually applies to her.

To return to the concern I had at the beginning of this discussion, about extrapolating too cleanly from what is, after all, a description of a very particular history of medieval European carnival, I think it is now important to ask how those carnival impulses translate in our contemporary moment. I suggest that they cannot possibly be as universal as they might have been in the moment Bakhtin describes. There is a violence to contemporary carnival in its racialized exclusions. But Obachan Naoe does much more than overturn it, when she rides bulls under the guise of the Purple Mask. A kind of collective agency is opened up in the sense that the Purple Mask is a reiteration of the name "Murasaki," which, as mentioned earlier, means "purple," and as a second racialized name for both Muriel and Naoe functions as a kind of mask. It is, in other words, the story telling itself again, opening up surprising new agencies for both granddaughter and grandmother that they could not possibly have in newspaper reality, in spite of the fact that it is newspaper reality that creates the conditions for their collective power. Further, an agency is opened up that does not reinsert the marginalized subject uncritically back into hegemonic social space, with all of that space's assumptions about what the marginalized subject is or is not. In fact, the space itself is transformed through this new cultural activity. The disguise donned by Grandma Naoe disguises, or rather re-guises, Alberta itself.

RE-GUISING ALBERTA/ FORMING THE INTERIOR

This re-guising of prairie space that Grandma Naoe inaugurates in *Chorus of Mushrooms* is deepened in Goto's second novel, *The Kappa Child*. Goto's carnivalization of space does more than renew, it radically transforms. When the father of the protagonist buys a farm in southern Alberta in order to grow rice, it alters the geography and climate of the prairie. Rice requires a lot of water, something the "natural" climate cannot provide. It is the father's wacky imagination that lays the possibility of rice paddies over an impossible landscape, just as the protagonist nurtures a strange pregnancy that both is and is not real. The material bodily principle of carnival is racialized. It is also intensified in the sense that it has broken the boundaries of carnival time to enter a perpetual raced present in which the wet fertility of both the land and the body (however painfully brought about) are material realities overlying the "hegemonic truth" of the prairie—that it is dry, desert-like, and white. Their dreams are, in a sense, carnival masks, laid not over their own faces, but over the land itself. The mask is a mark of culture but, because it takes the form of water, is natural at the same time. The "naturalness" of this cultural imposition[7] calls into question the naturalness of white, colonial impositions onto the same landscape.

What is interesting about this imposition, this re-ordering of prairie space, is that it is a joke, but one that the family materializes, however imperfectly, under pressure from the abusive father:

> "I will grow Japanese rice!" Dad proclaimed.
> "Ha! Ha! Ha! Ha!" Slither laughed joyfully. Mice ducked beneath the table. PG got up with her tumbler for more water, casually striding to the sink. My small eyes dodged around. I only had time enough to lean back in my chair as far as possible.
> "You're so funny, Dad!"
> He jerked out of his chair, grabbed the back of Slither's T-shirt, and tossed her outside before she could figure out he was mad. The door locked. I could hear her howling in the dust-heat tornado …
> What could Dad be thinking?! We were on the prairies. Everyone knew that the prairies meant undulating fields of golden wheat, the color of Mary Ingalls' hair. (113)

There is a violence in the materialization of the joke, one that re-inscribes patriarchal power. But this is a patriarchal power that is marginalized within the context of Albertan prairie space. The daughters, in turn, are oppressed by this power and yet are carriers of the hegemonic power of white superiority. They know what the prairies are supposed to mean. They mean golden wheat, not rice. They mean white skin and golden hair, like the Ingalls family in *Little House on the Prairie*, not Asian.

In externalizing the joke, in making it material, I argue, the father begins to give shape to the "propagandized inside" I discussed in my first chapter, the one that Miki says is radically silenced by hegemonic power, the one that the best-intentioned breaking of silence still cannot touch. In some ways, it is no surprise that this externalization is so misogynist and violent. It emerges from the unconscious, which is necessarily apolitical.

What I would like to suggest here is that through this reconfiguration of prairie space, this making external what was internal, the father opens up the possibility for the "silent interior"[8] of the protagonist to take a shape of its own. Her carnival pregnancy, which is both real and fake, is the form that the inside takes. The Kappa child insists itself. It kicks her from the inside. It demands that she eat Japanese cucumbers. It gives her interior a form in excess of the form bestowed on her by the racist gaze:

> I am not a beautiful Asian. I am not beautiful. There is a difference between petite and short; one is more attractive than the other. Don't get me wrong, I'm not bitter about my lack of physical beauty. My beauty lies beneath a tough surface, like a pomegranate, my Okasan is fond of telling me. Slither thinks all I need is a good orthodontist, a professional makeover, and a haircut done with a pair of toenail scissors. Maybe she's right, but I refuse to succumb. (51)

In recognizing the forms of beauty that "Asian" can take, the protagonist recognizes herself as not fitting. But the not-fitting is itself predicated on racialized expectations of beauty. Even as she recognizes this, without the kappa pregnancy, she can recognize her interior beauty only through the platitude "My beauty lies beneath a tough surface."

After the magical encounter with the kappa, however, that beauty becomes an entirely different thing. There is the possibility of a birth. But the pregnancy is not biological. The thing that presses on her from the inside speaks with the voice that is connected to a mythic past, one that holds no truck with Eurocentric conceptions of beauty. The kappa is, in a sense, the beauty that lies beneath the protagonist's tough surface, mythic, ancient, cosmological, and biological:

> *Light streams muted colors, speckles my shiny skin. Beneath the skin itself, my cells resound. There is a memory of the body, memory held with-in my ancient cells, always ever-present. My cells tell me what has passed before.*

I swim, here, in this liquid home and listen to the poetry of galaxies twined into double-helix strands. (105; italics in original)

As a part of the "pregnant" protagonist, the creature infuses her with this extraordinary and excessive beauty.

The material bodily principle of carnival is at work here in the sense that the pregnancy is felt. It is physical. The kappa child kicks and pushes and makes the protagonist crave cucumbers. And yet, it is not biological in the scientific sense. Here, I suggest that it is in fact cultural, and psychic. Or rather, as in classic carnival time, it is both biological and cultural. The biological and the cultural are rolled in one.

The presence of carnival is signalled through the establishment of the pregnancy itself. It begins with a carnival feast, in the form of a Chinese wedding banquet that the protagonist stumbles upon in Calgary's Chinatown, while looking for someone to watch the last lunar eclipse of the twentieth century with her. The feast turns out to be a magical fabrication of the lover kappa who later "impregnates" the protagonist. The bride celebrated at the wedding feast is none other than the kappa him/herself. The actual moment of "conception" is shot through with elements far in excess of the emotional and biological, though it certainly includes them. The kappa lover and the protagonist sumo wrestle naked on the tarmac while planes take off above them and the moon, sun, and earth fall into alignment. At the "moment of truth" where orgasm would occur in a conventional sex scene, liquid from the bowl of the kappa's head spills over the protagonist. The moment is shot through with elements of the technological, the mythical, the celestial, the biological, the sexual, the emotional, and the magical. These realms of life are themselves transformed in this strange, multivalent act.

In recognizing time as having "fabric-space," Goto acknowledges the multiplicity of political and cultural temporalities within the space of Alberta. Moments of profound recognition and connection can be held in a kind of perpetual present that exceeds the necessary passing of traditional carnival. The "still" in which the Stranger and the protagonist hold one another is both motionless and eternal, even as other temporalities flow around them.

What I want to suggest here is that the pregnancy that results from this moment is one that comes from the traumatic sites of white hegemony and the father's patriarchal abuses, and yet at the same time is more than mere reaction to oppression. The celestial, mythical, technological, cultural, and physical magic of the conception and pregnancy promise a birth that is more than a dialectic response to power. In a sense, it is an instance of the emergence of "the people to come," which I discussed in my second chapter.

The protagonist has emerged from a traumatic past, without being tied to or defined by that past. The future is as productive of this new subjectivity as history is.

Nancy Kang's suggestion that there are two forces at work in *The Kappa Child* is helpful here. Kang posits a utopian discursive mode that focuses on community-building and lesbian solidarity in contrast to a political mode that is "more combative, demanding a staunch, demonstrable commitment to overthrowing male supremacy" (Kang 3). While these modes are complementary, it is the utopian mode, particularly as it looks to the past in order to make the future, that marks the possibility for a "global sea change" (3). I agree with Kang and argue further that it is precisely because Goto's future-oriented, utopian impulses are non-dialectical that they offer the possibility of a generative break from hegemonic power and feed the potentialities of the concept that Roy Miki has called "asiancy." Nancy Kang notes further in a section of her essay entitled "Cosmic Corporeality" that the objects of desire in Goto's novel not only break the man/woman duality of heteronormativity, they break the bounds of the human. Desire in *The Kappa Child*, though it gestures toward both same-sex love and the auto-erotic, expressly stretches across species boundaries: "human with more-than-human, known with unknown" (Kang 3). The binary mirroring of self and other upon which so much of Western metaphysics depends is radically exceeded. Kang is right to note that Goto doesn't leave oppositional politics behind—the battle against patriarchy and racism are what ground the novel in the material world. But Goto's active engagement of the imagination seeks sublime possibilities beyond it.

There is indeed something of Kristeva's sublime, as it is attached to her conception of abjection, at work in this novel. Kang, Pearson, and others note the ways in which Goto re-valences as desirable precisely those figures that mainstream culture rejects—the alien, the fat, the foreigner, the old. In revaluing precisely that which Western patriarchal culture expels, the abject subjects of Goto's novels are necessarily caught in a complex relation to the sublime—both free and not free from the oppositional relations that still fixate them: "[T]he sublime is something added that expands us, overstrains us, and causes us to be both *here* as dejects, and *there*, as others and sparkling. A divergence, an impossible bounding. Everything missed, joy—fascination" (12). But what is missed in a psychoanalytic sense can be made again in a carnival sense that is materialized in language. The complicated relationship between language—newspaper language in the first instance, but stretching into the language of the Purple Mask—and practice does work to remake the world. Reading Karen Shimakawa, Sandra Almeida posits the category "Asian American" as produced through and in reaction to abjection (58). She emphasizes, thus, its productive potential—something Goto's work whole-heartedly embraces (58). In her carnival materializations of the sublime, Goto produces a radical alterity that exceeds the expectations of realism, assimilation, and heteronormativity. Her work is a deep refusal of contain-ment, and a spiral of making and remaking, as it were "outside the box."

What was generative about *Chorus of Mushrooms* was its entry, through the travels of Grandma Naoe, into carnival space. Goto actively produces culture in excess of simple response to racist name calling and its attendant violence. *The Kappa Child* further develops an alternative cultural space, one that is carnivalized, racialized, and open-ended, though it is not without its own violence. The most glaring political conundrum that *The Kappa Child* leaves open is the question of the relationship of the racialized immigrant subject to First Nations peoples, whose colonialist and imperialist oppres-sion Asian Canadians are complicit with, even as they/we are oppressed and marginalized by white mainstream culture. In purchasing the Rodney farm, for instance, the father figure in *The Kappa Child* accepts European con-ventions of land ownership, even though he chooses to farm it differently.

Goto addresses this problem through the introduction of the character Gerald. Through Gerald, a mixed-race boy with a Nisei mother and Blood father, the reader is brought into the complicated dynamics of complicity with colonialism. Goto is careful not to essentialize the position of First Nations people or that of Japanese Canadians. There is nothing "pure" about Gerald. In fact, he is presented to us as kappa-like and thus as a creature of culture:

> A webbed hand reached out and wetly tapped my cheek. Waft of algae drifted by. I sneezed. Wet, trickly sound, water over pebbles. Almost laughter. I rolled over onto my stomach and enormous eyes gleamed moist, bright, a color I couldn't name.
> "You fell asleep," Gerald stated. His slender hands clasped behind his head. A green blade of grass bobbed between his lips.
> My heart thudded. The shock of waking when I hadn't noticed falling asleep. I gasped and shuddered with a pull deep inside. Below my belly. I almost peed.
> "Shhhhh," Gerald whispered. And patted down my exploding hair. "Shhhh. It's okay." His honey-yellow eyes were sad and old. I could see myself inside them. I jerked upward and sat, back straight, my knees crossed. (168–69)

In this passage, there is a moment's confusion, between the protagonist's dream and waking, when we are not sure whether Gerald is indeed the kappa. The blade of grass between his lips and the prior moment of his having introduced the protagonist to the frogs in the pond already associate him with that mythical green creature. And like the kappa, his eyes are sad and old.

Goto is careful to refuse a racist, frontier stereotype of "Indians." She uses *Little House on the Prairie* as a kind of repository and example of all that is wrong about white colonialism and the myth of the frontier[9] but one that remains a fraught site of desire. The protagonist notes how very different Janice and Gerald are from the "Indians" represented in that novel:

> I could never figure out why Laura Ingalls wanted to see a papoose so bad. Or why her Ma didn't want her to. A baby was a baby. I didn't not want to see a Laura Ingalls Indian, but then I didn't want to see one either. When I met Janice and Gerald, I had to meet someone I'd never imagined.
>
> When we station-wagoned our way to the prairie, moving east instead of traditional west, I didn't really think about Indians, First Nations or otherwise. I didn't think. (189)

The protagonist acknowledges her own complicity in the romance of the West and the way in which it supports European colonialism. The power relation is addressed, but not resolved.

There are two instances at which the racialized power imbalance between the protagonist and Gerald are illustrated. The first occurs when they are playing "junken po" (also known as "Scissors, Paper, Rock"). In this variation of the game, the winner gets to smack the loser. The protagonist is more experienced at the game than Gerald. She beats him at it repeatedly and smacks him harder and with more enthusiasm the more excited she gets, until he is deeply and morally crushed:

> Gerald's eyes. Blink liquid. Oh no, oh no. I look away horrified.
>
> "I better get home now." Gerald stood up and brushed dust off his bottom before walking slowly back to his house.
>
> I jumped to my feet. A cry in my gut, almost to my throat. I had to yell but I didn't know which words to use, if I was sorry or if I hated him for his weakness.
>
> I didn't say anything at all. (191)

Goto does not let her protagonist off the hook. However, neither is there an easy sidestepping the inequity and the cruelty brought into play in this instance.

The second instance of cruelty is not overtly racialized, though I would argue that there remains a racialized undercurrent. Rather, the power imbalance acted out is based on questions of sexuality. Gerald shows sympathy to the protagonist's unpleasant and uncomfortable plight of having to help her father steal water from neighbours for the rice farm. She cries, and he gives her a gentle kiss to comfort her. But she is not grateful: "'Hey, sissy boy,' I sneered. 'I don't let sissy boys touch me. Ever.'" (200). Later, her father applauds her for turning away the friendship of a "weakling," and she realizes she has inherited his abusive impulses. Through this scene the complex intertwining of racism, sexism, homophobia, and emotional inheritance are illustrated. No happy alternative is offered, perhaps because there is none to be offered. All this illustration can do is help us to see the messy and complicated ways in which power works.

I want to return, in closing, to the scene of "conception" on the tarmac. While it clearly does not offer solutions to the complex entanglements of marginalization I have just been discussing, what it does do is open up a different kind of terrain in which hope is possible, though perhaps not without new abuses of as yet undetermined form. The conception scene is prescient in its recognition of the intertwining of the technological, the biological, the mythical, the cosmological, the sexual, and the emotional, as I discussed previously. It points toward the globalized, flowing extra-national sites on which current struggles against racism, capitalism, militarism, and fundamentalism must be fought.

Chorus of Mushrooms speaks to a very particular and very productive moment in Canadian cultural production. It grapples head-on with the problem of racist naming and attempts to find a liberatory space/time that works in excess of the master/slave dialectic. Its solutions are imperfect, as perhaps, all solutions to that problem must be. *The Kappa Child*, on the other hand, steers us into another terrain, beyond the nation-state. At this historical juncture, I think it is of tantamount importance that we think of ourselves and our political, intellectual, and creative work in global terms— that is, in terms of economics, technology, biology, travel, religion, and the military. In a way, though we didn't think about it in those terms then, the anti-racist work of the 1980s and 1990s involved a kind of nationalism. We believed in the possibilities of the democratic Canadian state and its ability to set history right.

That possibility is still there, but it has become complicated by the fact that the nature of the state itself is changing. Even before 9/11, and even as many of us were engaged in oppositional liberatory work, global capital was paving the way for its own international intensification. With Mulroney's implementation of NAFTA, the concentration of control in many industries into the hands of fewer and fewer individuals, the rise of fundamentalism, the orchestrated crashes of many national economies, the question of freedom inside the Canadian state, while still important, and still unresolved, could not possibly be enough. *The Kappa Child* does not ask these questions directly, but it gestures toward them through its opening up of extra-national discursive spaces. It is to these extra-national excesses that I wish to turn in my remaining two chapters.

CHAPTER 5

ETHNIC ETHICS, TRANSLATIONAL EXCESS
The Poetics of jam ismail and Rita Wong

HOPING FOR THE DISAPPEARANCE OF THE RACIST NAME

If the logic of the master/slave dialectic underlies the ontology "Asian Canadian," such that "Asian Canadian" has its being as an oppositional category always already tied to whiteness, and if, as Roy Miki teaches us, such an ontology is always a flickering one, always in danger of emerging into consciousness only to find void, rather than code, then it is not a fully habitable category. Writers whose lives cross through the terrain of "Asian Canadian," especially those who have an investment in it as a category necessary for social justice, need strategies to inhabit it or to write in relation to it. The subject who strategizes is, of course, also one that flickers. And further, as I hope I articulated in the last chapter, "Asian Canadian" is not a category from which justice in any pure form can be produced since any form of national belonging that it might supplementally provide is also attached to ongoing colonization and the oppression of Indigenous peoples. The question of language in general and poetics in particular becomes important if we take seriously Judith Butler's idea that subjects are produced through reiterative performance in language, the theoretical turn begun in Saussure's recognition of the non-coincidence of the signifier from the signified, and Derrida's elaborations of the notion of *différance*, that illustrate the play of non-coincidence. Language is a problem, further, given the tensions between the idea of subjectivity as *différance* and the necessity of what Gayatri Spivak has called "strategic essentialism." Should racialized writers admit poststructural instabilities into their work in order to destabilize master discourse? Or does an emphasis on linguistic ambivalence distract progressive writers, readers, thinkers, and activists away from real, material antagonisms that need to be worked out on a material plane?

In the Canadian context, jam ismail and Rita Wong are important poets, along with Fred Wah and Roy Miki, because of the ways they incorporate these questions into their work. In this chapter, I will illustrate the operation of a supplemental excess that not only operates within the work of both poets, but in fact founds their work and the possibilities that erupt from it. What emerges as excessive and productive in their work is not abstract. It is located with the social, historical, linguistic, economic, and translational specificities through which both poets come into subjectivity and writing practice.

It is important, then, to acknowledge also the queer and/or lesbian connections of these poets, as well as the feminist ones. Elena Basile, for instance, has written about the relationship between jam ismail's work and *écriture féminin* as it is associated with writers like Nicole Brossard, Gail Scott, and Daphne Marlatt. ismail's work, she notes, while it takes up the erotic transgressions of anglophone-francophone experiments in "transcultural reading-writing" among women, departs from another location, what Basile calls an "*already minor* English, specifically a *racially* minoritized relation to the imperial language, which she cannot inhabit freely without first taking stock of her own internal displacement in it" (161). Because ismail builds her work in a manner that is highly conscious of her fraught relationship to both language and the self, she is also aware of both the control and lack thereof that she has in relation to her own public presence. Thus her biographical notes are as much a part of her practice as her poetry itself. In a recent bio on softblow.org (accessed 28 August 2013), ismail describes herself like this:

> language-hobbyist jam ismail materialized in the british crown colony of hong kong, 1940. contexts past & present include: *koran, masculinities without men* (hongkong); ezra pound, *sacred texts of the east* (edmonton); frantz fanon, lisa robertson (vancouver); henry corbin, hamid dabashi (london); *gayatri mantram* (bangalore). jam studied & taught in hong kong & western canadian departments of english.

The first adjective, "language-hobbyist," clues us in to the fact that her relationship to the frames through which we might understand her and her work is already in question. She doesn't say she is a poet or a scholar. Rather, language is her "hobby," a site of play, pleasure, and ongoing attention. I would like to suggest that this claim is an overly modest one. ismail's work is hugely important to many writers in a wide range of contexts, some of which she does lay out in the second sentence of the bio. That she has wittily replaced the usual biographical expectation of declaring birth dates with the idea of materialization displaces the importance of biological and family genealogies in favour of all the possibilities through which she comes into presence, variously agented and variously aligned. The humour here is that she is not in the least concerned with the public knowing her age.

The date of her materialization—1940—is freely given. The way in which she introduces her contexts is also significant in the sense that she actively blurs texts, people, and places, recognizing the complex social and textual valencing of each in so doing. Her locations are clearly transnational. If we read carefully and assume just a little too much, we might trace a line through British colonial movement along Chinese, Muslim, South Asian (sometimes Hindu), and western Canadian vectors, which themselves are always gendered and always under construction. To claim Frantz Fanon, as she does, is to claim an anti-colonial analysis. To claim Lisa Robertson is to claim a feminist avant-garde, a querying of gender and cheeky language play. Like ismail, Robertson moves back and forth between the West Coast of North America and Europe, though ismail's geographies include parts of Asia, the so-called Near East, and the subcontinent as well. To claim Henry Corbin is to claim a relationship to a learned European tradition of Orientalism. Corbin was an important scholar of Iranian philosophy, Shiism, and Sufism from the 1920s to the 1970s (Jones 1983–84). To claim him is to claim a relationship to a learned Orientalism, one that, especially since the work of Edward Said, is very fraught for those who adopt an anti-racist stance. Nonetheless it is one that embraces a love of knowledge and admires the care and intelligence with which Orientalist scholarship approaches it objects. ismail understands the contradiction and holds it in order not to lose scholarship that is both brilliant and troubling in the sense that it calls Orientalist relations into being. To claim the contemporary Iranian-American professor Hamid Dabashi, especially his book *Brown Skins, White Masks*, is to claim a pointed critique of Orientalism, and particularly a critique of the figure of the "comprador intellectual" or "house Muslim" who deciphers the Arab world in the service of Western imperialism and colonialism (Choudry 40).

ismail's connection to Ezra Pound is important in the sense that she was a Pound scholar at Simon Fraser University in the 1970s, and in the sense that her own work continues his lineage at least in part. While it is beyond the scope of this chapter to trace Pound's influence on her work in detail, it strikes me that her writing continues and innovates on Pound's work in translation, especially as it pertains to the papers of Ernst Fenollosa that Pound received, edited, and published after Fenollosa's death. Fenollosa, of course, is known for the essay "The Chinese Character as Medium for Poetry" in which he understands Chinese characters as images compiled to produce meaning. As George Kennedy points out, he is mistaken in this. Meaning in Chinese is connected to the sound of words, and not the images that seem to comprise them:

What this all amounts to is simply that Chinese poetry was composed
in a language, as all poetry must be. And a poem of the eighth century
A.D. can be properly understood only if one knows the language of
the eighth century A.D. The assumption of the "etymological" trans-
lators—Fenollosa, Pound, Ayscough, Lowell, and others—is that the
meaning, connotation, allusion, perfume, concreteness of a given Chinese character has remained immutable from pre-historic times. But
this is inconceivable. The important question is, "What was the *word*
represented by a particular character in the eighth century, how did that
word sound, and what were its connotations?" To discover this is the
effort of philology. (Kennedy n. pag.)

Kennedy is quite indignant about the liberties that Pound takes, calling
them "fantasy":

For anyone who grants that Chinese is a language, elaboration is unnec-
essary. Chinese poetry, like any other, is to be sung, chanted, whispered,
recited, muttered, but not (God forbid!) to be *deciphered.* The association
of ideas that results from the dissection of a given character may produce a poetic thought. But this is a new thought, and it may completely
overshadow the thought that was in the mind of the writer. (Kennedy
n. pag.)

Michael Alexander has recognized, however, that a powerful poetics erupts
from Pound's (mis)translations or what he calls "remakes":

The Remakes begin with *Cathay,* after the volume *Lustra* (1913–15) in
which Pound had modernized his style and subject matter. *Cathay* is
freer because he did not know the language so well as to be possessed
by the delusion he had with Cavalcanti that by mimicry one can match
and achieve identity. The liberating difference, I am sure, is that Chinese
is outside the linguistic, cultural, and literary repertory of the European
languages Pound knew, so that even when possessed by the urge to identity, he could not copy language or form but had to translate, accepting
difference and seeking equivalence rather than identity. (24)

It is Pound's poetics of the remake that ismail takes up and, in a sense, inverts,
in taking up the generative possibilities of her own multilingual location,
to reveal repressed truths about relationships between the so-called East
and the so-called West, as well as between so-called women and so-called
men, often quite humorously, and always incisively. Her work reveals what
is embedded in the language itself, its misapprehension by the multilingual
speaker, or its misapprehension from more monolingual locations, or all

three at once. For example, the title of one of her works-in-progress is *scared texts*, playing of course on "sacred texts" especially as they are associated with Eastern mysticisms, which in the West cannot be divorced from a certain Orientalism, including that which infiltrates the work of Pound and Fenollosa, and in a sense then, many white American, Canadian, and British poets who practise precisely the kinds of appropriation that were so contested in the appropriation debates of the 1980s and 1990s. ismail offers us a riotous and joyful—though nonetheless very pointed—critique of those locations, without claiming any kind of purity or essence for own. For what might sacred texts, or their writers, be scared of except of being misunderstood, which is, in fact, an "always already" condition of Orientalism? ismail takes up this conundrum from her own embodied and culturally located position to re-ontologize imperial English and its various adoptions both as they are imposed or offered from imperial and neo-imperial sites and as they are taken up in racialized locations—Hong Kong, Dubai, Manila, or the Hudson's Bay Company. The interaction of these mobile Englishes and the ways in which they fall upon the body (and so determine how the subject is hailed into being) is exemplified in one of ismail's most quoted poems, "ratio quality":

> young ban yen
> had been thought italian
> in kathmandu, filipina in hong kong
> eurasian in kyoto, japanese in
> anchorage, dismal in london england
> hindu in edmonton,
> generic oriental in calgary, western
> canadian in ottawa, anglo-phone in
> montreal, métis in jasper, eskimo at
> hudson's bay department store,
> vietnamese in chinatown, tibetan in
> vancouver, commie at the u.s.
> border
>
> on the whole very asian. (*jamelie/jamila project* n. pag.)

"young ban yen" in this poem has no being outside of the variously mistaken ways in which she is apprehended and hailed. The last line of the poem, "on the whole very asian," gives us a tongue-in-cheek but nonetheless coherent subjectivity—one produced precisely through the variable list of misrecognitions that constitutes the body of the poem. On the interstices between the range of names and locations, a kind of self comes in to being. In ismail's work, names are also often puns—"ban yen" is one who abjures (bans) all yearnings and desires (yens). I suggest that young ban yen's yearning is for a coherent self, that is, for an essence that is unattainable and must thus be renounced. While banning her yens, young ban yen is at the same time a banyan tree, also known as a strangler fig because the young banyan germinates in the cracks and crevices of an older tree, sends its roots around the host, often eventually killing the host and thus becoming hollow inside. It thus bears a structural resemblance to hollow bamboo (*jook sing*), which is a derisive term in Cantonese for a second-generation Chinese Canadian who has lost her or his mother tongue and all sense of Chinese culture and protocol. The banyan is worse because it is actively unfilial. In order to grow and thrive, it must kill its parent. Through the association with *jook sing*, young ban yen is related to another of ismail's Chinese characters, bosan:

> in chinatown whenever bosan
> said (in cantonese): can't read
> chinese,   chinatown
> storekeepers would scold.
> in cheung chau* they would say:
> oh another (denatured
> returnee from overseas).
>
> *long island, an hour by ferry from hongkong (*jamelie/jamila
> project* n. pag.)

What constitutes disparagement is geopolitically dependent, and yet the specificities of location are transferable. Neither young ban yen nor bosan can settle, regardless of location. The naturalized space of chinatown displaces bosan even at the site of her assimilation.

As for young ban yen, one might also understand the hollow banyan as a metaphor for the absent signifier at the core of the sign in poststructural linguistics. Further, the roots of the banyan tree, as it matures, can spread out to cover a wide area. It is thus a tree of multiple roots and multiple belongings. And further still, the banyan tree is figured in the Bhagavad Gita as sending its roots to the sky and its branches into the earth. This makes it a figure of the spiritual world reflected in the material world and the material world reflected in the spiritual world. One might think of it as a philosopher's tree, or a language play tree, that reverses the relationship between signifier and signified, or at least recognizes the relative importance we give to language over that which it is supposed to represent. In figuring the hero(ine) of her poem as a banyan tree, ismail acknowledges the power of language to materialize bodily ontologies.

Elena Basile writes:

> Translation here inhabits the very constitution of the subject, it affects her agency within language(s) and needs to be productively put to use as a *generative* practice of interruptions, interrogations and reversals—a practice capable of enabling a different *dwelling* in language as a space of constant semiotic reshaping. (161–62)

For ismail, that semiotic reshaping is never innocent. The fragmented and multiplied dwelling in language that exposes the polycultural subject gives the lie to any chance of a coherent ontology, however much such a thing might be desired and politically expedient, especially in the face of oppressions that operate, as Frantz Fanon has taught us, precisely in linguistic terms.

Translation also inhabits the constitution of the subject in Rita Wong's work. Her writing connects to and builds upon jam ismail's work in the sense that it recognizes both the joyful and the abject possibilities of subject positions that abjure master discourse even as they depend upon it. An activist and writer with roots in the Pearl River Delta, Wong grew up in Calgary. She was a student of Fred Wah in her undergraduate years and was supervised by Roy Miki for her Ph.D. at Simon Fraser University. Miki's recent chapter on Wong's work in *In Flux* is particularly useful for recognizing how, in a moment after poststructuralism, the body comes back to us again, but already infiltrated and fragmented, now by the power of capital:

> *That body, the object of corporate biotechnology.*
> *That body, the matrix of desire, language and hope.* (192)

For Miki, the subject fragmented in language (which poststructuralism recognized) returns to us in Wong's work as the material body physically fragmented by corporate biotechnology. In Wong's work, there are reasons to desire both (bodily) human and (theoretically) humanist coherence again, but coherence that has passed through the poststructural crucible and emerged from it the same yet different. In other words, the poststructural turn does not cease to mark Asian Canadian ontologies, even if, now, we might desire to return to a simpler understanding of the way selfhood works. We can always have essentialized imaginations of ourselves, but only ever temporarily, no matter how much we might like to throw away those critiques that show us our instabilities. Further, the fragmentation of the self that occurs in language in at least partially productive ways in the post-structural turn has come back through globalization and the biopolitical in horribly physical ways that offer no recuperative possibilities.

Wong's earlier work, I would argue, already grapples with the desire for such a return. For her, especially in *monkeypuzzle*, the coherent subject is necessary for previously silenced Asian Canadian women subjects and Indigenous women subjects to be able to speak from a place of empower-ment and sometimes rage. But at the same time, she is aware that language leaks. Wong's work, like Roy Miki's and Fred Wah's, is important in this regard, though it has received much less attention. Christine Kim is particu-larly eloquent in articulating the new kind of human Wong calls into being:

> Instead of seeking ways to insert the subaltern into dominant positions within the economic and political order, *monkeypuzzle* implies that we must rewrite the structures that regulate the movement of labouring bodies between international spaces. The task then is not to make the marginal dominant, but to reterritorialize the dominant and transform it into what Rinaldo Walcott has called "a new universality." (69)

If Asian Canadian women are subjects whose being exceeds literary and political representation, then the question becomes what kind of writing is required to rewrite the hegemonic structures. As the complicated interac-tion between poststructural recognitions and anti-racist work deepens, the instability of named racial identities also deepens.

What was productive about cultural race politics as it is taken up by racialized cultural workers in Canada in the 1980s and 1990s is the accep-tance of the racist name—"Asian," "Oriental," "Chink," "Jap," etc.—as a site from which to begin to undo the name's racist effects. The acceptance is always contingent. The more creative, theoretical, and living practices move to inhabit the reclaimed racist name, the more evident both its pitfalls and its productivity becomes.

THE PASSIONATE VOID

Rey Chow's essay "Ethics After Idealism" suggests that it is only in accept-ing the push/pull nature of any racial term (including "Asian Canadian") that we can really inhabit it: "Understanding the immanent nature of this negative limit amounts to an ethics that refuses to idealize the reconcil-iation of social antagonisms and that, instead, accepts their permanence" (49). I would argue, in relation to the work of Wong and ismail, that it is through this acceptance that creative work gets made; in other words, the contradiction is vital to literary production. Toward the end of that essay, in a move that I think epitomizes the work of Rita Wong, Chow writes:

> [T]he apprehension of the world as void does not lead to existentialist angst and revolt, or thereby a new assertion of the meaningfulness of human endeavor. Rather, the void stands as a distinct form of passion, the passion of an indomitable "as if": although defeat is imminent, one goes on enthusiastically as if one doesn't know it—indeed, as if one's entire life force actually comes from this defeat. (54)

One goes on hoping that the need for one's anti-oppression labour will one day become obsolete, that the categories from which one claims a liberatory ontology will, if only one works hard enough, disappear and those whom we call subaltern will be free from their shackles and so no longer need the term "subaltern" or "Asian Canadian." Chow is careful here. She is critical of Gayatri Spivak's proposition about naming. Spivak says:

> The subaltern is all that is not elite, but the trouble with those kinds of names is that if you have any kind of political interest you name it in hope that the name will disappear. That's what class consciousness is in the interest of: the class disappearing. What politically we want to see is that the name would not be possible. (*The Post-Colonial Critic* 158)

Chow is critical of this argument because she thinks (borrowing from Spivak elsewhere, and pointing out Spivak's internal contradiction) that it gives the name—"subaltern"—a kind of originary status that properly belongs to experience. As value in Marx takes the place of labour, so the name takes the place of experience. This is dangerous because the work that one does in hopes of freedom from oppression is done for the sake of the name, instead of for the sake of the experience that the name always incompletely describes. A positivism erupts here, one that is attached to visuality and consciousness:

> This idealism functions as if the *conscious* level of articulation/representation is all there is: We say/show this (good image), therefore we are this (good). The success of such idealism comes from the collaboration of those who spontaneously identify with the things they consciously hear/see. (Chow 43)

This identification occurs without accounting for what Chow perceives as a kind of excess folded into the name as it is called into being. At the same time, Chow remains committed to a kind of material practice that values action over theory and is critical of Spivak's lapses when the latter allows "poststructuralism's discursivism" (Chow 47) to take a privileged position.

The contradiction between the need to act in the material world and the recognition of both the necessity and the excesses of the name in order to do so is a contradiction that Rita Wong and jam ismail are highly conscious of in their own poetic practices. The uncontrollable excess that manifests in the spaces between language and the material world also sometimes operates in ways that entangle capitalist economics with racial locations.

Reading Spivak and Žižek, Chow draws our attention to the problem of excess at the site of the production of value. In classical Marxist terms, value is a direct representation of labour. To say that value is a representation, however, is to analogize economic relations to narrative or linguistic ones and thus to abstract it away from its "irreducible materiality" (Chow 34). Spivak proposes a notion of value as difference. In other words, she suggests that there is an excess produced in the conversion of labour to value. While Chow seems reluctant to analogize value to writing at the level of materiality, she does note that they have something in common, namely that while they are supposed to be secondary—value to labour, and writing to speech—they act as primary determinants (Chow 35). Like writing, value raises the question of whether labour actually precedes it, or whether there is something originary about value (or writing) itself.

To read an originary openness into value is, then, to insert the economic into the textual. Spivak writes: "The method of *Capital*—the title of a book—is the method of capital—the value form (as Marx points out) not by special dispensation but because making theory has something in common with capitalization (as Derrida points out)" (qtd. in Chow 36). Namely, what theory and capitalization have in common is a production of excess—at the site of writing in the first instance and at the site of the production of value in the second.

This is important for a poet such as Rita Wong, who is conscious of writing as labour. We see the production of this excess at work in the opening poem of her first book of poems, *monkeypuzzle*. "sunset grocery" opens with the eight-year-old speaker making change for corner store customers, and then, a few lines later, working out the monetary value of her own labour and that of other family members:

> ... the store is where i develop
> the expected math skills: $60 net one day divided by
> twelve hours is $5 an hour, divided by two people is
> $2.50 an hour, or divided by five
> people $1.00 an hour. (11)

It is hard to imagine how any profit is produced from this labour. Between labour and the exchange value produced there lies an inarticulable excess, hinted at by the ways in which race is negotiated in the store, from customers faking "snotty chinese accents" to the child speaker's humorous but discomfiting play at being "inscrutable" until she realizes "i am read as inscrutable by many customers with no effort on my part" (Wong 11). But the articulable playing out of racialization in the poem, perhaps as some form of Althusserian "hailing" combined with Butlerian "performance," is not the full extent of the excess. Located in the night, and in the sounds of sleep, there is still something unsaid that remains, something perhaps, that cannot be said. Wong writes:

> ... our dog Smokey often sleeps by the bunk bed.
> she snores. my sister talks in her sleep. down the hall
> my father snores too. some nights, it's hard to tell
> who snores louder—the dog or my dad. the nights are
> noisy with all the things never said in the day. (12)

But even the not-quite-silent rumblings of the night are not the extent of all that takes place in excess of the racist name. Wong writes about fire on two occasions in the poem:

> the summer that i am afraid of fire, i always have a glass of
> water near my bed. not enough to put out flames, i can at least
> drink when I awaken, throat dry, sweating & fearful in the night. (12)

Later she writes:

> ... i know the power of fire ...
> ... how it rests hungry within me
> waiting for the tinder of another body. the fear stems from fire's power
> to destroy
> to erase an existence eked out from penny nickel dime tedium. (13)

In this poem, fire is a particularly volatile kind of excess that rages between labour and value. In this stanza it is figured as desire, and as the incendiary will to destroy.

Reading Spivak, Rey Chow (36) locates this excess within a catachrestical notion of *différance*, an excess that is at once outside the system and, at the same time, keeps it functioning. Žižek, she notes, locates the asymmetry

between capital and labour as "the symptom." Chow points out that there is
an abstraction at work between labour and capital, an abstraction located in
social relations among people at the site of commodity exchange. It is only
possible for it to function, however, when there is a certain non-knowledge
or non-awareness at work (Chow 37). As lived experiences, as part of the
flow of (unsettled) daily life, the night noises behind the store, the child
speaker's fear of fire, the latent desire that "rests hungry within me / waiting
for the tinder of another body," and the unresolvable negotiations around
race and racialization that occur in the store might all be read as symptomatic of this unknowable excess that cannot quite be grasped.

Žižek suggests that this abstraction, in fact, is not purely abstract, but
has a kind of materiality to it. It is neither purely of the mind, nor purely of
matter, but contains elements of both; this is his "sublime object" (Chow 37).

We can observe this materiality asserting itself in an untitled poem by
Wong, which begins: "write around the absence, she said show / its existence /
demonstrate / its contours." The lines fall down the left-hand side of the
page making a concave shape—a sort of hollow. The materiality of the words
themselves outline an absence. On the far right-hand side of the page, making a fat, convex shape is a sort of riddle, an aporia, an absence:

> this is
> *the sound of*
> *my chinese tongue*
> *whispering:* nei tou
> gnaw ma? *no*
> *tones can*
> *survive this*
> *alphabet* (29)

Italics, used conventionally to indicate foreign words, are used for the
English words. Wong's rough transliteration of Chinese sounds (which,
interestingly, are not written according to any of the systematized methods for romanizing Chinese) are printed in non-italicized plain text. But
without any tonal indications, their meaning is unclear. They might echo
the Chinese characters ghosted between the two text-shapes. These might
be translated as *Are you hungry?* But they also might not. The language, the
hunger itself, is loosened from its capacity to mean by the conversion to the
roman alphabet. So there is both an abstraction and a materiality at work,
but the materiality is itself one that indicates absence—something lost in
translation—an undecipherable question that remains unanswered, and at
the same time an indication of hunger, itself an emptiness, an absence.

ABSENCE/THE EMPTY ORIGINAL

Returning for a moment to my discussion in Chapter 1, about the inartic-ulable interior of autobiography, I would like to suggest that, by noting the absence as central to her work, Wong is able to speak to it in a way that Lau, for instance, is not. Her writing supplements the absence rather than attempting to define it and make it secure for the white mainstream that wants to be sure that the inscrutable other is named and defined so that it can "understand" race.

In the work of jam ismail, the excess also occurs within grammar, at the level of the word itself. In an untitled piece in *sexions*, a cluster of the definite article "the" hangs off the poem at the beginning and end like excess fabric that could easily be sheared away:

>   the
>
>   the
>   the   the
>   the
>
>   the
>   the
>   the
>
>   the
>   (ooo
>   blue   frequency
>   reclamation innervates .   un image , a vol.
>
>   wel abov sealevel : <u>landfill</u>   times
>   harbor
>   sky   affix

The cloud of "the's" that hovers above this text could be read either as waste or as a material reclamation of the definite article at the edges of meaning, a surplus, but also a kind of material certainty that sparks feeling, that is visual, that takes up space (vol-ume) or that flies (Fr. *voler*) or that robs. It is an excess that might be in the process of being pulled to the body of the poem, or driven from it.

Insofar as ismail locates this poem in Hong Kong, it is important to note that there is no definite article in Chinese, a fact often parodied with racist (or sometimes merely exoticist) intent by Westerners. To associate the defi-nite article in English, the language of the colonizer, with the landfill that

makes up much of the Hong Kong waterfront, is to ask about the displacement of the harbour/water and of the indigenous tongue (which is more
fluid, more referential and infinitely more flexible for the purposes of pun-
ning).[1] In Chow's terms, the harbour becomes the original (though a watery,
empty one)—like "labour" in Marx or "the Real" in Lacan. The landfill is the
stand-in, the representation that contains the traumatic excess. The landfill is
like the name, attempting to define and, in the process, obliterating the productively empty space it fills for the purposes of capitalist production. When
water is translated into land, a vital absence is lost. When nouns that did
perfectly well on their own are modified by the definite article, something
of their perfection is lost. In English translation, the complete functionality
of Cantonese becomes deficient. A market is created for English articles
that no one needed until the English said they needed them. The placement
of the two little pockets of "the's" function visually as landfills displacing
the blankness of the page on either end of the poem. The definite article
becomes then a (raced) site of traumatic excess or waste—the (alienated)
labour in the harbour.

On the facing page, ismail engages traumatic excess again:

> These tumours are un common in   Ahmerica
> Theyy are common in Japan
> The radi ation is ad minster ed over a wi de port al (n. pag.)

It remains vague as to whether the tumours are of the body or of geography.
It is possible, however, to read the gaps that break the words up in the third
and first lines above as tumours in the poem. This time, it is space that is
excessive, rather than content. When, then, can we tell those moments in
which we are being injured by some kind of translational corruption apart
from those moments in which we are being helped? Or when, indeed, we
are encountering a moment of purity?

Chow posits the abstract excess I have been discussing at the site of an
"impossible encounter between rationality and trauma" (38). Žižek suggests
that there exists a traumatic kernel that the subject cannot comprehend.
However, the subject's very survival depends on her or his not-knowing. We
survive because we don't know. Knowledge is lethal. This lack of knowledge
that guarantees our ability to function is Žižek's "symptom," which, Chow
suggests, might be figured as a "nauseous, verminous open wound" (Chow
38). To understand the surplus we ought then to be vigilant for the moment
when "the symptom erupts"—in other words, when paradox reveals itself
(Chow 38). The (occasional) collapse of meaning, in Wong's work certainly,

but especially in ismail's, can be read as a self-preserving blindness. Or if not blindness, then a wilful re-envisioning, a misrecognition that is both knowing and not knowing, and therefore one that flirts with the collapse of survival.

For example, earlier in *sexions* is a short question and answer piece in which "Q" asks:

> in concentrating so long on sex ratios, we hav ignored the broader question of sex-allocation. how long do you think a sex-changing fish should function as male & how long as female?   how should a hermafroditic plant divide its resources between production of pollen & ovules? (n. pag.)

Rather than replying directly, "A" responds elliptically by suggesting, first of all, that the question is too singular, too logocentric: "all this data is one datum um um m" (n. pag.). "Um" is an Arabic word for "mother." In English, it is a colloquial expression of hesitation. For "A," then, the logocentrism of positivist knowledge is undermined by matrilineal hesitation that, in embracing uncertainty, is more true to "nature" than the singular, fixed knowledge of God-the-Father. The next chunk of text describes an experiment in which inverting goggles are placed on a monkey and right-left reversing lenses placed over the eyes of hens. The monkeys are immobilized for several days and finally begin walking backwards. The hens become "severly disturbed & show no impravement after 3 months of waering the sprims" (n. pag.). As her response continues, A's language itself deteriorates to a random flow of letters. The initial syllable of her made-up word "impravement," the part suggestive of "improvement," gives way to the second syllable that points towards madness, or "depravity." The specificity of the question has blinded A, or else she has taken on the symptoms of the monkeys and hens she has been discussing. It is a kind of survival in the face of the linear/logocentric that depends on non-knowledge, or on misrecognition. In other words, there is a different kind of power and a different kind of freedom in the production of knowledge that is not entirely recognizable, that is disoriented and visually impaired.

A page later we are presented with an image of what appears to be a rooster with the distorting prisms over its eyes! On either side of its image are references for a number of texts on evolution, gender, and experiments on light and vision. ismail is both poking fun at and playing with the truth regimes of science and the visual:

Figure 1

The substitution of the rooster-like image playfully throws the gender of the previously discussed hens into question. Or else, it raises the question of why the viewer sees a rooster in this image, and not a particularly "butch" hen! What we understand as nature or the natural is thrown into question. Or else nature and culture are more deeply intertwined than we usually imagine them to be.

It does not fully make sense, then, to say that Wong and ismail are writing with a non-knowledge of traumatic excess that allows their "vision" to survive intact. On the contrary, both poets have a consciousness of what they are doing, of how their language is working. ismail is certainly able, however, to point to the eruption of the symptom at sites where power coalesces. For instance, in a piece called "Casa Blanca" in the *Jamelie/Jamila*

Project, a bookwork consisting of loose sheets that can be ordered any way
the reader wishes, which ismail produced with visual artist Jamelie Hassan
in 1992, she writes:

> 'the westward creep of the ontario scenario,' premier vander
> zalm warned, describing first, as it turns out, himself. (n. pag.)

And later, quoting CNN's coverage of the 1991 Gulf War in which the
United States invaded Iraqi-occupied Kuwait:

> '... killed, by friendly fire ...'
> (uhh. lucky other side) (n. pag.)

The apparently straight truths of contemporary media or politics are recon-
textualized to reveal a repressed content, a surplus unknown and unintended
by the original speaker that perversely permits not only the speaker's survival, but his/her/its ability to thrive. In the first instance, Premier Vander
Zalm believes he is describing the movement of a particular relationship to
politics from Ontario to British Columbia, unaware of how this description in fact names his own damaged, unknowing subjectivity, through the
double meaning of the word "creep." His survival, his potency as a politician
depends on this not-knowing. In the second instance, the news anchor and
the machine that feeds him/her is so invested in their constructions of the
enemy they don't see the violence they commit against their "own side" even
when the result is death. This not-knowing, even in the face of the wound's
final symptom—death—is the blindness that allows the American media/
industrial/military complex to survive. The power of non-knowing has no
partisan alliances.

Chow points out that proper deconstructionists like Paul deMan find
language's most truthful revelations in the misreadings, aporias, and fail-
ures of language. What happens, then, to the voice of a poet like Wong or
ismail, who is conscious of her own revelatory activity—the double and
triple meanings, the multiply-hailed subjects? The ethical deconstructivist,
Chow suggests, must be forever mindful of her own slippages in language
to guard against unintended meanings, but the result can become an obsessive, unreadable self-referentiality that reinforces a kind of elitism that both
Chow and Spivak want to avoid. Spivak suggests two solutions: a move to
metalanguage that materializes its own possibility through paradox on the
one hand, and the strategic risk of essentialism on the other. This is precisely
what both Wong and ismail do.

Of course, these risks are real risks. Žižek is critical of essentialism as idealization, which functions very effectively in the service of totalitarian regimes (Chow 41). It works through the identification of the "good" image with good governance. We have already seen in ismail's paradoxical "screen-play" with the Socred government in British Columbia and with the major television networks how this kind of idealization, uncritiqued, has a fully oppressive underbelly. ismail is aware of the complicated play of projections that makes the absurd surface masquerading as "truth" possible. Chow takes up Althusser's notion that hailing interpellates the subject and points out its derivation from Pascal's analysis of how we come to "know" the existence of God: "Pascal says, more or less: 'Kneel down, move your lips in prayer and you will believe'" (Althusser qtd. in Chow 44). The existence of "God" or the "Great Leader," then, resides not in any actual quality of that entity, but in the submissive practices of believers (Chow 44). Žižek argues that the "People" on whom the power of the Leader is based do not exist, except in the form of a fetish (Chow 44). Chow notes that Žižek borrows from antidescriptivist philosophy to invoke the notion of naming. Chow explains how it works:

> In the phrase "the people support the Party," the word "support" operates linguistically as well as symbolically ... *naming* ... depends for its authen-tication on something more than the objective properties of the thing named.... ["N]ames" ... [refer] to an external causal link, which allows things to be transmitted from subject to subject. (Chow 44)

What Žižek finds useful here is the notion that there is more than a simple correspondence between naming and the thing named. This excess, he calls "desire." Through desire, identity is constructed retroactively. The name is a sublime object that has a materiality constructed for it after the fact of naming (Chow 45).

The notion of the name, then, is the crux of Chow's new ethics. Material practice can bring names into being. There may be nothing at the root of the name, but it is the practice that matters. The unfolding of that material practice, fuelled by a desire to make something from nothing, produces the symptom. This is not a bad thing. The symptom, perhaps painful, is none-theless generative.

ETHICAL EXCESS

What then of the writer who recognizes these problematics and who has an interest in undoing the tidy functioning of ideology? Spivak notes: "[I]f you have any kind of political interest you name it in hope that the name will disappear" (qtd. in Chow 46). At the same time, this produces anxiety, since the politicized agent becomes invested in her struggle at the level of identity. Žižek finds a solution in the notion of immanent negativity—to think of an ethics with a negative limit, that is the edge of the moment at which the name would disappear. To understand that moment's immanence is to accept that social antagonism is permanent (Chow 49).

jam ismail's "Poeisis" plays on the edge of the name's disappearance. In many ways it is a strategic essentialism of the most productive kind, since it calls into being a multiplicity of sexes, joyously invoked. This prose poem has a narrative. A young boy called Sami, whom jam is babysitting, asks her: "are you a girl, a mummy, or a Japanese?" The child inadvertently calls attention to the arbitrariness of classificatory systems. The excess, the desire to name is present, but it is also being pointed at. If the arbitrariness of these gendered and raced modes of naming come into the full light of day, they could be shattered, though whether such a shattering would be productive for the child or not remains questionable. jam and Sami's play at the "negative limit" is turned around at the moment when Sami asks jam, "Do you have a johnny?" From this question, a plethora of individually raced/gendered names for human genitalia are called into being. jam has a "jammy-whammy." Sami, since his name isn't "John," doesn't have a "johnny." He has a "Sami-yami." In the end, though, this dissolution of the binary conventions of gender with its always already racialized undertones is reduced to the inconsequential, through the invocation of capital:

> On the Planet Earth, five billion human genitalia stirred,
> unwilling to take on the headache of namehood.
> Prime Ministers moan: "How are we going to handle this,
> Michael?"
> Finance Ministers foam: "Taxonomy, Brian, taxonomy." (n. pag.)

ismail's word play both allows the possibility for this multiplicity of names and at the same time erases them, in the invocation of tax ("-onomy" or "-ation"?). But either way, the calling into being of a free-flowing multiplicity is contained, either through a new system of classification or through the subsuming of raced/gendered categories under the neat and homogenous category of citizen as taxpayer (within a capitalist economy).[2] Chow's qualification of ethics would suggest, however, that this is not necessarily disempowering, since there is a void at the root of all systems of naming, including the one that makes taxation possible.

ismail, as we saw in "Poeisis," plays with the intertwining of raced and gendered concerns. What, then, of her tidy clipping away the extraneous "e" (for "excess"?) and the occasional "l" from the ends of words? One might note the absence of the letter "e" in the word "abov" in the "harbour" piece I discussed earlier. This is a tactic that ismail employs extensively, in both *sexions* and *from the diction air*. It works to produce a differently gendered speaking/writing subject, tending toward the masculine (if one thinks in terms of the French convention of adding the letter "e" or sometimes "le" to the ends of nouns in order to feminize them, or the use of specific linguistic forms that gender not the noun, but the speaker, in many Asian and European languages). One might conceive of it as a self-affirming excision of the traumatic from language, in the sense that the excision genders the speaker, if not as male, then as butch. It materializes the body. It materializes the (partial) truth of gender. The pressure to "act feminine" is relieved. The speaker makes for herself a joyous entry into the materiality of language.

In "Poeisis," ismail writes: "wat's sauce for the goose ,[*sic*] is source for the gender." If one thinks of all those saucy e's she has removed as gender's source, then obliterating them potentially removes gender from language. But ismail doesn't remove all the "e"s from her text, only strategically placed ones. She does not want to obliterate her femininity so much as relieve some of the social pressure placed on it. To remove all of the e's could theoretically dissolve gender as a system of naming. The existence of gender is a primary source for the poet's wordplay. But there is pleasure in the play. As vowels are the source of gender they are also the source of meaning, with all of its traumatic excesses. ismail doesn't want to give up on these just yet. She points toward the dissolution of gendered language, but, as Spivak might encourage, she also defers that dissolution. There is passion and pleasure in the excessive void. What harm is there in hanging on to it a little longer?

To investigate further how the void is generative, Chow discusses two Buddhist monks in contention to succeed the Fifth Patriarch of the Dhyana School in the seventh century C. E. Chow notes that the Patriarch chooses not the one who emphasizes changing the world through action, but the one who recognizes the "no-thing-ness of the world," the one who sees that life is beyond human intervention. This recognition is a fraught one, surely one that is very difficult to accept. Chow suggests that the symptom arises through desire: "But as we also learn from the ancients, the void is unavoidable. That is why desire, which is often the desire to possess (things) as such, is always insatiable" (Chow 53).

Spivak, Chow suggests, recognizes this and thus emphasizes postponement, deferral, failure, non-fulfilment, and "impossibility" while at the same time emphasizing the historical and the social as the site of struggle (Chow

53). Spivak writes: "any really 'loving' political practice must fall prey to its own critique" (qtd. in Chow 53).

Likewise, Žižek advocates an "enthusiastic resignation" with regards to the primacy of nothingness. In her final move, Chow posits an ethics that is both ambivalent and paradoxical:

> [T]he void stands for the source of a distinct form of passion, the passion of an indomitable "as if": although defeat is imminent, one goes on enthusiastically as if one doesn't know it—indeed, as if one's entire life force comes from this defeat.[3] (Chow 54)

Wong's "writing around the absence," then, becomes an acknowledgement of the absence at the root of race. The tonal excess of spoken Cantonese, which colonial English wants to "steamroller," is a no-thing-ness (tones can't exist without syllabic utterances) in excess of race, one loaded with the boisterous passions of the people who produce these sounds, these meanings. For Wong, "grammar, like wealth, belongs in the hands of/the people who produce it" (29).

PUSHING THROUGH THE ABSENCE TO THE OTHER SIDE OF THE NAME, OR FROM APATHY TO ANARCHY

Wong is not as pessimistic as Chow. She recognizes the defeats of daily life. And she goes on enthusiastically, in the face of those defeats, with the hope that they can be pushed through:

> In my daily life, I do not consent to the sweatshop labour that made the clothes I wear. I do not consent to unlabelled genetically modified foods forced upon an ignorant market. I do not consent to the colonization of the First Nations land on which I live. I do not consent to Canadian tax money funding environmentally destructive projects like overseas mines and hydro-electric dams through the Export Development Corporation....
>
> I think that recognizing my entanglement in oppressive systems is one way to begin changing it [sic]. It's like how alcoholics have to admit there's a problem before they can stop drinking. There are many people organizing against sweatshop labour in unions and in groups like the Maquila solidarity network. There are environmental groups and consumers' rights groups organizing boycotts of genetically modified products. First Nations people have been fighting for their survival for centuries, and continue organizing to do so. These efforts value the body, the imagination, the possibility of longterm peaceful co-existence. These efforts give me hope and inform my writing, not always in obvious or direct ways. (Restless Bodies 11)

While a part of this articulation is clearly, and necessarily, oppositional, her poetic writing practice opens up another kind of relationship to the void. What is interesting in her poetry is that the "I" is no longer the focus of the project. Rather, a kind of psychic space is opened up, one in which violence and hope are embedded in one another, and subjectivity is a node along which these elements come into play. We can see this embedding at work in her poem "chaos feary":

> pyre in pirate bio in bile
> mono in poly breeder in
> womb pull of landrace allo
> me poietic auto me diverse
> trans over genic harassment
> over seas genetic as pathetic
> as engine of disease (*Restless Bodies* 6)

The "pyre in pirate" is not equivalent to the "bio in bile," in spite of their grammatical equivalence. While Wong has described this poem as a "rant," it is actually loaded with an ambivalent multiplicity in which names exceed themselves producing endlessly productive catachreses. The "pyre in pirate" may, on the first pass, appear as a blazing deathbed. But what dies? On the first pass: species, diversity, working people. However, because the piracy of the corporate world depends on the very things it destroys for its own survival, its violence cannot last. Wong is right to see this mutual destruction as a horror. But because "pyre" is itself a living force, it is full of possibility far in excess of the "piracy" that contains it. "Pyre" is related to the fire of her earlier poem "sunset grocery." It is fire that she rightly fears for its power to destroy. But it is also the fire that burns within her:

> how it creates heat in
> cold prairie winters, how it simmers, boils & stirfries countless
>   meals
> in the steaming kitchen, how it rests hungry within me, waiting
>   for the
> tinder of another body. (*monkeypuzzle* 13)

The fire is a nurturing and generative force as much as it is a destructive one. Like the name "subaltern" or "Asian Canadian" it is sometime productive and sometimes destructive, and often both at once. Value depends on experience and not any absolute quality of the thing.

Even more so than the fire in the pyre, the "bio in bile" contains the possibility for endless catachrestic difference. Certainly the biological is something that the large biotech corporations are interested in patenting, genetically modifying and containing for the purposes of profit. But the biological terrain is infinitely larger or more unpredictable than corporate attempts to contain it. Wong's dismay on recognizing the new territory corporations have found to colonize leads rightly to fear and anger. But the excessive creatures that emerge from corporate abuse, such as the "jellypo fishtato" in "nervous organism" have already been set loose and have a power of their own. They are not innocent or pure. They are fully products of the military/prison/industrial/religious context that spawned them,[4] and yet they are endlessly mutatable and still capable of protest.

In "domestic operations 2.0," a poem about three nuns who disarmed a missile silo in Colorado in 2002, Wong recognizes a space for hope:

> from apathy
> to anarchy in a few consonants. somehow witness does
> not equal resignation. locating hope in the unpredictable
> and the shared. assembling to conjure up a larger spectre
> than fear. larger than greed. larger than marx even.
> sudden bearded lady apprehensions. missile apprehensions.
> monstrous attention scarlet alert weather and consumption
> patterns transform property into commons. (*Restless Bodies*
> 8–9)

The name "apathy" can, through a small linguistic twist, be transformed into a hopeful and generative "anarchy." As Wong shows us with "pyre" and "bio," all language is loaded with its own catachreses, its own possibility for repetition with a difference, for mutation against the grain of corporate drives toward terminator technology and profit. It will not do, then, to go on as though defeat is imminent. Rather, it is important to recognize that the horror is all too likely, but then so is random mutation that empowers, and so is protest and dissent.

Writing about Lawrence Chua's *Gold by the Inch*, Wong notes a moment when Martina, a computer chip assembler in Malaysia's Free Trade Zone, scratches "bad words" on microchips (14). She sees hope for a new kind of relationship with technology and the marginalized, racialized women who produce it, through such actions as the scratching of protest on microchips: "The image of angry, microscopic curses embedded within the computer on which I type makes me re-imagine my relationship to the computer" (*Restless Bodies* 14).

One might read Wong's later work as a more sophisticated "writing around the absence," in which the copious traumatic excesses of naming are taken up, pointed out, dissolved, and rewritten or re-imagined. When she says "allo / me poeitic auto me diverse," she opens up the possibility for the creation of a new kind of self, greater and more multiple than the system that produced it.[5] The play with sound, pun, and shifting meaning illustrates the endless catachrestical possibilities proliferating beneath the surface of the name. While there is "no sense in food or rhyme," she clearly engages both. This is a dancing on the edge of disappearance. But there is also the chance that something productive will come of the dance in excess of nonsense, food, or rhyme. The line "Dinner a roulette" refers to the deaths, the obliterations, the losses of livelihoods and lives that lie behind Western eating patterns. But one could also conceive the notion of "dinner" itself as a name that could be obliterated through a game of roulette, a name that we might or might not want to erase, since dinner feeds the "hunger" of Wong's earlier untitled "absence" poem. The keeping or the giving up of these traumatic names is a gamble. In her most hopeful moments, Wong recognizes the possibilities inherent in a flickering having and not having of the name. Certainly the hour is late, and Wong calls for us to understand the horror of our moment. Her work clearly calls for awareness, even as that awareness is painful. She quotes Lu Xun:

> Imagine an iron house without windows, absolutely indestructible, with many people fast asleep inside who will shortly die of suffocation. But you know that since they will die in their sleep, they will not feel the pain of death. Now if you cry aloud to wake a few of the lighter sleepers, do you think you are doing them a good turn? (qtd. in *Restless Bodies* 11–12)

Wong insists that she would want to be awake. She is less certain that it is right to wake those who might rather sleep. She feels it is unethical to impose one's decisions on others. But nor is she able to keep silent. Instead, she proposes to make "a steady stream of sound that can be easily overlooked by the sleepers but encodes your questions and impressions to those who are actively listening for them" (*Restless Bodies* 12). The sound is full of play that includes the name but is loaded with possibility in excess of it. Some of these excesses, I argue, might find and press open cracks in the walls of the iron house. The name is not so much something to be had or denied, as it is something that can be open, and that can spill unpredictable possibility, for both better and worse.

In this chapter, I have attempted to recognize the productivity and playfulness of the name and its excesses, even as one might long for its disappearance. The racist name may well be the source of an originary trauma. To reclaim the racist name and to play with it relocates the trauma. Through reiteration it produces a new kind of violence, but it also brings the name to the brink of disappearance. In so doing, I argue, the name is transformed, or rather, made to open. Once open, it spills catachrestical excess that does not resolve the original violence but makes continuous space for other ways of living, being, and thinking that were not part of the original violence. The marginalized subject is pulled into a kind of liveliness and possibility it did not have before. These recognitions do not resolve the conundrum of naming I posed in my Introduction, but rather open other possibilities for writing, reading, and acting in excess of that "oolemma," even as it remains a question.

CHAPTER 6

THE CAMERAS OF THE WORLD

Race, Subjectivity, and the Spiritual, Collective Other in Margaret
Atwood's *Oryx and Crake* and Dionne Brand's *What We All Long For*

THE POROUS CHORUS

The second half of the twentieth century brought with it many challenges to the Enlightenment humanist subject from a range of disparate quarters—feminist, anti-racist, postcolonialist, and poststructuralist, just
to name a few. With those challenges, agency, coherent subjectivity, and relation (with the Other, or within the subject herself) have been destabilized
with unsettling consequences for those thinkers interested in a politics of
liberation. In this chapter, I offer readings of the character Oryx in Margaret
Atwood's *Oryx and Crake* and Quy in Dionne Brand's *What We All Long
For* to propose an imagining of a kind of agented subject, one that is abject,
multiple, dangerous, and damaged, but not necessarily as radically Other
and silent as the subaltern Gayatri Spivak famously theorized in "Can the
Subaltern Speak?" The subject I propose is more porous and more collective
than the subject of liberal humanism. I offer the glimmering of an ethics of
relation that might be useful for breaking out of or, at least, partially exceeding the Subject/Other dichotomy that has been such a problem for Western
critical theory and the politics of cultural belonging for such a long time.

POSTMODERN SURFACES, GLOBAL FLOWS, AND SACRED MAN

In "Notes on Globalization as a Philosophical Issue," Fredric Jameson suggests that in the last decades of the twentieth century we have entered a
new stage of multinational capitalism that is fundamentally different from
anything that has preceded it (54). He sees this new stage as marked by and
inseparable from that thing that theorists have for some time been calling
postmodernity. Jameson posits globalization as a continuation of colonialism, in which the world market, as the "ultimate horizon of the capitalist
project" (54), figures as the primary focus. Suggesting that our current late
capitalist conditions are new and different from what went before, Jameson
says that there are two ways of dealing with change. One is a modernist

mode that mourns "the disappearance of History." He sees the present as the end of a modern period in which political struggle took place on the ground of grand ideologies carrying great, quasi-religious authority. The other is the postmodern mode, which is to celebrate the "end of History" (55). Jameson sees postmodernity as having broken away from linear time, as being marked by spatial rather than temporal categories, that is, synchronic rather than diachronic categories ("The Cultural Logic" 16). He offers the synchronic postmodern moment in terms of a number of impulses—the emergence of a kind of Utopianism focusing on everyday objects, mimicry as pastiche, schizophrenia resulting from the de-linking of the signifier and the signified, the radical eclipse of nature accompanied by a celebration of the machine, and finally mutations in built space. With the advent of the cybernetic revolution, the rate of information exchange is quicker and its directions more multiple. Economic transfers become embedded in communicational ones. Advertising and American TV are exported faster than new information comes in from "exotic" locales. It is this massive and rapid movement in the rate of exchange, facilitated by the new communications technologies, that Jameson sees as the major marker of "newness." Communication and economics have, in a sense, collapsed into one another ("Notes on Globalization" 56).

Another theorist of globalization, Arjun Appadurai, has termed these simultaneously interacting, synchronic forces "global flows." Appadurai sees the global economy as a "complex, overlapping, disjunctive order" (32) in which a variety of forces can play out in an endless number of combinations that must be theorized in their particularity.[1] Appadurai suggests the new rapid movement of information creates "communities with 'no sense of place'" (29). He writes:

> The world we live in now seems rhizomatic, even schizophrenic, calling for theories of rootlessness, alienation, and psychological distance between individuals and groups on the one hand and fantasies (or nightmares) or electronic propinquity on the other. (99)

As aesthetic descriptions of contemporary conditions, the notion of the postmodern surface or the idea of global flows gives us a vision of an unsettled present in which the agency of the humanist subject plays the role of stylistic anachronism. But what the humanist project offered and continues to offer, in spite of imperialist and faux universalist abuses of the term, remains the possibility of justice. If theorists like Jameson and Appadurai see our moment correctly, it is difficult not to throw one's hands up and surrender one's humanist agency (the imagination of which, somehow, persists) to whatever entity enthralls us—the state, the corporation, style, or global flows.

To rethink subjectivity in terms of citizenship might help. A justice-minded thinker like Giorgio Agamben, however pessimistic, still has something to offer us in the possibility of the cleaving together of *bios* and *zoe*, the life of the citizen and bare life. Agamben recognizes that the modern state is founded on the state of exception in which some human beings must be reduced to *homo sacer*, the sacred man who can be killed without being sacrificed. The paradox of the modern democratic state is that our civil rights can be suspended at any time in the service of preserving, paradoxically, none other than those same civil rights. Through contemporary state legislation like the War Measures Act in Canada or the Patriot Act in the United States, those whose civil rights are in most need of protection are precisely those who are interned, deported, rendered, or imprisoned without trial or recourse in the name of civil rights—Japanese Canadians during World War II, for instance, or, in the awful present that we dream will soon pass, prisoners at Guantanamo Bay. If Agamben does not offer a solution to this state of affairs, he at least offers a sense of its extreme injustice, an injustice that does not disappear, in modernist mourning or otherwise, beneath a postmodern surface.

SCOPOPHILIA IN THE AGE OF DIGITAL REPRODUCTION

As Laura Mulvey taught feminist spectators in the 1990s, the camera of Hollywood's Golden Age relies on vision as the sense through which knowledge-power is produced and perpetuated. Hollywood's emphasis on the gaze produces and intensifies the power of men's (and whites') subjectivity and renders women (and other others) as objects to be desired and controlled (399). The problem under the conditions of neo-imperialist neoliberal capital, or what Hardt and Negri have called "Empire," is that the conditions of image production have changed. The Western subject is no longer the voyeur in the dark cinema, but instead views its others over the Internet or, at the very least, on TV or in the glossy reports sent to generous donors who give to humanitarian organizations. (I acknowledge, of course, that the gift, under the distribution systems of globalized capital, is a complicated entity.) The people photographed by the cameras of globalized postmodernity, like the demons of Beelzebub, are dark and legion. And related to "us," citizens and humanist subjects—by love and by blood. Horribly, this doesn't undo relations of power imbalance. It doesn't displace the "Third World" from its othered location, although, I argue here, the conditions of otherness are unsettled. They waver; difference is returned to sameness as kinship, and the Western subject must then be accountable, not just for reasons of right or wrong, but for reasons of relation. The postmodern moment returns something like humanist subjectivity to us in the Derridean sense of *hauntology*, in which the spectre of more idealistic ways of being—Marxist and/or humanist—still hangs over us, as that which seems to have been relegated to the past, but which might return in a hopeful future, one that still remembers the violent conditions of the present's founding.

Or to put it another way, "the cameras of the world" photograph ghosts. Those who suffer in refugee camps, extra-territorial prisons, or as migrant labour—the people captured in "the cameras of the world"—can be understood as the remainder of humanity after the violent production of states. In *Ghostly Matters: Haunting and the Sociological Imagination*, Avery Gordon (reading Laura Kipnis) notes that on the postmodern surface, "hypervisibility is a kind of obscenity of accuracy that abolishes distinctions between 'permission and prohibition, presence and absence'" (16). In high-tech culture, hypervisibility puts the world on view. Dedicated to ghostbusting, it shines its light into every possible crevice. In Gordon's terms, hypervisibility gives us the impression of seeing and knowing, but in fact such vision is "punctuated alternately by apparitions and hysterical blindness" (17). "*I see you are not there*" (16). The ghosts insist themselves, or rather, even though the First World subject cannot see herself in the glossy print, a haunting kinship pervades the image. She knows herself, but in an uncanny way. Guiltily, she shells out cash to feed the hungry ghosts. But as the ultimate abstraction of the postmodern surface, the cash donation only deepens the haunting. Gordon writes:

> Hypervisibility is a persistent alibi for the mechanisms that render one *un*visible.... [T]he mediums of public image making and visibility are inextricably wedded to the co-joined mechanisms that systematically render certain groups of people apparently *privately* poor, uneducated, ill, and disenfranchised. (17; emphasis in original)

The ghosts can be understood as *homo sacer* upon whom the production and perpetuation of the state depends. But they are also our family members. To insist on relation is not to deny difference. The subjects of First World privilege are also shifting, through privileged states of exception. Aihwa Ong notes that in our neoliberal present, exception can be deployed to include citizen-subjects, still extra-juridically, but for the purposes of privileging, for instance, high-tech knowledge workers. The serendipity of fortune plummets close kin into wildly disparate futures, which then draws us rapidly back together in its new conditions of global flow. A new, or at least "improved," politics of recognition and relation is necessary to address these new forms of uncanny kinship built outside the bounds of national and democratic politics, but upon which such politics and the illusion of democracy depends. The uncanny has not escaped its connection to trauma or to haunting. Imperialism is not over, but it is being re-embodied. And the bodies are not the same as the bodies of the old (as opposed to the present) colonial moment. Race still matters, as much for the history it carries as for the way it is being redeployed under the present global order.

Beneath the surface of this text, rights also matter, rights both within and outside the bounds of the state. If there is something to be salvaged from the wreckage of democracy in order to make it anew, it is the concept of justice. That justice, I argue, depends desperately on an ethics of relation across borders, one that can meet the violence of globalization. That justice depends on ethical practice by different kinds of subjects with different kinds of agency from secular humanist agency, with all its blindness to history, difference, and multiplicity. I explore a new kind of agency here, through a reading of Margaret Atwood's character Oryx from the novel *Oryx and Crake* and Dionne Brand's character Quy from the novel *What We All Long For*. What I would like to suggest is that while Atwood offers us an imagination of the postmodern condition as one in which we are doomed to the excesses of patriarchy, mad science, and global capital, Brand offers us a glimmer of hope through a recognition of kinship that remembers difference and traumatic history, but through which it is still possible both to see and to speak.

ORYX'S LOOK BACK

One might read Atwood's novel *Oryx and Crake* in terms of a postmodernism that celebrates the "end of history" ("Notes on Globalization" 55). But it is at the same time a fully modernist text that mourns the "end." Its crisis, embodied in the character of Snowman, is a humanist crisis—the crisis of the end of individual agency in the face of science and capital gone mad. The implications for the racialized Other, figured most clearly in the character of Oryx, are marked by a strange kind of ambivalence. Without clearly formed individuality, Oryx is deeply disempowered in liberal human terms and, at the same time, strangely empowered through an ironic hyperactivation of a particular stereotype of Asian women. Unlike Offred, the white woman protagonist of Atwood's earlier post-apocalyptic novel, *The Handmaid's Tale*, she cannot mourn. Oryx needs a white man, however clownish, to do it for her. *Oryx and Crake* is not a feminist novel nor an anti-racist one. In some ways it is a throwback to an earlier moment, when free will and agency were valuable ideals, returned to us tongue firmly planted in cheek but nonetheless

still the only option, and one only available to straight white men. Without
the discrete consciousness bestowed by Enlightenment subjectivity, and also
without the capacity to feel pain, Oryx acquires a kind of collective bodily
power that might throw open our thinking of what freedom can mean in
the moment of late capital. Whether this kind of freedom is desirable or
not, however, is fully open to question.

Atwood constructs the figure of Oryx as an unindividuated subject in
postmodern terms. Oryx is, for all intents and purposes, a white man's fantasy of the racialized, sexualized Other. And yet she also has a kind of subaltern power that is open-ended and ambivalent. I will interrogate how, and
to what extent, this construction works, on one hand, in the service of capital
and, on the other, in the service of a kind of post-identity anti-racism—in
other words, one that uses all the language of an anti-racism that once made
a material difference to people's lives and has now been appropriated by a
complex of mediatized and mainstream political discourse that reiterates its
terms but not its liberatory effects.

We first meet Oryx on the Internet, as one of a number of young Asian
girls featured on an Internet kiddie porn site that protagonist Jimmy (a.k.a.
Snowman) and Crake, his scientifically brilliant but morally vacant friend,
visit on a regular basis. For Jimmy these visits are a daredevil sort of thing,
acts of youthful rebellion. For Crake, we discover later, it is part of something much more serious and sinister. The key moment in this scene occurs
when Oryx looks up from the pornographic tableau, in which she and two
other little girls are working over a naked white man with a bag on his head!
She looks directly into the lens of the camera. It seems to Jimmy that she is
looking straight at him: "*I see you*, that look said. *I see you watching. I know
you. I know what you want*" (*Oryx and Crake* 91; italics in original).

This scene and its fallout are fully shot through with Jameson's econom-
ic-in-the-cultural or, alternatively, all five of Appadurai's "scapes." The girls
are commodified to provide a crass entertainment. The boys watch across
vast geographical distance. Oryx's location isn't even all that specific. We
know only that it is geographically far away:

> They then went to HottTotts, a global sex-trotting site. "The next best
> thing to being there," was how it was advertised…. The locations were
> supposed to be countries where life was cheap and kids were plentiful,
> and where you could buy anything you wanted. (*Oryx and Crake* 89–90)

Not only does it occur over a great distance, but the interaction is inter-
racial, financial, broadcast ready, and loaded with ideological significance.
Further, there is a kind of indeterminacy to the location, such that we aren't

really sure whether it is geographical at all, or purely virtual. I shall return to this problem presently.

First, I'd like to discuss Oryx's look back in terms of the status of the image. Hardly the Enlightenment paradise provided by a journalist-hero, HottTotts[2] is the postmodern nightmare flip side of the modernist communications dream. One might argue, however, that its possibility was always present as the repressed of the colonial project, which claimed to be a civilizing mission, but was, in fact, as Edward Said has taught us, one of producing the other as exotic, murderous, sexual, and different, as a way of knowing "our" (European) selves (*Orientalism* 205). But there is one feature that marks this moment as different from any one of a number of exemplary Saidean instances at which a white man or woman looks on a dark other in order to recognize his or her own superiority. Oryx looks back at the camera. It is as though she is looking back at Jimmy, or even as though she is looking through him. This is an effect of the technology—the camera presents a lens that can be looked into. But then, so did the modernist camera, technically speaking. (One might still argue that the impulse to look back is a postmodern impulse.) Certainly, in Oryx's look back, there is the possibility of simultaneity. (Was it a live broadcast?) The technology for the instantaneous return of the gaze across vast distances exists at present, with any one of a number of available softwares. Atwood narrates Oryx's gaze as though it is an actual return, though we understand it as an effect: "Then she looked over her shoulder and right into the eyes of the viewer—right into Jimmy's eyes, into the secret person inside him" (*Oryx and Crake* 91). We know the return can only be an effect of technology, and yet we are left with a creeping feeling that the gaze has been physically and personally returned. HottTotts is a site meant for the voyeur to look on anonymously. The racialized, sexualized other is not supposed to look back. But there is something interdeterminate about power relations on the Internet, such that this relationship is destabilized.[3] Oryx achieves a measure of scopophilic power in the illusion (or real possibility) of her having returned the gaze.

Further, Atwood narrates another kind of instability and contradiction in this situation of gross power imbalance. She describes in lurid detail the staging of the pornographic scene. The action takes place over a soundtrack of moans and giggles, one that Jimmy thinks must have been recorded because the three young girls all look frightened, and one is crying (*Oryx and Crake* 90). But even this loaded, disturbing vision of dubious pleasure and certain suffering cannot escape its own overdetermined textuality:

> Jimmy knew the drill. They were supposed to look like that, [i.e., crying and scared] he thought; if they stopped the action, a walking stick would

come in from offside and prod them. This was a feature of the site. There were at least three layers of contradictory make-believe, one on top of the other. *I want to, I want not, I want to.* (*Oryx and Crake* 90)

Racialized, sexualized, exploited, and dubbed over to boot, Oryx could easily stand as a figure of Gayatri Spivak's much-discussed subaltern:

Here are subsistence farmers, unorganized peasant labour, the tribals, and the communities of zero workers on the street or in the countryside. To confront them is not to represent ... them but to learn to represent ... ourselves. ("Can the Subaltern Speak?" 290)

Spivak echoes Said's notion of the Oriental as the other through which the European "Self" is constructed. In this pornographic scene, dubbed over with moans and giggles, Oryx truly cannot speak. She is deprived of her voice. But in this case, it seems, that while the subaltern cannot speak, she can at least *peek.* As I suggested earlier, there is something double and indeterminate about the location from which Oryx gazes (at Jimmy? Or at us?). It is any one of a number of countries "where life was cheap and kids were plentiful" (90) and it is no country at all, but only, and perhaps solely, a virtual site—one that exists only in cyberspace. It is Jameson's "ultimate horizon of the capitalist project." It is geography collapsed to the economic collapsed to technology collapsed to the labouring Third World body, collapsed to exchange itself—economic, cultural, financial, and sexual.

THE SAME PERSON, OR SURFING THE SIMULACRUM

In his chapter on postmodernism, Jameson notes that the individual subject disappears as a consequence of the unavailability of personal style ("The Cultural Logic" 16).[4] The black humour of pastiche takes over from a lighter, derisive, mimetic parody. Pastiche is still mimetic, but

without any of parody's ulterior motives, amputated of the satiric impulse, devoid of any laughter and any conviction that alongside the abnormal tongue you have momentarily borrowed, some healthy linguistic normality still exists. Pastiche is thus blank parody, a statue with blind eyeballs. ("The Cultural Logic" 17)

One might read the nonspecificness of HottTott's "real" location as symptomatic of this narrative's descent into pastiche, such that the virtuality of its location, in other words, its mimesis, is more significant than its physical geography. And not only is geography up for grabs, but so too is the pleasure of the situation enacted, not just as sex, but as scene and as scene of scene. There is, Jameson argues, still a certain humour and a certain passion possible in pastiche:

> [I]t is at least compatible with addiction—with a whole historically original consumers' appetite for a world transformed into sheer images of itself and for pseudo-events and "spectacles." ... It is for such objects that we may reserve Plato's conception of the "simulacrum," the identical copy for which no original has ever existed. Appropriately enough the culture of the simulacrum comes to life in a society where exchange value has been generalized to the point at which the very memory of use value is effaced. ("The Cultural Logic" 18)

It is easy enough to read HottTotts as a site of the simulacrum. I argue here that the "use value" of a commodified little girl has, on the HottTotts site, been converted to exchange value. Indeed, Oryx herself, during a flashback in which her departure from her indeterminate village of origin is narrated, contemplates the emergence of her own exchange value:

> The children cried at night, not loudly. They cried to themselves. They were frightened: they didn't know where they were going, and they had been taken away from what they knew. Also, said Oryx, they had no more love, supposing that they'd had some in the first place. But they had money value: they represented a cash profit to others. They must have sensed that—sensed that they were worth something. (*Oryx and Crake* 126)

One might read the Oryx of Jimmy and Crake's Internet adventures as a sort of automaton, animated by the power of capital moving at rapid speed over a vast electronic network.[5] She is as fluid as cash itself, a figure of pure transaction. At the same time, in a contradictory doubleness, her body is foregrounded in a manner that is both intimate and debased. In this horrifying instance of synchronic postmodernism, her biology is completely saturated by the cultural in the economic. She is what Donna Haraway in "A Manifesto for Cyborgs" calls "new flesh," both machinic and biological, fully implicated in the workings of patriarchal military industrial capital and yet radically outside it at the same time.

If this strange cleaving of the violent sexualized biological to the techno-economic that Oryx embodies is not disturbing enough, I'd like to point further to the fact that she is also a racialized figure of the "generic Asian" type—country of origin indeterminate, sexual exploitation certain. She is a kind of hyperactivation of the much discussed and much derided notion that "all Asians look alike." She embodies the Oriental Other of financial excess and violence-enacted-elsewhere. Atwood presents this image ironically. But what for me is disturbing about this construction is that the abject body presented to us suffers violently, repeatedly, and as a class. At same time, our (Western) reading of its plight is, through this kind of analysis, abstracted to the point of its evaporation into the ether of the virtual.[6] This, for me, is the ethical problem of postmodern reading and writing strategies.

Just in case we don't get it, Atwood nails home the point that Oryx is not an individual in the self-enclosed, Enlightenment democratic sense of the individual that we have inherited from Western philosophy. Oryx may not be Oryx at all because her individuality is highly unstable. Crake makes a printout of Oryx's look back and gives it to Jimmy, who "saved it and saved it" (*Oryx and Crake* 91). When Jimmy and Oryx become lovers many years later, he shows it to her:

> "I don't think this is me," was what she'd said at first.
> "It has to be!" said Jimmy. "Look! It has your eyes!"
> "A lot of girls have eyes," she said. "A lot of girls did these things. Very many." Then, seeing his disappointment, she said, "It might be me. Maybe it is. Would that make you happy, Jimmy?" (*Oryx and Crake* 91)

Atwood tells us nothing about what Oryx's eyes look like to Jimmy. Do they slant? This conversation, in fact, is precisely an argument about the specificity of subjectivity, which Jameson says disappears in the postmodernity of late capitalism ("The Cultural Logic" 16). When Jimmy says "It has your eyes!" he is pointing toward a kind of individuality that Oryx is unable to claim. For Jimmy, the liberal humanist figure in the book, the eyes are still that clichéd "window to the soul," of an earlier, modernist past. "A lot of girls have eyes," she responds. The eyes that Jimmy sees as proof of her individuality are for her merely evidence of her own genericness, her own indistinguishability from a multitude of other girls. In an earlier moment Atwood indeed describes her as one in a trio of "soulless pixies" (*Oryx and Crake* 90). She is, in a sense, the constructing and accepting agent of her own psychic dismemberment. This is the only agency she has. It matters little to her whether the image "really is" her or not. She is not invested in her individuality in the way that Jimmy is.

If, as Jameson (reading Lacan reading Saussure) suggests, meaning is no longer a one-to-one relationship between the signifier and the signified but rather is generated in the movement from signifier to signifer ("The Cultural Logic" 26), then Oryx is a figure of this movement. She becomes not Oryx, but a sort of Oryx-effect: "that objective mirage of signification generated and projected by the relationship of signifiers themselves" ("The Cultural Logic" 26). Jameson tells us further, "[W]hen that relationship breaks down, when the links of the signifying chain snap, then we have schizophrenia in the form of a rubble of distinct, unrelated signifers" ("The Cultural Logic" 26). Which Oryx is Oryx? The little girl who looks back from the HottTotts site, the young woman who loves Jimmy, the woman who loves Crake, or just some girl somewhere exploited by a vast and anonymous system of patriarchal global capital that doesn't care who she is, that will just sell her and sell her until there is nothing left to sell? Or is she, like the character Fevvers in Angela Carter's novel *Nights at the Circus*, a figure of pure text, a wet dream desperately imagined by Snowman on one of his lonely nights of self-loathing, after the apocalypse?

> Sometimes he can conjure her up. At first she's pale and shadowy, but if he can say her name over and over, then maybe she'll glide into his body and be present with him in his flesh, and his hand on himself will become her hand. But she's always been evasive, you can never pin her down. Tonight she fails to materialize and he is left alone, whimpering ridiculously, jerking off all by himself in the dark. (*Oryx and Crake* 110)

Does it matter whether all of these are the "same person" or not?

ONE OR LEGION: THE MULTITUDE

Later in the novel, Snowman thinks of Oryx in a synchronic time of no time, a strange perpetual present in which her integrity as "the same person" is up for grabs and ultimately irrelevant:

> Because now he's come to the crux in his head, to the place in the tragic play where he would say: *Enter Oryx*. Fatal moment. But which fatal moment? *Enter Oryx as a young girl on a kiddie porn site, flowers in her hair, whipped cream on her chin;* or, *Enter Oryx as a teenage news item, sprung from a pervert's garage,* or, *Enter Oryx, stark naked and pedagogical in the Craker's inner sanctum;* or, *Enter Oryx, towel around her hair, emerging from the shower,* or, *Enter Oryx, in a pewter-grey silk pantsuit and demure half-high heels, carrying a briefcase, the image of a professional Compound globewise saleswoman?* Which of these will it be, and how can he ever be sure there's a line connecting the first to the last? Was there only one Oryx, or was she legion?
>   But any would do, thinks Snowman as the rain runs down his face. They are all time present, because they are all here with me now. (*Oryx and Crake* 307–08)

Oryx is both one and legion. The options of diachronic time become the smorgasbord of synchronic time. Snowman can have it all, but cut loose from history, cut loose from linear time, having it all means nothing. To have everything he wants is not the ultimate joy but the ultimate sorrow.

One might read Oryx as the movable feast of Bakhtin's work on carnival, *Rabelais and His World*. She is an embodiment of the carnivalesque material bodily principle, in which the individual body is merged with body of the collective. The difference here is that her collective bodily being is not restricted to a moment of festive reversal, but rather caught in an endless synchronic present, the grotesque nightmare of carnival that never ends.

The Oryx whom Snowman hears talking to him, in his post-apocalyptic fantasies, laughs at her own multiplicity and her own dissolution. It could be carnival laughter, in the Bakhtinian sense of the celebratory upside-down world, or the radical outside laugh of the Medusa, or it could be the laughter of the pure victim, lacking self-awareness and identifying with the oppressor. These options, like all the options that confront us as we attempt to understand Oryx, are wide open. We could take none of them, or all of them. They all lack human and humanist agency. But even this is an undecidable virtue. If one were to read Oryx radically, one might say that she frees us from the Western individual subject. Whether or not her subjectivity is an empowered one is, however, an entirely different question.

In one of the more idealistic moments in their much discussed book *Empire*, Michael Hardt and Antonio Negri propose "the multitude" as a liberatory concept that is both a product of "Empire" and a potential for escape from its violence. They suggest that the multitude radically reconfigures space such that "[a] new geography is established by the multitude as the productive flows of bodies define new rivers and ports" (397). Further,

> Through circulation the multitude reappropriates space and constitutes itself as an active subject. When we look closer at how this constitutive process of subjectivity operates, we can see that the new spaces are described by unusual topographies, by subterranean and uncontainable rhizomes—by geographical mythologies that mark the new paths of destiny. These movements often cost terrible suffering, but there is also in them a desire of liberation that is not satiated except by reappropriating new spaces, around which are constructed new freedoms. (397)

Oryx works as a representative figure of Hardt and Negri's one and many, though whether the new freedom she offers is desirable or not is entirely open to question. It may well be freedom-under-the-gun, freedom imposed on the subaltern body by the demands of the religio-military-industrial complex. She moves from her non-specific Asian country of origin into Crake and Jimmy's First World; she also moves through cyberspace. Her topography is both real and virtual. Rhizomatically, she self-replicates in her genericness, and at the same time remains singular, in the possibility that she is the same person. There is nothing particularly heroic or revolutionary about this singularity however. It is fully ironized in her status as love object for both Crake and Jimmy. In Avery Gordon's sense she is a ghost—invisible in her hypervisibility.

Jameson notes that our entry into the spatial logic of the simulacrum shifts our relationship to "what used to be historical time" ("The Cultural Logic" 18). The past itself is modified. It becomes a "vast collection of images, a multitudinous simulacrum" ("The Cultural Logic" 18). We have entered, in other words, a kind of continuous present marked by a nostalgia that is in fact incompatible with a modernist, linear sense of history ("The Cultural Logic" 19). Jimmy notes a feeling of precisely this kind of nostalgia on the afternoon of Oryx's look back. He and Crake are somewhat more (Atwood doesn't tell us how much) than twelve years old. As the scene opens, they are watching porn in Crake's room as they have regularly done for years.

> Already it felt like old time's sake, already it felt like nostalgia—something they were too grown-up for, like middle-aged guys cruising the pleebland teeny clubs. Still, they dutifully lit up a joint, hacked into Uncle Pete's digital charge card via a new labyrinth, and started surfing. (*Oryx and Crake* 89)

Crake and Jimmy are canny children, living out a perpetual, jaded adulthood in a time of no time collapsed to a space of no space. Oryx's look back, captured on the printout Crake makes for Jimmy, who "saved it and saved it" (note here that Atwood implies duration without actually naming time—she doesn't say "saved it for years"), also belongs to a sort of perpetual present from which a perpetual but indeterminate loss is continuously regarded, like Orpheus looking back at Eurydice and remaining forever in that moment. The smooth, endless synchrony of this postmodern time is intensified after the apocalypse, when Snowman's watch ceases to work and there are no other people left around to keep time for him.

For such a postmodern text, the novel's concern is a strangely modernist one. It is a liberal humanist mourning for a world lost to the violent, sexed-up madness of technoscience. Its paranoia is fear of the machine. It is fully dependent on traditional race, class, and gender categories in order to work as a coherent novel. Still, there is a certain dark, decidedly pastiche pleasure in reading Atwood's Oryx. It strikes me, however, that at a more political level, the figure of Oryx does not tell us as much about globalization as material force as it does about postmodern reading and writing strategy. While they may be connected, I am not convinced, as Jameson is, that the two are coterminous. Random House's website on Atwood provides a reader's guide for the novel, and one of the questions it asks is "How might the novel change if narrated by Oryx?" As I've suggested above, *Oryx and Crake* is a fundamentally liberal humanist project. I'm not convinced that this is a story that could be told from Oryx's point of view, because I think this novel can work only with a stable, singular, individual humanist protagonist, however carnivalized, in order to maintain a coherent narrative.[7] For all that it mourns the passing of liberal humanism, it also functions as a marketable object in a globalized consumer society, which sells liberal humanism as an ideology.[8] That is the difference between our present and the future sketched out for us in the novel itself.

Is it possible to narrate/represent a globalized present that is more than just descriptive of an intertextual, synchronic postmodernity? I admit, as a dyed-in-the-wool activist, I still long for the text that is also a call to action. This may well be a naïve, modernist desire. And, as Jameson has noted, a return to older ideologies is not an option. He points to the collapse of the socialist experiment in various formerly socialist countries. Nor do older traditionalisms once vibrant in the so-called Third World offer a real alternative ("Notes on Globalization" 67). Only fundamentalism, he argues, has that power ("Notes on Globalization" 67). This is not encouraging! Hardt and Negri propose a notion of the multitude that is a delightful and possibly productive idea, but in many ways it is merely the antithesis of Empire, the dialectic in disguise.

If Oryx is a subject of a fundamentally different order than Jimmy, she cannot, as perhaps Offred in *The Handmaid's Tale* could, step in and begin to narrate as though she did have an equivalent kind of subjectivity that is "merely" marked by difference (of the same order) in race and gender. The question then becomes whether Oryx can be some sort of model of Asian women, or cyborg women that a practice (of writing, of acting?) can be gleaned from, or whether she is pure construction, pure text, hypervisible object, and thus pure subaltern, who, in spite of her ability to look back, still cannot speak.

THE SNOW OF HUMANKINDNESS

While I've argued that Atwood's Oryx does present a liberatory possibility, in her break from humanist subjectivity, I'd like, in this final instance, to return to the body of racialized experience. My hope, in other words, remains with some variation of the human. I do think that to read Oryx as the multitude, or as pure text, is to confirm in postmodern terms an Orientalist suspicion and desire that Asian women are indeed fundamentally and irredeemably Other. Further, I think that to conceive of liberation there does run the danger of a kind of immaterial, discursive excess that many anti-racist critics, including Rey Chow and Gayatri Spivak (at different moments), are critical of. For now, I'd like to leave open the possibility for liberation at that site of pure Otherness[9] and pursue modes of thinking that keep the materiality of the name in a more oppositional kind of way, even as they seek another kind of ontology beyond it.

The problem of representation (who speaks for whom) that was so important in the identity politics moment remains pressing. How are we to value the particularity of experience against the necessity of collective action in any kind of liberatory moment? Dionne Brand's characters Tuyen, Binh, and Quy in her novel *What We All Long For* are interesting in this regard. As brothers and sister, they are foils for one another. But Tuyen and Binh, who were born and raised in Canada, are presented to us with coherent, singular subjectivities in ways that their lost brother Quy is not.

In this novel, Tuyen's experience, as Asian, as woman, as lesbian, is presented to us in all its individual particularity. It is as though the snow—of liberal humanism and of whiteness—infiltrates all inhabitants of the city. The snow remains, no longer exactly as the white universal, but as some remnant of it taken on by all the inhabitants of the city regardless of racial origin. It still belongs to a kind of whiteness, but whiteness paradoxically inherited by those who are not white—the "bananas" and "oreos" of second-generation immigrant experience. The snow of Canadian whiteness, which might also be read as the snow of Eurocentric humanism, is a matter of fate, but it is also mutable. Like the weather it affects all inhabitants of the city (or the country) but differently each time. And it can melt, become water that flows. I argue here that the snow of liberal humanism has, in the case of this novel, gotten under the skin of the four young people of colour whose lives the novel traces, particularly Tuyen.

The first time we see her, she is given to us from a distance. We watch her from the point of view of a bus rider, as she crosses the city with her friends Carla and Oku on her way home after a night of partying. Like Oryx she is presented to us as the object of the gaze: "[S]he's wearing an oilskin coat, and you want to look at her, she's beautiful in a strange way" (*What We All Long For* 2). But unlike the kiddie porn star Oryx, Tuyen carries a camera. She is a photographer and, we discover later, an artist, who takes the power of representation into her own hands. The art project she carries out through the course of the novel, the building of a lubaio, or public message post, is one in which she empowers herself and her fellow city dwellers to ask and answer a deeply human and humanist question: What do you long for?

The notion of longing as an emotion that shapes community is interesting because it is multidirectional. The longings of the city dwellers who participate in Tuyen's project stretch into the past, circle the present, slant in to the future. Their longings bind them and, at the same time, drive them into crisis, and into separation from one another.

In denial over the particular loss of her brother, Tuyen feels the longings of the whole city. And the whole city is built on longing—for another home, for lost loved ones, and also for the future and for potential new loved ones, which it promises but never offers up completely. It is this incompleteness itself that makes Toronto the city that is, like Tuyen's art projects, looking to a traumatic past lived out elsewhere, always under construction. Caught between their parents' nostalgia for a lost homeland and their own longings for a future that is full of promises as yet unfulfilled, they are bundles of anger, restlessness, unfocused discontent. The nostalgic, traumatic sleepwalk of the parents is a tragic one, caught in a time that is neither past nor present. But the time of the children is dendritic, stretching its fingers in multiple directions. It has a relationship to history, but it is separated from it at the same time. This separation makes a kind of newness possible. One might conceive this newness as an imagination of democracy and youthful possibility that stretches beyond the borders of the state. It stretches into another space that is real and yet cannot be made singular and material in the way that the lives of the Toronto characters can.

Reading Deleuze and Guattari, John Rajchman asks: "What would it mean to introduce this 'city to come,' which is that of our singularities, our 'originalities' without origin, into our idea of what a democracy can be?" (52). In other words, what if democracy is not a social construct but a way of being yet to be imagined? Tuyen, Carla, Jackie, Oku, Binh, and Quy are citizens-in-progress—unruly, messed up, and incomplete, but full of possibility for the democracy-to-come.

SINGLE TRUTH, MULTIPLE ERROR

Of a traumatic past, but born in the city, Tuyen is born into liberal individuality in a way her brother Quy is not. Historic trauma unifies, but only after the fact. After the trauma is over, a common history of social brutality can be constructed to remember and mourn. In the case of this novel, it is Quy who is subaltern. He never escapes the trauma of war and flight but is, in a sense, stuck in a strange, stateless kind of Middle Passage, in which the horror of war never ends but rather becomes a part of his person. There is something not-individual about him, something collective, sad, violent, and spiritual that, like the character Priest in *At the Full and Change of the Moon*, never leaves him.

Quy loses his singularity at the moment he is set down by one of his family members, as a child, in the middle of the family's flight from war-torn Vietnam:

> My sisters walked in a small knot, holding each other, my mother held me, my father held me, they passed me between them time and again. One of them put me down. I won't say who. (*What We All Long For* 7)

In not naming and not blaming the one who abandons him, however accidentally, Quy loses himself. He loses grip on the truth of his identity through the loss of his father:

> I jumped up and down looking for my parents. I made out my father's legs. I followed him. Someone lifted me into a boat. I sat next to my father's legs. I said nothing.... We were in the middle of the South China Sea when I understood I was alone.... I didn't belong to anyone on board. I followed the legs I had mistaken for my father's. (*What We All Long For* 7)

The father's legs and the mistake are one. In the conflation of truth and error, Quy loses his chance for, or hold on, an individual self. In losing the body of his father, he loses his entry into Western subjectivity. The truth of his father's legs, the father's most mobile part, becomes the first error in a lifetime of errors that are increasingly less attached to any moral or ethical commitment. In a sense he is reborn—or rather, half-born—in violence and loss on a boat at sea. Édouard Glissant describes such a boat in *Poetics of Relation*:

> Yet, the belly of the boat dissolves you, precipitates you into a nonworld from which you cry out. This boat is a womb, a womb abyss. It generates the clamour of your protests; it also produces all the coming unanimity. Although you are alone in your suffering, you share in the unknown with others whom you have yet to know. This boat is your womb, a matrix, and yet it expels you. This boat: pregnant with as many dead as living under sentence of death. (6)

Glissant is, of course, describing the Middle Passage. I would like to suggest here that Brand constructs the South China Sea in this novel as a kind of Middle Passage. I understand this as Brand making and claiming a kinship between Black and Asian diasporas. It is a generous gesture of relation-making on her part, one made quite profoundly.[10]

After his loss at sea and without a family to care for him, Quy is relegated to a place outside social acceptance or expectation. There is no justice for Quy, nor does he himself have a sense of justice. He remarks:

> I was fortunate, I learned later, that I wasn't thrown overboard by the others. Though I was mistreated, beaten back when I reached for the good water or when I cried for food. Well, it would surprise some, I suppose, that people running to democracy are capable of such things. Why? You would think I would've turned out better myself. I didn't. (*What We All Long For* 7)

In these perpetual sites of injustice, like the refugee camp at Pulau Bidong, produced through a permanent "state of exception,"[11] liberal human individuality is also lost. Like Oryx, Quy is photographed, and like her too, his individuality is denied at precisely the moment when the camera ought to capture it. Both are hypervisible ghosts. In Said's terms, we know ourselves as Western subjects in the knowledge that we are not Oryx, that we are not Quy. But Quy himself has no access to this kind of self-knowledge:

> When you look at photographs of people at Pulau Bidong you see a blankness. Or perhaps our faces are, like they say in places, unreadable.... We look as one face—no particular personal aspect, no individual ambition. All one ... Was it us or the photographer who couldn't make distinctions among people he didn't know? (*What We All Long For* 8–9)

Indeed, the crisis of identity in *What We All Long For* is a crisis of vision and its technologies. The looker whose vision matters most in this novel is Tuyen, the sister, whose sexuality is not directed at the radically subaltern Quy, but rather at her cat-like, distant friend Carla, who, interestingly, is unavailable to Tuyen largely because of her preoccupation with her own brother, Jamal, a small-time troublemaker and petty criminal in downtown Toronto.[12]

THE CAMERAS OF THE WORLD

The chapter in which the complicated power of this gaze emerges is the one in which Tuyen unexpectedly sees her Canadian-born brother Binh, and the newly arrived and newly "discovered" Quy on the street in Koreatown, just as Korea beats Italy at the World Cup Soccer finals. There is euphoria in the air as the Korean community and its supporters celebrate this surprising upset. The key scene begins with Tuyen photographing Binh. She doesn't recognize him immediately. He is uncanny to her, both familiar and unfamiliar, a strange guide leading to an even stranger encounter with the truly uncanny brother, Quy:

> She spun around, her camera clicking off shots. She didn't yet know how she would use them. Through the lens, she saw a familiar face and stroked the button to open the aperture; she clicked twice, trying to remember who it was. Binh! She hadn't expected to see him there, so the face of her own brother was familiar and unfamiliar to her. She was shocked and ashamed at the same time at not recognizing the sibling with whom she had so many recorded and unrecorded fights. Perhaps there was something in her misrecognition that told of those battles, how a brother was both a stranger and a loved one, more than a loved one, the same as you; and seeing his face outside of yourself, of the family, was to see him anew. (*What We All Long For* 207)

Binh has done in a local way what Quy has done in a global way—shown up in the wrong neighbourhood, one where he was not expected, only for it to turn out that the "wrong neighbourhood" had been his home, or rather, his shop, all along. He is uncanny in the sense that Brand articulates, as the familiar in the unfamiliar, and also in the sense of "everything that ought to have remained hidden but has suddenly come to light" (Freud 224). This appearance of the brother in the wrong neighbourhood gives Tuyen a sense of unhomely self-recognition, a chance to see herself as external to herself. As the textual focus moves from Binh to Quy, that externalized self is smashed open to include a violently uncanny "home in the world" as Bhabha has famously reformulated Freud. The unexpected appearance of Binh in the wrong place becomes the unexpected arrival of Tuyen in the wrong place. She realizes she has been photographing Binh outside XS, the store in Koreatown that he owns and runs. This recognition of her own displacement occurs simultaneously with her first sight of Quy: "Binh was grim-faced, talking to another man whose back was to Tuyen" (*What We All Long For* 207). There is no recognition yet. Quy is purely Other. She cannot see his face.

The presence of Quy is a kind of excess (signalled in the name of Binh's store—XS) to the uncanny doubling of Binh and Tuyen. He is still familial and familiar, but he is also strange to Tuyen in a way far beyond the strangeness of Binh. Quy's entry into the family's visual field is an entry that must draw him into individual subjectivity, and yet it cannot quite. As the long-standing object of loss, as a ghost of both a person and an irretrievable moment, the material appearance of Quy presents an incomprehensible conundrum. He is supposed to belong to the invisible, imaginary world of pure loss:

> It must have been a milky evening: the water was grey milk, the sky was stone grey, the boat was disappearing in a noisy rush, and Tuyen's mother and father must have seen Quy like this—slowly, slowly moving away. Floating, floated away in the China Sea without a trace. Her mother's insomnia was caused by this sight. When she closed her eyes at night, she herself saw Quy floating away. So Tuyen kept clicking. She kept looking at what wasn't being seen, as her brother must have been unseen, and her mother noticing too late, harried with irrational fear. (*What We All Long For* 206)

The technology of the camera, with its uncanny relationship to time, allows for the kind of vision that mere eyesight does not. The lens and frame make specific and draw into focus that which we would prefer to turn away from. It makes eternal, or at least perpetual, that which otherwise would get away because we did not see it the first time—the original loss of Quy. The lacuna has substance. Or rather substitute, since the image and the experience are not the same precisely because one is marked by intense absence while the other is marked by intense presence. Tuyen's photographs of Quy stand in for an earlier, unregistered (and unofficial) moment of traumatic loss that cannot be retrieved and yet is fundamentally transforming, a loss that is a direct consequence of the fact that it belongs to an unregistered moment. The moment outside XS is a substitute for the moment of loss, and the photograph is a substitute for the moment outside XS—two links in a chain of signifiers leading back to an absent, but nonetheless founding, original.

In *Specters of Marx*, Derrida proposes a concept of *hauntology* in which a different kind of subject is produced through a ghostly relationship to history and the necessity and impossibility of setting time back on the right tracks. He is speaking specifically of the spectre of Marxism as a politic of the past that haunts Europe, and yet, because it has never been enacted (in spite of many pragmatic abuses of the term) already belongs to history: "At bottom, the specter is the future, it is always to come, it presents itself only as that which could come or come back …" (19).

As a product of loss and error, without a human or humanist ethics, Quy is both a ghost of the past and a harbinger of the future. The challenge here lies in how to understand what that future might look like. What does a character like Quy mean in relation to the citizen of liberal democracy? Like Oryx, there is something collective and indeterminate about Quy. He might or might not be the same "Quy" who was lost that night on a boat in the dark. The stories he has told, regardless of their truthfulness, have all become a part of him. They are all true and they are all false. Or rather, their truth or falsity is irrelevant—they are equally constitutive of his subjectivity.

Identity is arbitrary: "There are times when I've said to myself, Who the hell are you? That's a dangerous question. And this [Toronto] is a dangerous city. You could be anybody here" (*What We All Long For* 310).

It is only upon entering the city that Quy becomes a problem. The conundrum he poses is one of relationship to citizenship. Quy is conscious of reinventing himself for the city and for the family. Not only does he not know if he is the "Quy" who was lost, he doesn't care. Brutal, damaged, and utterly uninvested in the truth, he is simply seeking material advantage for himself, not even to any greater end, but only because it is what he understands he must do to survive in the strange temporality he introduces to the city. On the laptop he has stolen from another corrupt, human-trafficking monk, Quy finds his own story, or at least, the story of "Quy" and decides to use it:

> By some coincidence, if you believe that kind of thing, I come to the name of some guy, Vu Binh, in the monk's emails. Young guy, M.B.A., all the money he wants, all the pussy he needs. And by some stranger coincidence, this one perhaps love, he's looking for a man who was a boy named Quy. Well, see for yourself. I already put two and two together. I appear. The guy is either very cunning or a *lo dit*. I arrive; he's convinced. I'm convinced. He turns out to be my brother. Isn't my name Quy? Wasn't I lost so he could come to me in his expensive shoes, in his silk shirt, his mouth slow and vulgar on his mother tongue, with his silver Beamer?... I say to myself, Fine, let it play. (*What We All Long For* 311)

The moment of play is a moment of transformation. Playing is precisely the point. Insofar as he is a postmodern subject, like Oryx, Quy can do nothing but play. Paradoxically, playing is the only way he can regain entry to the "truth" of his lost childhood and his birth family.

At a point in the novel when Tuyen apologizes for being suspicious of him and reluctantly welcomes him to Canada and back into the family, Quy responds in broken English: "No I" (*What We All Long For* 300). At the level of English as a second language, this response is meant to say: "No, it is I who am happy and honoured to be re-united with you." But at deeper, parapractic level, it is the denial of self, the denial of a coherent subjectivity, which was in fact lost that night on the South China Sea, on the boat in the mist. Everything is play, everything is story. He is without a singular humanist self, and there is no coherent truth to his story. But what is more disconcerting about Quy is that there is something viral about him. Because he is, in a sense, the masses, or the multitude, he is also one of us. He is one of us in his anger at injustice, in his jealousy of his brother Binh who has all that he does not, and in his recognition that in spite of his loss of everything, including a self-enclosed, identifiable self, that he has just as much of a right to the material comfort as anybody else, but especially Binh:

> I'm so full of rage of a kind I've never felt before, and I want to take a swing at him and I want to hug him as my brother. But I know that I'm going to take him for everything he's got. It's the things that were mine, and he got them double. He's got my mother and my father and my two sisters. He's got the world in front of him. He's got the store, and we're in the store when the World Cup match between Korea and Italy is playing. He's got happiness like the people outside in the street when the Korean redhead scores the goal that beats Italy. He's got everything.
>
> I look at the crowd outside and I say to myself, How come, how come this can't be me? And I say to myself, Quy, it is you. (*What We All Long For* 311–12)

To recognize that Quy and Binh are alike, that they are brothers, that they could be the same person is to recognize the level at which citizenship, and good fortune, are arbitrary. Insofar as we recognize that Binh (as kin to Quy, and also, through his underground activity, to Jamal) is up to illegal or extra-legal practices, we must also recognize the multiplicity of the state of exception. The boundaries between discrete subjects dissolve, at least, in the strange alternative temporality of *homo sacer*. Had he been born in Vietnam, Binh could just as easily have been lost that night on the boat. And because Binh, like us Canadian readers, is a First World citizen we are forced to recognize that Quy is also like us, that he isn't purely Other, and that we are responsible to and for him. The edges of our humanist individuality are also rough. We too tell stories about ourselves that are not the same each time we tell them. Our own violence toward the Other [as in our complicity in the Vietnam (and Korean and Iraqi) War] turns out to be a violence against ourselves. We must carry the trauma. The repressed returns from both inside and out. Interestingly, here, it returns not as the home in the world, but as the shop in the world.[13]

The question of representation becomes newly pressing. If Binh is a stand-in for both Quy and Tuyen, or the signifying link between them, and Quy is a representative of the collective mass of humanity out there against whom things are done (one need think only of the countless Iraqi victims of the recent war, who are seldom discussed and almost never individualized in the Western media), then there is an elision between those of us with all the privileges of the Western world and those without. Indeed, with the War on Terror in the United States, and all its erosions of human rights, it is clear that those differences are very small. What then, is one to make of one's

Western democratic privilege, fragile though it may be, if our individuality is not so fixed, if we are all stand-ins for one another?

At the height of his uncanny doubleness in which he is both a highly spiritual and a highly corrupt and corrupted figure, Quy is attacked and left for dead by Carla's brother Jamal, who sometimes calls himself "Ghost," in an act of random violence, in which Jamal and his friends mistake Quy for a wealthy, privileged Asian, adding to his character the last in a battery of tropes concerning the Asian Other.[14] The city ghost Jamal mistakes the extra-territorial ghost Quy as occupying the privileged state of exception (that Aihwa Ong writes about) instead of the abject state of exception (that Giorgio Agamben writes about). It is as though the city, soaked in the melt-water of the snow of humanism, cannot, in fact, contain Quy. Here again, he embodies Agamben's *homo sacer*, in the sense of a "bare life" that does not belong to the realm of the (socialized) human, even as it founds this realm, and therefore can be killed without being sacrificed (*Homo Sacer* 9). But as uncanny kin, Jamal also embodies *homo sacer*. The paradox of a life lived between "truth" and play, individuality and multiplicity, sameness and difference is more than the novel structure can uphold. Quy is beaten to the brink of death, by the dysfunctional Jamal, whom one might read as a reflection of Quy, radically enclosed by the city rather than radically excluded from it. This happens just as Quy is at the brink of returning to a subjectivity that is singular and human, just as he is being returned to his mother and father. Quy is left for dead, but he doesn't die "on stage." Like Oryx, he belongs perpetually to liminal space—between material embodiment and pure simulacra, between master and slave, between undocumented migrant and citizen, between hypervisible and invisible, between life and death.

Interestingly, insofar as he is dead and a victim, Quy is returned to his human subjectivity. The love "we all long for" is returned to him, as tragic loss. Insofar as he lives, he remains simulacra, multiple, liar, ghost, thief, and priest, existing outside the nation "in the cameras of the world" (*What We All Long For* 287). It is there that Quy is free to be multiple and excessive, to "let play" the forces of capital, religion, state, and love. But of course, insofar as the *homo sacer* is human, this is a site of tremendous pain. We feel for Quy in a way that we don't for Oryx because Brand gives him his humanity, without irony, in snips and glimpses. Like Oryx, he is both human and radically outside the human at the same time. But through his connection to his brother and sister, through Jamal, and through his speaking voice, we are given a route to identification with him that we are not given in Oryx's case.

AN IDEALIST'S CODA

In this chapter, I have been concerned with the question of how to write about marginalized experience from a feminist, anti-racist point of view within the contemporary context of global capital and unjust war. If how we construct the Other has everything to do with our actions toward her or him, then, in this moment when human rights and the rule of law are not enough to bring justice to those deserving of it, it is important to ask why. While I recognize the European and Eurocentric roots of liberal individualism, I still see it as a useful ideological construct. What I have been attempting to interrogate here is what happens to those who fall outside of the liberal humanist conception of the subject. I have asked whether other models of subjectivity are viable, and if so, what liberation might look like for "the multitude" or *homo sacer*. I have asked whether other models of time might offer other kinds of freedoms. I have suggested that there is something viral about the spiritual, violated, collective Other that makes her or him one of "us." There are no easy answers to the questions I ask, and much of how one answers depends on who holds "the cameras of the world" that photograph our alternative selves, which alternative selves we are asked to identify with, and for what reasons. To my mind, this is one of the major crises in writing Canadian literature at the present moment. I'm fairly sure that the market does not recognize this, but that does not mean that Canadian writers cannot.

CONCLUSION

COMMUNITY ACTION, GLOBAL SPILLAGE
Writing the Race of Capital

THE LONG NOW

As a close to this project on the cultural organizing of the 1980s and 1990s, I think through the 1994 conference Writing Thru Race, firstly as an event that I helped organize, participated in, experienced, repressed, and remembered, and secondly as a historical moment in which the discursive and culturally productive roles of "race" radically shifted in the national imagination. I want to begin, however, by talking about a politics of time and a time of politics. The reason for this is that the discursive terrain upon which I will shortly embark feels to me contradictorily dated, forgotten, and yet still overdetermined. In thinking through "writing thru," I find it very difficult to analyze without repeating syntactical and ontological coding that produces both writer and readership in a strange temporal space in which we are hailed into a moment that has passed, and yet a moment that remains constitutive of how activists, academics, writers, and citizens have our social, political, and discursive being in the present. The articulation of categories I recognize as constructed through language and yet also as historically, experientially entrenched remains uncomfortable in the way it hails all players into a particular narrative, and yet I recognize the necessity of such articulation as a bulwark against a naïve universalism that works in the service of hegemonic power.

In particular, I want to think about the notion of archive, as Deleuze reads it in Foucault. If how we research and articulate the past constructs us in the present, then it is important to understand the present we are living in and what its stake is in seeing the past in the ways we do. There is imaginative possibility here—if we can read the past for that which is hopeful, then we can produce the present in terms that allow for those productivities that Roy Miki has called "asiancy" or "ethics," or which Fred Wah has called "generative." These terms are, of course, themselves up for grabs. In recent years gestures to notions of "citizenship" or a politics of "affect" have been other ways of imagining both epistemologies and ontologies of the present that might give way to a more hopeful future than the one offered to us by neoliberalism, high capital, or "empire." I'm intrigued by the return in the last few years to Foucault's archive, and also to the notion of the biopolitical, which has variously been taken up by Giorgio Agamben, Michael Hardt and Antonio Negri, and David Harvey to understand the ways in which free-flowing capital under a neoliberal agenda mobilizes populations and politics as statistical entities to be manipulated, bypassing the "individual" of Enlightenment humanism at both macro (population) and micro (e.g., such as organ donation, genome mapping, genetic engineering) scales.

In the face of these large, orchestrated movements of capital, ideas, and bodies, the smaller movements concerning social justice and a politics of representation, inside the bounds of the state, remain important, but the vantage point from which we view them at this historical moment is necessarily different from the vantage point from which we saw them in the moment of their enactment.

If a conscious politics of the archive involves looking back in order to produce a desirable future, then the question becomes how to look back. More specifically, for those of us who work in language, how does one articulate that past—in what terms and using what kind of discourse? To me, it seems respectful to write foregrounding the discourse and political priorities of that moment. But it also seems necessary to articulate the past in the terms of the present, not just because the distance in time allows for hard emotions to be addressed, or for that which has been repressed to now be "released" or "worked through," but also with an understanding that the political priorities of the present are necessarily different. It is important not to be righteous or derisive. I think that to say identity politics are "over" is too simplistic and dismissive of important, and often excruciatingly painful, work done at that time, the goals of which have not been achieved. Also, it is important to acknowledge that the work continues in the present and remains productive. It is important to ask what was achieved—both in terms of what was desired, but also in terms of the unpredictable art, freedom, ethics, and asiancy that "knocked at the door" and may even have been answered.

In a recent talk on the work of Fred Wah, Jeff Derksen invoked the notion of scale as a way of thinking through Wah's work, and as a way of thinking about the relationship between the local and the global. Derksen writes:

> Wah's space is not globalized from a central Cartesian "master of all I survey" point of view ... but rather is globalized from below in a sense,

in his investigation of the local (in early works) as also distinctly part of a global economy. (1)

Thinking about the local, cultural specificity of Wah's work, Derksen recognizes its implications at the level of capital—particularly in relation to the classed alterations of Vancouver's neighbourhoods through the interference of global capital. I'd argue that the question of Asianness reads in complex and contradictory ways through a range of global/local scales that reflect and refract one another. Through Derksen's scalar lens, then, I'd like to think about Writing Thru Race as historically productive in the way it returns different spatial scales to us (at different historical moments), in ways that indicate the need for a different kind of practice, although the form that that practice might take is not totalizable or prescribable. The question of agented citizenship then, at local, national, and global levels, is deeply problematized.

To read Writing Thru Race at the scalar level of the nation is productive in historical terms. To understand it in archival terms is to try to understand it from the point of view of a globalized present, one in which the hopefulness for national democracy is that much more intense because it is that much more under siege.

WRITING THRU RACE

Let me begin, then, by revisiting the anti-racist cultural gatherings of the 1980s and 1990s. I am thinking of such disparate events as the 1989 women's film and video festival InVisible Colours; the 1990 film, video, and photo-based exhibition *Yellow Peril: Reconsidered*; the 1992 Writers' Union of Canada conference The Appropriate Voice; and the 1993 ANNPAC gathering It's a Cultural Thing.[1] That moment was also marked by the gathering of First Nations people and their supporters at Oka in response to attempts by the municipality of Oka to expand a golf course on Mohawk burial grounds in 1990. The Canadian government sent in the army, threatening a violent putdown of the Native protest. The Oka protest was different from other anti-racist actions of that moment in the sense that the First Nations struggle is a struggle for sovereignty. It is not caught up, as other racialized struggles must be, in complicity in European colonialism and in its relationship to land. (It is beyond the scope of this project to address that complex historical/political situation here, except to acknowledge that it is the necessary ground on which this work lies. A good coalition-building project might be one that looks at cultural projects emerging from solidarity building projects between First Nations and Asian Canadian cultural workers, such as the Earth Spirit Festival or Imagining Asian and Native Women:

Deconstruction from Contact to Modern Times, a gathering at Western Washington University in 2002, organized by the writer Lee Maracle.) To articulate an ethical means by which an Asian Canadian subject could approach and support an action like the Oka protest (beyond merely showing up for it, which a few of us did as a gesture of solidarity) would be a truly radical and productive endeavour. For it is in fact the histories, complexities, and communities such as those addressed by the Earth Spirit Festival and Imagining Asian and Native Women that are so buried in the construction of Canadian national community. Those connections remained repressions in the moment I am writing about (and, for that matter, the current moment). In order to explain why, I would like to look in some detail at both the "controversy" and the community building that occurred around the 1994 Writers' Union conference Writing Thru Race. As an organizer and participant in this conference, I experienced it as a devastating turning point in anti-racist cultural organizing in Canada.[2]

It is precisely such discursive spaces as these that the organizing committee of Writing Thru Race intended to open, before its agenda was hijacked by incendiary comments[3] from the reactionary right, and the subsequent last-minute withdrawal of funding by the Department of Canadian Heritage. The potential for opening up more complex understandings of the space of the nation was shut down at the public level. Those two conservative moves drew the discursive context of the conference quickly back into the terrain of white hegemony, and a Eurocentric imagining of the nation, before much substantial coalition-building work could even be laid on the table.

In "The Haunt of Race," Scott Toguri McFarlane documents the ways in which the original organizing committee of Writing Thru Race was invisibilized both by the Writers' Union itself and those who attacked it for its support of a "no whites" policy. It is important to note that the conference policy never used the formulation "no whites," but rather limited enrolment in the daytime session to First Nations writers and writers of colour. The "no whites" formulation originated in the mainstream press. Attendance, in other words, was predicated on self-identification and not the systematic, discursive production of marked bodies from an outside location (of colonial authority, for instance, or even from a site of injured righteousness). McFarlane documents (and I remember) how the policy actually came about:

> The first pitch of the conference was followed by a series of meetings throughout the summer, during which a core group formed the conference planning committee. Input at these initial meetings came from

approximately sixty people including community activists, artists, film-makers, critics, writers, curators, performance artists, students and teach-ers. The vast majority of these people were not members of the Writers' Union, and many expressed discomfort with the conference's association with the Union and its race politics. It was at these summer meetings that the policy of including only First Nations writers and writers of colour was established. (27)

The fact that the impulse for the conference structure came from outside the Writers' Union, outside the Racial Minority Writers' Committee of the Union, and outside of the mainstream backlash is important because it points directly to the existence of a community in need of precisely the kind of space the policy demanded—one in which white guilt, anxiety, anger, and apology did not need to be attended to. Those of us who imagine the nation differently may also have seen how reimagining community configurations could be opened up to address the movement of bodies, labour, technology, money, and other financial products in ways that the neoliberal agenda was actively opening up for the benefit of capital in the same historical moment. McFarlane notes that official state multiculturalism in fact depends on a "ghostly other community" that haunts multiculturalism without actually speaking, in order for multiculturalism to work (28). The conference rep-resented a chance for that community to speak, listen, and begin to know itself, not as a ghostly force outside the nation, but as agented and acting both within and beyond it, though not necessarily following its rules.

To my mind, a great source of the burnout and disappearance under-ground of many of those cultural workers was a direct consequence of the hijacking of the discourse of race in the public arena. The discourse had become (once again) about the assertion and production of whiteness. This assertion reproduces "white people," bizarrely, as figures of rights abuse. (Note, for instance, an incendiary headline from the *Vancouver Sun*: "Feds won't fund writers' workshop that bars whites.") And who tramples on the rights of these freshly reproduced "whites"? No one but the ghostly Others, the evacuated subjects Miki discusses in *Broken Entries*. Of course it was impossible for those without a voice, who could not even be acknowledged as active subjects in the midst of this discussion about whites, to trample on the rights of those who had privileged access to all the major channels of public discourse. But there was nowhere for us to say so. McFarlane's article is extraordinary for the way in which it is able to articulate this contradiction.

THE GLOBAL AFTERMATH

These dozen or so years later, and now that this particular evacuated subject has found a channel or two, it is possible to say something. But in the time it has taken to garner that power and that analysis, the terrain has shifted again.

The late 1990s, I think, were a moment of burnout, exhaustion, reflection, and going underground for many of us who were active as critics, activists, and cultural organizers earlier that decade. It does seem as though we are entering a moment where it again becomes possible to act, though how and in what direction is not fully clear. Certain things have shifted, not just what sits on the global stage, but its actual form, most notably in the aftermath of 9/11 and the fall of the Twin Towers in New York. But in fact, these shifts have been piling up for some years. The shifts that stand out in my mind include the fall of the Berlin Wall in 1989, the "return" of Hong Kong to the People's Republic of China in 1997, the U.S. invasion of Kuwait in 1990, and U.S. invasion of Iraq in 2003, the likely U.S. coup in Haiti in 2004, and the likelier Republican coup in Florida that brought George W. Bush to power for the first time. (One might point even further back to the Iran-Contra scandal, the U.S. backing of the Contras in Nicaragua, and their backing of General Augusto Pinochet to topple Salvador Allende's democratically elected government in Chile in 1973.) In tandem with these political changes the great power brokers of the world have massively reorganized the global economy. Free trade agreements such as GATT and NAFTA have opened the possibilities for the international flow of goods and money, though not necessarily labour, producing a new kind of abject body—that of the "illegal" migrant worker. These symptomatic bodies are accompanied by other symptoms of this massive reorganization—the Asian financial crash of several years ago being a major one. It is this situation of global flows and global disjunctures that I scratch the surface of in my chapter on *Oryx and Crake* and *What We All Long For.* I am particularly interested in the mutations of the "Asian" body as it figures within the trope of the "illegal" migrant on the one hand and the moneyed, monster-house-building "astronaut" on the other.

In Canada, those of us with citizenship privilege experienced this global economic shift in financial cuts to social organizations necessitated by the sudden, urgent need to balance the budget, spearheaded by then Canadian finance minister Paul Martin. The deficit was brought to zero at a breakneck pace. Whatever some of us may think of him, this act was read as heroic enough to bring him the prime ministership in short order. The deficit reduction struck me as arbitrary at the time, though it may have been necessary from the point of view of a certain conception of the autonomous state within a rapidly changing, increasingly brutal global politic, if the massive financial crash in Argentina is any example. What has decidedly changed is that the state as a unit that once held considerable sway over the movements of capital no longer has the clout that it once had. The state in which some of us were fighting for our rights, in other words, was changing its shape in the midst of and through that struggle. Just at that moment when it looked possible that the voices repressed by the old (not-quite) democratic state might be admitted into that old (not-quite) democratic state, the old (not-quite) democratic state began to morph into the neoliberal state we have today.

In my second novel, *Salt Fish Girl*, I imagine a world in which the power of the state has devolved to almost nothing, while corporations run small city-states in various parts of the globe, which affect the material structure of people's lives differently and more deeply than the state could ever hope to. The notion of the citizen has elided with the notion of the consumer/worker. (It would be worth examining the play of "will" in relation to "desire" to think about how the subject is hailed by the old state as opposed to contemporary, hyped-up capital, but that is beyond the scope of this project.) Prior to the election of the second Bush and his War on Terror, it seemed to me that this was the way the world was headed. In Canada, Ralph Klein's and Mike Harris's "Common Sense" Revolution was sweeping the nation with its apparently populist ideals. Through the deployment of such terms as "reverse racism" and "politically correct," the conservative right managed to shut down much of the productive anti-racist discussion that was taking place at that mid-1990s moment, at the same time bringing in a conservative economic agenda that pushed for a devolution of powers from the federal level to the provincial level. While it seemed that power was being transferred from the hands of the elitist feds and into the hands of the people, it might more properly be read as moving from democratically elected officials straight into the hands of big business and those it has seduced or bullied into accepting its highly undemocratic world view. What seemed, in other words, to be a downscaling of power was actually an upscaling, neatly disguised in populist language.

The grain of truth in the conservative critique of federal government, which became all too obvious during the reign of Paul Martin, is that, in spite of the fact that officials are elected, they come from privileged backgrounds that afford them both the social and financial capital to mount and win campaigns. However, the federal system, for all its flaws, provides greater possibility for anti-racist action and the support of so-called minority groups than conservative populism, which is a kind of tyranny of the majority, does. It may well be, however, that more working-class white voices get heard in the latter system. How to theorize this tension? I suggest, joylessly, that liberalism has evacuated the state and rushed into the arms of capital, while the state rebuilds its power on those medieval staples of religion and the military.

REVERSE DEMOCRACY

While anti-racist artists, writers, and activists were pushing to get their voices heard within a liberal democratic federal system, the conservative right was pushing for the weakening of that system in favour of "common sense" populism; that is, the power of global capital masquerading as the power of the people. That moment in the House of Commons when Reform MP Jan Brown called for the repeal of funds already granted to Writing Thru Race by the Department of Canadian Heritage marks a head-on collision between the rising politics of neoliberalism on the one hand and the local specificity of Canadian cultural race politics on the other. As Andrea Fatona explains in an interview with Monika Kin Gagnon in *13 Conversations about Cultural Race Politics*, the terrain for anti-racist cultural workers was clear: "[T]here were issues of funding, access to institutions, and a real push for structural change" (41), where structural change meant a re-articulation of the place of racialized subjects in Canadian cultural institutions. But in the meantime, the place of these institutions was shifting in relation to the larger neoliberal agenda, not just of the then rising Reform Party but of Canadian politics, both electoral and cultural, and on both national and international planes. It seems the "old liberalism" of an institution such as the Writers' Union of Canada could not grasp this and so fell neatly, though contradictorily, in line.

The "controversy" around Writing Thru Race focused on the conference policy that restricted its daytime events to First Nations writers and writers of colour, a practice that had been used, in various configurations, in social justice movements from the 1970s onward to create discursive space for those historically marginalized by the forces of racism, sexism, classism, homophobia, colonialism, or other oppressions. The 1991 Writers' Union sponsored conference, The Appropriate Voice, was its most recent predecessor. While the limiting of attendance for The Appropriate Voice drew ire from certain quarters, the extent of the backlash was minimal in relation to that unleashed against Writing Thru Race. I want to explore the reasons for that here.

Reading David Harvey's *A Brief History of Neoliberalism*, I see Writing Thru Race and the backlash against it in relation to a neoliberal reconfiguration of the state, in which gatherings such as Writing Thru Race are pushed, literally, beyond the pale. Harvey argues that in the United States, Reagan and the forces of American neoliberalism managed to commandeer the religious right in the service of an agenda that reconsolidates power in the hands of a new financial elite at the expense of social services and state-controlled enterprises of any kind. In Britain, where socialist ideals were more deeply embedded in the fabric of society, Thatcher broke the power of the unions in order to pave the way for neoliberal policy. In Canada, it seems, it took partly the galvanization and rise of the Reform Party and an entrenchment of a new Right, in addition to the co-opting of an older liberalism—the only one we could see from where we were standing in 1994. While Reform's agenda may have been primarily global and economic, anti-racist movements provided a useful punching bag against which the term "politically correct" could be popularly deployed in order to consolidate the hold of neoliberal power in uncritical white middle and working-class communities—communities that don't necessarily stand to benefit from the shift in power, but who could support it in a putdown of that which was clearly Other, and therefore a convenient scapegoat for the ills arising from intensified neoliberal economic and political practices. It's now evident that the "whiteness" many anti-racist activists perceived as monolithic was in fact composed of a fabric of related forces pushing the Canadian state into a very different imagination of itself. The loss of federal support for the conference might be read as a symptom of the waning of federal power—to support or deny cultural projects and movements. While at the time it seemed a great accomplishment that the conference recouped the value of the Canadian Heritage grant, and more, from "private" sources, the greater loss may in fact have been the loss of a strong national public, a loss hastened, ironically, by those who claimed to care for it the most—old liberals like Pierre Berton and Margaret Atwood.

For indeed, their arguments fell neatly in step with the neoliberal agenda. Pierre Berton argued for the right of organizers to put the conference on, but against the spending of public funds on such an endeavour: "Have a meeting! Have many meetings! Just don't ask for taxpayers' money!" (Berton qtd. in Tator et al. 90). To back up their convictions that such an event should exist, but in the private realm, he (and Margaret Atwood, who shared his stance) donated personal money to the conference (Dabydeen 25). The gesture was meant to say "I don't include your conference in my idea of a national public." But in the end, the power of the public is itself eroded by such narrow-minded and mean-spirited exclusion, however generous one individual might be from his or her personal coffers. If Berton really believed the conference was racist and ethically wrong, then it is worth asking what his donation of private money signals. Either he approved of racism in private, or perhaps, at some level, he recognized that while such a conference might go against his personal interests, it was, in fact, a democratic project.

The political stance of many Writers' Union members is embedded in a well-meaning, if curmudgeonly and patronizing, ideal of individual freedom. The problem, however, as David Harvey says, is that to hold individual freedom sacrosanct is to make oneself vulnerable to unwitting incorporation into the neoliberal agenda (41). It was indeed this connection between "the exclusion of whites" and taxpayers' money that Jan Brown used in the House of Commons to instigate the withdrawal of democratically approved funds by the Department of Canadian Heritage from the conference. In spite of the fact that the stance taken by the Reform Party and the stance taken by such Writers' Union stalwarts as Berton and Atwood was the same, I'd argue, that their intent was different. That while a combination of self-interest, shame, misperception, and honest (if uncritical) commitment to the concept of universalism guided the "old" liberals, Reform was guided by something infinitely more sinister—an agenda intent on removing social justice issues from the public forum.

The charge of "reverse racism" on the part of the Reform Party and many white liberals was deeply damaging to many people of colour, conference organizers or otherwise, because of its refusal to recognize historic racisms and the deep embeddedness of white privilege into Canadian society. At a pre-conference panel held at the Writers' Union AGM in Toronto that year, Roy Miki organized a panel to keep the union informed on the storm brewing around the conference. The final speaker, Makeda Silvera, began her talk like this: "I hate this kind of forum—to have to explain to a group of white people why we have to have this conference" (Racial Minority Writers' Committee 16). Berton denounced the meeting on the basis that it used the money of non-consenting taxpayers. When the audience applauded Berton's "taxpayer" comment, Silvera pointed out that people of colour also pay taxes, then left the stage and went to sit in the audience (Tator et al. 90). This was a more ambivalent gesture than it might have seemed. Visibly a protest against Berton and those who supported him, it was also an under-the-table critique of Miki, who had, in good faith, organized the forum in the spirit of working with the Writers' Union, an organization with which he himself had an ambivalent relationship. What the white writers in the audience could not see was the tension between Black Canadian and Asian Canadian communities, having to do with the differing modes through which they had been racialized and exploited under European colonialism. I am not here attempting to judge the actions of either Miki or Silvera, except to note that most racialized people in the room would have immediately noticed the strain. The cry of "reverse racism" worked precisely to invisibilize this and other related tensions deeply in need of discussion and healing. By producing "colour" as monolithic, whiteness strong-arms shut the possibility for discussion and negotiation necessary to heal the wounds that whiteness as a subject location (and one that could be let go of at any time, as Lenore Keeshig-Tobias has pointed out) is too arrogant, self-absorbed, and self-interested to see.

It was, in fact, on this frustrating binary discursive plane that the battle for the conference was fought. While many readers, positioned all over the spectrum of race and gender, could see how disingenuous the outcry of "reverse racism" was, this nonetheless remained the dominant discourse. The outcry depended on misapprehension and misrecognition to work, as indeed the term "reverse" symptomatizes. The only way in which, for instance, Robert Fulford, who wrote the first reactionary *Globe and Mail* piece against the conference, could talk about Writing Thru Race was by equating it with apartheid, a trope that Michael Valpy repeated and elaborated just over a week later in the *Globe*'s Classroom Edition. The fact that white supremacy was apartheid's hallmark goes conveniently unremarked in both pieces, even as they appeared in Canada's dominant national paper. There is a symptomatic duplicity in Fulford's text—it accuses the Other of all those things of which Fulford himself is most guilty, as Dionne Brand notes in her book *Bread Out of Stone*:

> [W]hen ... Robert Fulford ... says that colour is his least important feature, he is, of course, disingenuous. He could not exist without it. It is responsible for his entry and location in the myth-making intellectual elite of the nation-state and for his role in the debate on racism in the arts.... He is doing the most important part of his job as a member of the white cultural elite by using all the discursive strategy—implying that race does not exist, emptying "skin colour" of its acknowledged political meanings, invoking liberalism, appealing to rights won through Black struggle as if he had a role in their accomplishment, paternalistically warning those whom racism affects the most that they are going down the wrong path in how they choose to organize against it, positioning himself as an objective and omniscient observer with no politico-racial interest—and means—the *Globe and Mail* ... —to attack outsiders, to defend the elite and organizing characteristic of the nation-state. (175–76)

Brand recognizes precisely what Fulford does not—the specificity of racialized experience. She makes material what for Fulford is fully discursive and abstract.

Miki's response to Fulford's attack is similar to Brand's in the sense that he foregrounds the historical materiality of racism in Canada—racism directed against First Nations people and people of colour by the Anglo-European establishment. It is not abstract, although it is rooted in linguistically constructed categories. In the face of historic fact, the principle of universality disguises white supremacist farce:

> Mr. Fulford's attack fails to recognize that the governing bodies throughout Canadian history have resorted to "race" categories to exclude certain persons and groups—beginning with the Indian Act, a colonialist document used to construct the "identity" of First Nations in order to dispossess them of their lands, languages and cultures. This same history would include the withholding of franchise from persons of Asian ancestry (until the late 1940s), the Chinese head tax, the 1914 Komagata Maru incident [in which more than 300 Sikhs on a Japanese-owned freighter were refused entry to Canada and held off-shore in Vancouver harbour without food or water for two months], the internment of Japanese Canadians in British Columbia, and the injustices suffered by African Canadians in Nova Scotia. (n. pag.)

Miki's was the only pro-conference response by a writer of colour that the *Globe and Mail* published, in spite of other submissions, notably one from the much respected cultural critic and video artist Richard Fung (Sehdev 84). He is made to visibly and monolithically embody the racialized Other in this context, whether he chooses it or not. The historical wrongs Miki describes above are not news, though they are perhaps not widely known, and are certainly not part of the founding myth of the Canadian nation. If anything, they constitute its founding repressions. By the same token, their listing is not for the benefit of social-justice-minded First Nations people and people of colour. It does not deepen our healing or critical analysis. In a sense, Silvera's under-the-table "comment" is correct. Here, Miki is talking back to whites. He is forced to, as indeed she is also, for not to do so is to allow the absurdity of Fulford's comments to stand in the national public forum. In coercing the speech of all players to address only whiteness, whiteness again asserts its hegemony. This is the unacknowledged victory of white supremacy in Canada. It makes the marginalized Other talk back to whiteness and whiteness only, and in so doing, produces the Other as monolithic, homogenous, and largely silent. Miki's articulation is, however, also sophisticated in excess of mere dialectic response. By articulating these traumas, even for those of us who "know," he counters the abstraction of "reverse racism" by placing material, traumatic, and constituting difference on the table. If difference has been historically materialized through racist violence, then the subjects of that difference cannot be vindicated through the Band-Aid of discursive but not materialized universality. The open wounds require redress. The work of the conference, partially at least, might have been imaginative work to articulate the shape of restitution.

Both Scott Toguri McFarlane and Sourayan Mookerjea have argued that the production of the multicultural Other is in fact necessary to the constitution of the Anglo/Franco Canadian state. McFarlane argues that Canada is haunted by the spectre of multiculturalism, which produces a body of living ghosts—present but rendered mute by the Constitution itself. The heterogeneous and silenced organizing committee of Writing Thru Race in a sense embodies these ghosts—present, unheard, and different from one another in ways that there was no space to articulate, far more different from one another than we were different from the white subjects so affronted by the one thing the committee could agree upon. All of us are called to fixate upon and mimic whiteness as much as we are called upon not to see or recognize a violently disparate and heterogeneous "one another." This problem of a disparate, incoherent, and non-cohesive "one another" is exactly what Sourayan Mookerjea recognizes in his piece "Some Special Times and Remarkable Spaces of Reading and Writing Thru 'Race,'" published in *West Coast Line* the same year as the conference. Mookerjea worries that the affirmative action techniques of the organizing committee do indeed re-inscribe race in precisely the way official multiculturalism intends it to be inscribed (122). Mookerjea writes:

> We can now begin to specify what exactly is at stake in our policy which is exactly what our praxis puts at stake: "For a brief but concentrated period of time" ... "to be able to converse with each other without the mediating screen of a binary 'white'/'coloured' dichotomy." What does this mean, to be able to converse without controversy? Are we now without the controversy?... To be without the mediating screen of a binary "white"/"coloured" dichotomy then would mean among other things to have suspended, as if by a spell cast by our policy, "for a brief and concentrated period of time" the discursive logic in which the either-or of the "white"/"coloured" dichotomy governs and organizes all possibilities of speech. By inscribing this space exclusively under the conjoined sign of "First Nations and Writers of Colour," by specifying and particularizing in this way, by repeating and multiplying a nationalism and a pluralism in a nationalism and a pluralism, in other words, other possibilities for speech, governed by other kinds of logics, are to be made free. But is this not just what Robert Fulford found in his example of Orwellian double-think? (121–22)

He is posing the same conundrum that Monika Gagnon and others have articulated: the problem of the master/slave dialectic. Mookerjea asks what kind of space Writing Thru Race might produce in the absence of the master's surveilling gaze (not to mention recrimination, guilt, and tears), as long as it exists in the language of the master narrative, the binary split. It is, after all, that gaze, and that construction of Otherness, that necessitated the gathering to begin with. It is that gaze that constructs the common experience of race and racialization, as Miki articulates in his *Globe and Mail* article. Perhaps what was not visible for such a close vantage point was the kind of productivity that could emerge, ironizing the conundrum, exploring it, or exceeding it, as much of the cultural work in the following years attested to. It would be interesting to revisit the discussions that took place during the conference itself for the seeds or already growing vines of this productivity. In other words, it may well be that to meet under the banner of First Nations writers and writers of colour does indeed reproduce colonial systems of race. The question becomes whether such reproduction could work as a sort of "repetition with a difference," that is more honest and less repressive than the whitewash of assimilation. Where productivity lies is not in obliterating racism but in accepting its history and exceeding it, as many of the writers, editors, and organizers before and since have done, in more or less perfect ways. The idea was never to make the space of Writing Thru Race a state of permanence. Limited as it was in its attendance, it was also limited in time, unlike the indefinite time of white supremacy, or indeed the permanent "state of exception" in which our civil rights are perpetually and legally vulnerable to suspension in the name of the War on Terror.

SCALES OF SUBJECTIVITY

In the final session of Writing Thru Race, tension arose between the non-union members of the organizing committee and the Racial Minority Writers Committee of the Writers' Union. The latter were eager, in good union form, to appropriate the work of the organizing committee and to take recommendations back to the union as outcome. The former were less unified but more open-ended in their desires and not particularly interested in speaking back to the union. The silencing endured by the organizers from such disparate locations as the media, co-opted writers of colour (most notably Neil Bissoondath and Evelyn Lau), the Department of Canadian Heritage (under pressure from the Reform Party and the House of Commons), and, in addition, the Racial Minority Writers Committee was enough to shatter the heterogeneous and tenuous coalition, at least for the time being. There is no question that the work was democratic work, but between the

Hegelian conundrum on the one hand and the motley repression from disparate loci of power on the other, it was nearly impossible for that particular group of marginalized subjects to remain intact. In a sense, cut loose from the master/slave relationship, without a "synthesis" of any kind to turn to, the group could only dissolve. At the time, the dissolution felt to me to be one drenched in despair and disillusion. In reading the cultural productivity that followed, however, I suggest that in fact it opened the floodgates to the possibility of not one synthesis, but many. These "synthetic" solutions[4] remain open-ended, but are also full of all kinds of (admittedly imperfect) possibilities. Perhaps indeed, their imperfection is to be celebrated rather than mourned, since hard pushes to idealized states lead only to fascism. In other words, the irresolvable nature of Gagnon's "other conundrum" is precisely what makes it productive.

It is important to recognize the temporal specificity of the event, as I said earlier, even as its conditions remain present. The notion of palimpsest is useful here to recognize that the form of that struggle re-emerges constantly in the present moment, but that it is layered over by a different and frightening redeployment of race categories within the context of the War on Terror, with its attendant tortures and abuses of human rights. It is not enough that a few of us have achieved a small measure of "representation" when race categories are still used to profile, detain, deport, or torture. Indeed the capacity for our voluntary or involuntary tokenization is greater than ever at the scale of global capital. It may be worth asking to what extent an apparent making of space for racialized people is in fact a making of space for capital that just happens to be racialized. The deeper question of what constitutes justice and redress remains.

I'd like to close by thinking of the shattered, collective malaise of the organizing committee in relation to the shattered state of the racialized subject brought about by changes in the global economy and the shattering of the old liberal democratic state. I think it is still important to look at the work of writers and artists for answers to the question of how we can know ourselves, and therefore how we can organize at the present moment. Dionne Brand's traumatically globalized character Quy, in tandem with his traumatically localized foil, Jamal, in her recent novel *What We All Long For*, offers us a fraught possibility for imagining subjecthood across a range of scales. We might now think beside her to work out how to counter the ills of the not-so-new world order. Both violent and violated, spiritual and deeply amoral, Quy and Jamal offer us a vision both of what we have been and what we might become inside the bounds of national and city space, and beyond its borders, as both sacrifice and agent. Denied human rights and

subjectivity and yet constructed through those rights and subjectivity, Quy
and Jamal seem to provide a way forward in thinking about subjects, both
singular and collective, that can pressure, ride, and mutate global capital.

There is a relationship, then, between the figures of our imaginations and
the "imagined community" of the nation, to borrow from Benedict Anderson, that needs to be thought through and engaged in terms of productive
and creative practices of both national and global citizenship. The relationship between figures like Quy and Jamal and the practice of everyday life
for those of us who imagined ourselves as equal citizens in another more
just iteration of the democratic state also requires further thinking, both
in relationship to the current form of the state and within a larger, mobile,
mediatized, technologized, militarized, and financially hopped-up global
arena. The space of race has become concomitantly complicated. As a site
of oppression it is as deep as ever, but can also be a site of strange privilege
(depending upon how one is racialized) that must be attended to, to avoid
misuse and perhaps to deploy for social justice reasons.

In this book, I have attempted to trace an open-ended liberatory impulse
through a period of anti-racist work in Canada from the late 1980s through
the 1990s as it circulated around the term "Asian Canadian." I have focused
in particular on the "oolemma" of reclaiming the racist name for the purposes of self-empowerment. I have addressed a range of collective and individual strategies of subject production, including the autobiographical tactic
of "breaking the silence," the special issue and the anthology as community-building projects, storytelling in the work of Hiromi Goto, the possibility
of pushing through the racist name and opening it to multiple catachreses
in the work of jam ismail and Rita Wong, and finally the production of
extra-human subjectivities in *Oryx and Crake* and *What We All Long For*. This
last chapter, I hope, moves the conversation out from questions of national
belonging to questions of globalized subjectivities, still raced, classed, and
gendered, but in more fluid, mobile, and overlapping forms.

My purpose has been to attempt to understand the trajectory of political
engagement for progressive creators and thinkers of my own generation.
Inspired by such vital events as Race to the Screen, The Appropriate Voice,
It's a Cultural Thing, Racy Sexy, Writing Thru Race, and the Oka Crisis, we
were also casualties of burnout and the conservative backlash that followed.
Since that extraordinary political moment, the people I have organized with,
written about, written for, or otherwise worked with have branched out into
many divergent practices and modes of living. The ground on which we were
able to organize and produce in that late-1980s/early-1990s moment has
radically shifted, as I have described above. In spite of the War on Terror
and its attendant propaganda, torture, and abuse of human rights, and in

spite of massive economic shifts, human displacements, species extinctions, and earth disruptions, I remain hopeful that there are other ways for imaginative and progressive people to work together, against the forces of the prison-military-religio-industrial complex (or sometimes through or around them) and with one another.

NOTES

NOTES TO INTRODUCTION

1 In that period, *Parallelogramme*, the magazine of the Association of National Non-Profit Artists Centres/Regroupement D'Artistes Des Centres Alternatifs, collapsed and gave way to *Mix Magazine*. The collapse was a consequence of deep disagreements and bitter struggle over questions of race and racialization.

2 The latter two were published by Sister Vision Press in Toronto, with Makeda Silvera as managing editor.

3 I take up the term "First Nations" here because it was the term that the conference Writing Thru Race used. A better term would have been "Indigenous" because "Indigenous" includes those usually understood as First Nations, Inuit, and Métis. That said, I also want to acknowledge both colonial production of these terms and the experience of those whose lives are contained and produced by these terms. I recognize and support the individual nations whose traditional territories precede the legal construction of Canada.

4 Our generation was certainly not the first to recognize this problem. Albert Memmi and Frantz Fanon also address it. It is, in essence, the problem of the Hegelian dialectic.

5 Quoted in Gagnon (22). It is interesting to note that it is the English translator's word "dilemma" that Gagnon takes issue with. The original French states: "*Le terme de race, déjà, nous plonge dans la perplexité*" (Memmi 21).

6 Interestingly, Gagnon's move toward ismail's coin resonates with Memmi's original "*perplexité*" in the sense that both words allow for a multiplicity of solutions, rather than the mere two of "dilemma."

7 Many readers will also understand Chow as an Asian American critic in the first instance. Her arguments in "The Fascist Longings in Our Midst," however, are absolutely a propos vis-à-vis the politics of Asian Canadian literature in the late 1980s and through the 1990s.

8 I stick with the original title of the *Maclean's* article because it is so clearly illustrative of the intractable racism in Canadian society.

9 It is important to remember that the evolving narrative of the state unfolds on land that was previously inhabited, and from which many other people including those we now describe as "Asian" have been coming and going, perhaps for centuries. The model of the state is a recent European imposition.

10 Copyeditor Wendy Thomas notes that Toronto.com erroneously reported the character Sundance as being of Chinese and aboriginal heritage, when in fact Zhang describes Sundance as being of "Indian" and English heritage. It is worth noting further that Zhang's depiction of Sundance is troublingly under-researched, but that is the subject of another project.

11 I use the term "Native" here because it is the term Keeshig-Tobias uses. However, where an inclusive term encompassing First Nations, Inuit, and Métis people is intended, I will usually use "Indigenous."

12 I have always thought it strange that no one has ever accused Sarah Sheard of appropri-
    ation for her novel *Almost Japanese*. It came out in 1985, just as the appropriation debates
    were flaring, though admittedly from a small press—Coach House. Some racialized
    writers in my acquaintance were quite upset about the orientalism of Peter Oliva's *The
    City of Yes*, but no major national media scandal ever erupted over this. I might conjecture
    that appropriation was a "hotter" issue for First Nations people because it is continuous
    with the unresolved and unjust theft of land, but this would be a subject to address in
    another book or essay.

13 This is indeed what Bill Schiller at the *Toronto Star* (11 Feb. 2011) called Lee, Choy,
    and Yee in one of the first English-language pieces to break on the *Gold Mountain Blues*
    scandal, echoing the language that racialized people used to describe white authors with
    privileged access to the channels of publication during the appropriation debates. *Quill
    and Quire*'s Stuart Woods repeated the designation in the headline for an article on the
    same subject published later the same day: "Chinese Novel Alleged to Have Stolen from
    Canada's 'Literary Elite.'"

NOTES TO CHAPTER 1

1 That the ideal of affirmative action in hiring practices rose and became prominent at this
   time is no coincidence. In some progressive circles the notion of "optics" also became
   salient. Workplaces and organizations were challenged to find hiring and recruiting
   strategies to literally up the count of brown bodies in their makeup, as concrete praxis to
   begin undoing the unjust historically entrenched privileging of white bodies through the
   ideology of colonialism. These strategies challenged the notion of meritocracy, not as an
   ideal per se, but as one that could be put into practice without privileging certain already
   privileged histories, thought systems, and bodies—the white, the European, the male.
   Liberation politics claimed a gap, and a hypocrisy, between the theory of meritocracy and
   its practice. They also pointed to the particularity and historical specificity of the white
   body in ways that those used to thinking of their literatures and experiences as "universal"
   often found quite difficult to stomach. Within these politics, strategies like affirmative
   action were always recognized as contingent, as arising out of historical circumstance
   rather than the Western philosophical notion of first principles, which posits the ideal
   before the body. Lest I appear to be claiming a pure outside to "Western philosophical
   notions," however, let me remark that these are fully Marxist strategies, emerging from
   Marx's observation that politically aware people can build their own histories, but not
   under conditions of their own choosing (15).

2 It is important to note here that body politics are oppositional only within the flow of
   Western philosophical and literary discourse. As the title of Miki's book suggests, for
   the Japanese Canadian subject, one both does and does not enter racialized subjectivity
   within a linear flow. Her emergent subjectivity is thus a "broken entry." Insofar as she
   is other, it is perpetually present. It cannot have a past. Insofar as she is assimilated, she
   belongs to Western discourse and is thus a (continuous) product of it.

3 I am not arguing here that her claims are false, only that they do not tell us everything
   about the "true identity" of the author.

4 I mean this in an associative, poetic sense. Milk is a fluid associated with motherly love
   and nurturance. One might read the horse's mouth, psychoanalytically, as a kind of
   feminine opening. Its associative attachment to milk in Choy's system of images makes
   it doubly feminine. Of course, there is room here if one wants to play with words, for
   other kinds of gendered associations—the milkman as a man with strong attachments
   to the mother, the horse as a figure of virility, the horse's mouth as a source of truth, etc.,
   but this is beyond the scope of my argument.

5 Writing of a moment in Samuel Delaney's *The Motion of Light in Water*, in which he
   witnesses gay male sexuality at a bathhouse, as an epiphany of sorts, Scott says:

   > For Delaney, witnessing the scene at the bathhouse (an "undulating mass of naked
   > male bodies" seen under a dim blue light) was an event. It marked what in one kind
   > of reading we would call a coming to consciousness of himself, a recognition of his
   > authentic identity, one he had always shared, would always share with others like
   > himself. [This is the kind of reading that Scott eschews.] Another reading, closer
   > to Delaney's preoccupation with memory and self in this autobiography, sees this
   > event not as the discovery of truth (conceived as the reflection of a prediscursive
   > reality), but as the substitution of one interpretation for another. Delaney presents
   > this substitution as a conversion experience, a clarifying moment after which he
   > sees differently. But there is a difference between subjective perceptual clarity and
   > transparent vision; one does not necessarily follow from the other even if the
   > subjective state is metaphorically presented as a visual experience. Moreover (and
   > this is Swann's point), "the properties of the medium through which the visible
   > appears—here, the dim blue light, whose distorting, refracting qualities produce
   > a wavering of the visible," make any claim to unmediated transparency impossi-
   > ble. Instead, the wavering light permits a vision beyond the visible, a vision that
   > contains the fantastic projections ("millions of gay men" for whom "history had,
   > actively and already, created … whole galleries of institutions") that are the basis for
   > political identification. "In this version of the story," Swann notes, "political con-
   > sciousness and power originate, not in a presumably unmediated experience of pre-
   > sumably real gay identities, but out of an apprehension of the moving, differencing
   > properties of the representational medium—the motion of light on water." (66–67)

6 It is interesting that he uses the Western convention of naming (personal name followed
   by family name) when declaring his authorship (Wayson Choy) but the Chinese convention (surname followed by generation name followed by personal name—Choy Way
   Sun) when he is the object of his own text. In another project, it would bear interrogating
   how voice and silence are enacted through these uses of the name.

NOTES TO CHAPTER 2

1 I argue that subjectivities are produced in the act of writing, publication, reading, and
   circulation of texts; that if, as Benedict Anderson says, nations are imagined communities, then the imaginative work of its citizens necessarily reproduces them, sometimes as
   identical to what they were before but more often, as Judith Butler has taught us, with
   a difference.

2 It is beyond the scope of this book to address the work of the 1970s in detail. But if this
   chapter had the space to be fully historical, it would go back to the progressive period-
   icals of the 1970s—*The Asianadian* and *Inalienable Rice*, or even further back to look at
   the histories of community newspapers, which still proliferate in many marginalized
   communities at the present time. Paul Yee's *Salt Water City* documents some of these
   publications, as does my article with Jean Lum in the catalogue for the 1990 film, video,
   and photo exhibition *Yellow Peril: Reconsidered*.

3 While I argue for the "specialness" of *Awakening Thunder* and its production of a special
   and different present, as I have already suggested, its moment of publication was just one
   among other groundbreaking anti-racist cultural texts and events that filled the lives and
   imaginations of many racialized cultural workers. In the late 1980s and early 1990s, it
   was possible—not without great personal cost but nonetheless possible—to speak about
   race and racialization in public Canadian fora that simply were not available to racialized
   cultural workers until that point. Beyond SKY Lee's *Disappearing Moon Cafe* (Vancouver:
   Douglas and McIntyre), published in 1990, the same year as *Awakening Thunder*, other

texts attesting to repressed histories began to emerge. For example, in 1989 in Vancouver, Zainub Verjee and Lorraine Chan put on *InVisible Colours*, a women-of-colour and First Nation women's film and video festival, while in 1991 Paul Wong launched *Yellow Peril: Reconsidered*, an exhibit featuring twenty-five Asian Canadian artists working in contemporary media. These, and other events and publications too numerous to list here, all contributed to the production of a particular kind of anti-racist present that, to my mind, offered a distinct break from the past, even as it built on it.

4 Interestingly, the *Komagata Maru* incident of 1914 is not invoked in the introduction to *Awakening Thunder* as a founding trauma for Asian Canadian identification. In that year, approximately 376 Punjabi migrants (the number is disputed) were denied entry into Canada on the basis of the fact that their journey from the Punjab was not continuous. They were turned back, and many died on the return voyage. Twenty were killed on their return arrival in Calcutta during a skirmish with police. Insofar as more radical Asian Canadian identities are imagined (in Benedict Anderson's sense) as founded in the uprooting and exclusion as traumas that place us in a fraught relationship to the Canadian state, the *Komagata Maru* incident has been of great importance for Asian Canadians who identify specifically as South Asian Canadian. At the Anniversaries of Change conference organized at SFU Harbour Centre by Chris Lee and Henry Yu in 2007, for instance, the *Komagata Maru* incident was recognized along with other moments of violence against Asian Canadians, specifically, for that conference, the 1907 anti-Asiatic riots in Vancouver, as well as the Japanese Canadian internment and the Chinese Head Tax and Exclusion Acts. What I would like to recognize here is not so much an act of intentional exclusion from what Gagnon, in the *Yellow Peril: Reconsidered* catalogue, has called "Belonging in Exclusion," but rather to note that the early 1990s were a moment in which the recognition of community and kinship through shared experiences of trauma was itself at a moment of formation. Subsequent work in racialized trauma and memory solidifies this recognition over the course of the 1990s and into the new millennium. There is a full essay, if not a book, to be written, I think, on the movement through imaginings of community in relation to histories of trauma as they evolve through this period.

5 Here I acknowledge that I feel tempted to read a kind of progress into the motion from one special issue to the next. However, in the final instance, I note that there is a discursive moment to which each issue belongs, not necessarily in a linear or progressive relation to other special issues but certainly in relation to a particular way of thinking about race, class, gender, and sexuality.

6 These "posts" are, of course, relative and depend on acceptance of the linear trajectory of Western philosophy. Given the diverse and fragmented backgrounds of the editors and contributors, I argue that there are many possible ways of situating this special issue in terms of time and tradition. To explore this multi-pronged temporality would, in fact, make a very interesting project.

7 In *Broken Entries*, Miki explains the problem of self-knowledge and articulated subjectivity for Canadian artists and writers of colour growing up in assimilationist Canada. He suggests that, for such subjects, subjective interiority is rendered speechless and devoid of content, so much so that the racialized subject does not even recognize the absence (110).

NOTES TO CHAPTER 3

1 "Quality" and "representativeness" were buzzwords in the late 1980s and early 1990s, often used as reasons for not including women, people of colour, and gays and lesbians in anthologies, art exhibitions, or other mainstream forms of collective representation. The Eurocentric norms through which creative work was judged went, for the most part, unquestioned.

2 From my personal experience with him, I recognize Jim Wong-Chu as the primary editor for this anthology in spite of the fact that he is named second and does not write a preface or introduction. In an odd way, then, this poem becomes Wong-Chu's spare but telling introduction, expressing his own uneasiness around living between languages and cultures.

3 That said, my critique of Lau's work in Chapter 1 stands, not so much for its obsessive self-exoticism, as for its inability to recognize the vast gap between text and experience. Further, unlike Lee and Wong-Chu's work, Lau's closes out revolutionary potential, as her 1994 article in the *Globe and Mail* against the work of racialized writers shows more overtly.

4 What does remain a problem are its investments in progress and universality. I have discussed these as issues more generally in my own Introduction.

5 It would be productive here to ask questions about the constructions of "home" and "family" in Foucauldian terms. I would argue, however, that regardless of whether such categories are "natural" or "socially constructed," they are deeply felt.

6 The anthology's full title is *Premonitions: An Anthology of New Asian North American Poetry*. "North American" and "American" seem to be conflated on the dust jacket. Lew himself is conscious of using the term "North American" or "Canadian and American" throughout. It would be worth examining (somewhere else) U.S. usage of the term "American" with regards to texts and writers originating in Canada. It would also be worth examining the different parameters and struggles regarding self-definition and location in Asian American and Asian Canadian literary contexts. While it may seem odd that I am taking up a text edited by an "Asian American" editor here, and published by an "Asian American" press, I do so because this anthology is exceptional in both Asian American and Asian Canadian contexts for the editorial strategy it takes up. Further, many Asian Canadian writers are included in the text: Roy Kiyooka, Joy Kogawa, Evelyn Lau, Roy Miki, Gerry Shikatani, Fred Wah, and Jean Yoon.

7 These venerable forebears include anthologies from both sides of the 49th parallel. Among them are *The Big Aiiieeeee!*, *The Open Boat*, *Strike the Wok*, *Red Silk*, *Making Waves*, and *The Very Inside*, to name a few.

8 I consider myself to be one of those bodies, and my texts to be some of those writings. This question is thus for me also a question of my own institutional responsibilities. For the sake of my own ethical practice, I feel I need to ask how one can do liberatory work from the inside. As I ask that question, however, I do think and hope that it will be useful to other marginalized subjects who nonetheless are privileged in different kinds of ways.

NOTES TO CHAPTER 4

1 I consider myself to have been nurtured by this history.

2 I am not suggesting here that the trope of the storytelling grandmother cannot be progressive, but only that its circulation, after a certain point, tends to evacuate it of its original power. Further, I believe there are ways of repeating traditional tropes that can be layered and duplicitous in a productive way. What I am arguing is that Goto sees the pitfalls of this strategy and writes against it.

3   In casual conversation, Goto has noted that she disagrees with this reading. "Why must mushroom signify cloud?" she asks. "Why can't a mushroom just be a mushroom?" For her, to make this connection overdetermines and closes down the wide variety of possible connections "mushroom" can make. While I certainly respect that fact that such a reading was not part of her authorial intention, and am sympathetic with the need to open our social and metaphoric connections, I do think that Beauregard's reading captures a tension in the text between older and newer metaphorical associations, though he may close those readings down more than Goto would like.

4   In the official, daylight world, young men drink beer, old women drink other drinks—tea perhaps. For Grandma Naoe, to drink beer is to enter into carnival time by reversing the order of the daylight world.

5   Bakhtin is writing about a traditional European society during the medieval period. It would be an interesting project to analyze how carnival might function differently in that moment as opposed to one we currently inhabit. Such historical changes as the Industrial Revolution, the computer revolution, extensive migrations, the rise of the city, airplanes, the Internet, the military–industrial complex, intensified capitalism, and fundamentalism have brought about radical changes in social relations, but such a discussion is beyond the scope of this dissertation.

6   Indigenous people do participate in the Stampede and, thus, in a sense have some "voice" in how they are represented. Nonetheless, the framework remains a Eurocentric one. It would be a useful and interesting project to investigate Indigenous self-empowerment strategies in relation to the Stampede.

7   Indeed, Goto is highly conscious of immigrant complicities with white settler colonialism. The novel presents, though does not resolve, this conundrum.

8   In *Broken Entries*, Roy Miki proposes this "silent interior," as that voiceless, oppressed place inside the marginalized or "evacuated" subject. It is the place that the anti-racist reclamation of the racist name cannot touch or articulate. I discussed this at some length in my chapter on autobiography.

9   At the same time, she still recognizes its beauty and seductiveness, and plays with these.

NOTES TO CHAPTER 5

1   Since 1997, Mandarin has been replacing English as the language of incursion. It would be interesting to think about China's large engineering projects such as the Chek Lap Kok Airport, more landfills, and an extensive bridge to connect Hong Kong with the airport at its Lantau Island location, with regards to its linguistic impositions (fewer tones, simplified characters, a smoothing down of Cantonese's rude, rough edges).

2   Through this pun of "tax," value and naming are conflated with one another.

3   Incidentally, the title of Roy Miki's recent book, *Surrender*, is interesting in this regard. Rather than suggesting defeat, it suggests empowerment precisely at the border of defeat, at the border of no-thing-ness, the disappearance of the name.

4   Donna Haraway has described such subjects as cyborgs in her famous "Cyborg Manifesto."

5   According to Wong, allopoiesis is a process whereby a system produces something other than itself, or in excess of itself.

NOTES TO CHAPTER 6

1 He coins the term "scapes" for these forces and ascertains five varieties. Ethnoscapes are constituted of people in a constant state of shift and migration—tourists, immigrants, refugees, exiles, and guest workers. Technoscapes refer to the communicational networks I've been discussing above—the fluid global configuration of technology moving at high speeds across previously impermeable boundaries. Finanscapes are economies linked through a grid of global speculation and capital transfer. Mediascapes are landscapes of images that flood our consciousness through newspapers, magazines, television stations, film. Ideoscapes are concatenations of images that are often directly political—the ideologies of states in addition to counter-ideologies of various movements (33–36). Appadurai's concerns are not so different from Jameson's in terms of the range of concerns they address. I think that bringing his theory into the discussion emphasizes the quality of embeddedness that Jameson articulates.

2 There is an odd racial conflation here, of a kind of manufactured Asianness covering over a manufactured Africanness, if one thinks, for instance, of how Saartjie Baartman was exhibited as "the Hottentot Venus" in nineteenth-century Europe. The HottTotts of *Oryx and Crake* are all underage Asian girls.

3 Consider, for example, adware, the type of junk advertisement that pops up from time to time when one surfs the Internet; and spyware, those small programs that watch our Internet activities without our necessarily being aware of it. Consider the ways that adware often invokes our fear of spyware as a ploy to get us to download harmful programs or annoying content. Consider also the recent revelations made by Edward Snowden about the extent to which the US government surveils our Internet activity.

4 There is room here, I think, to suggest that in the new global order, race has been reduced to style, at least in certain cynical quarters. I think of ads for The Gap or Benetton.

5 I am reminded here of Olympia, the automaton in Hoffman's *Sand-Man*, with whom the protagonist Nathaniel falls in love as part of an anxiety about the loss of his eyes. Freud reads Olympia as a figure of the uncanny (*The 'Uncanny'* 227–33).

6 Donna Haraway's notion of the cyborg might be useful here, as new a way of conceiving subjectivity, one that would allow for both the virtual and the physical to exist in contradiction. But I have discussed Haraway elsewhere and so will not take her up here. French feminist approaches might provide another useful tack. I am thinking in particular of Kristeva's notion of abjection, which conceives of the subject before the mirror stage, when the separation between conscious and unconscious is not yet complete. While her site of the abject is not a particularly pleasant place, it does offer possibilities for a conception of the subject that allows quite a radical swinging back and forth between inside and outside, individuality and sociality.

7 It would be interesting to write a comparison of Jimmy to Offred, the protagonist/ narrator of Atwood's earlier post-apocalyptic novel *The Handmaid's Tale*. It strikes me that there has been a step backwards made in terms of women's subjectivity and women's ability to tell their own stories. In the move from a modernist moment of grand ideology and grand narrative to a postmodern one of local politics and fragmented narrative, has the power of speech again reverted to the straight white man? Must women writers ventriloquize in order to be heard?

8 In the face of the War on Terror and the American drive to market democracy abroad, this cannot be innocent.

9 Could Atwood have written Oryx differently if she had supported writers of colour and First Nations writers at the height of the identity politics movement? If she had, for instance, supported Writing Thru Race? What has she given up, as a feminist, by clinging, however ironically, to the cold white Snowman doomed to melt?

10 Though it is beyond the scope of this chapter, I also read Quy as a story-brother to the beautiful and dangerous character Priest in Brand's *At the Full and Change of the Moon*.

11 Referring to such locations as Abu Ghraib and Guantanamo Bay, Giorgio Agamben writes: "[M]odern totalitarianism can be defined as the establishment, by means of the state of exception, of a legal civil war that allows for the elimination not only of political adversaries but entire categories of citizen who for some reason cannot be integrated into the political system.... [T]he voluntary creation of a permanent state of emergency (though perhaps not declared in the technical sense) has become one of the essential practices of contemporary states, including so-called democratic ones" (2).

12 Jamal is also closely related to the character Priest in Brand's *At the Full and Change of the Moon*. It would be interesting, in another project, to read Quy and Jamal as foils for one another. Jamal is repeatedly and violently hailed by the city, while Quy is repeatedly and violently shut out.

13 Another project, though one beyond the scope of this book, might look at the ways shops are represented in racialized fictions—as uncanny spaces, as spaces of transit, as figures of homes in the world, and as loci of desire.

14 Gang violence is itself also a trope. There is in this scene an odd sense of one collective, representative body with "No I" attacking another. Through this association, Jamal also becomes *homo sacer*.

NOTES TO CONCLUSION

1 Monika Gagnon has written movingly about this event in "How to Banish Fear: Letters from Calgary," in her groundbreaking book *Other Conundrums*.

2 To examine the linear trajectory of a number of related gatherings might be one way of thinking through the massive change that, in a felt way, seemed to occur at that moment. It would be a historicizing project of the kind that that early-1990s moment called for.

3 The most disingenuous and incendiary of these was a *Globe and Mail* article by Robert Fulford entitled "George Orwell, Call Your Office," in which he said that the conference was a reinvention of apartheid and marked the end of liberal pluralism in Canada, replacing it with a "multiculturalism" that focuses on the rights of special interest groups. A few days later, in the *Globe and Mail* Classroom Edition, Michael Valpy reiterated Fulford's anxiety about apartheid and pushed as a problem the fact that public funds were being spent on the conference. Neither noted that the Bantulands of apartheid South Africa is based on the Canadian reserve system, nor the fact that public funds come as much from the racialized citizens of Canada as from those who imagine and privilege themselves as unmarked.

4 The pun is intentional. Conscious artifice, as that embraced by the queer practice of drag, can be a highly effective way of producing future selves without forgetting history but also without being reduced to it.

BIBLIOGRAPHY

Abraham, Nicolas, and Maria Torok. *The Shell and the Kernel: Renewals of Psycho-analysis*. Ed. and trans. Nicholas T. Rand. Chicago: U of Chicago P, 1994.

Agamben, Giorgio. *Homo Sacer: Sovereign Power and Bare Life*. Trans. Daniel Heller-Roazen. Stanford: Stanford UP, 1995.

Almeida, Sandra. "Strangers in the Night: Hiromi Goto's Abject Bodies and Hopeful Monsters." *Contemporary Women's Writing*. 3.1 (2009): 47–63.

———. *State of Exception*. Trans. Kevin Attell. Chicago: U of Chicago P, 2005.

Ahmed, Sara. *The Cultural Politics of Emotion*. New York: Routledge, 2004.

Alcoff, Linda. "The Problem of Speaking for Others." *Cultural Critique* 20 (1991–92): 5–32.

Alexander, Michael. "Pound as Translator." *Translation and Literature* 6.1 (1997): 23–30.

Appadurai, Arjun. "Disjuncture and Difference in the Global Cultural Economy." *Modernity at Large: Cultural Dimensions of Globalization*. Minneapolis: University of Minnesota Press, 1996. 27–47.

Arnold, Matthew. *Culture and Anarchy: An Essay in Political and Social Criticism*. London: Cornhill Magazine, 1869.

Asia Pacific Authors on the Prairies. (No editor named.) Spec. supplement to *Prairie Fire* 18.4 (1997–80): 1–40.

Atwood, Margaret. *Oryx and Crake*. Toronto: McClelland and Stewart, 2003.

———. *The Handmaid's Tale*. Boston: Houghton Mifflin, 1986.

Bakhtin, Mikhail. *Rabelais and His World*. Trans. Helene Iswolsky. Bloomington: Indiana University Press, 1984.

Bannerji, Himani. *Thinking Through: Essays on Feminism, Marxism and Anti-Racism*. Toronto: Women's Press, 1995.

Bannerji, Himani, Ed. *Returning the Gaze: Essays on Racism, Feminism and Politics*. Toronto: Sister Vision, 1993.

Barbour, Douglas. *Lyric/Anti-lyric: Essays on Contemporary Poetry*. Edmonton: NeWest, 2001.

Basile, Elena. "Scars of Language in Translation: The 'Itchy' Poetics of Jam Ismail." *Literature for Our Times: Postcolonial Studies in the 21st Century*. Ed. Bill Ashcroft, Ranjini Mendis, Julie McGonegal, and Arun Mukherjee. Amsterdam: Rodopi, 2012. 151–64.

Battiste, Marie, and James Sa'ke'j Youngblood Henderson. *Protecting Indigenous Knowledge and Heritage*. Saskatoon: Purich, 2000.

Beauregard, Guy. "The Emergence of 'Asian Canadian Literature': Can Lit's Obscene Supplement?" *Essays in Canadian Writing* 67 (Spring 1999): 53–75.

———. "Hiromi Goto's *Chorus of Mushrooms* and the Politics of Writing Diaspora." *West Coast Line* 29.3 (1995–96): 47–62.

———. "What Is at Stake in Comparative Analyses of Asian Canadian and Asian American Literary Studies?" *Race* Sp. Issue of *Essays on Canadian Writing* 75 (2002): 217–39.

Bhabha, Homi. *The Location of Culture*. London: Routledge, 1994.

Blanchard, Marc Eli. "The Critique of Autobiography." *Comparative Literature* 34.2 (1982): 97–115.

Brand, Dionne. *At the Full and Change of the Moon*. Toronto: Alfred A. Knopf Canada, 1999.

———. *Bread Out of Stone: Recollections, Sex, Recognitions, Race, Dreaming, Politics*. Toronto: Coach House, 1994.

———. *What We All Long For*. Toronto: Alfred A. Knopf Canada, 2005.

Browning, Janisse. "Self-Determination and Cultural Appropriation." *Fuse* 15.4 (1991): 31–35.

Butler, Judith. *Bodies That Matter*. New York: Routledge, 1993.

———. *The Psychic Life of Power: Theories in Subjection*. Stanford: Stanford UP, 1997.

———. "Subjection, Resistance, Resignification: Between Freud and Foucault." *The Identity in Question*. Ed. John Rajchman. New York: Routledge, 1995. 229–50.

Cabri, Louis. "'Diminishing the Lyric I': Notes on Fred Wah and the Social Lyric." *Open Letter* 12.3 (2004): 77–91.

Canadian Press. "Authors Sue Gold Mountain Blues Writer for Copyright Infringement." CBC.ca. 28 Oct. 2011. Web. 12 June 2012.

Canclini, Néstor Garcia. *Consumers and Citizens: Globalization and Multicultural Conflicts*. Trans. George Yúdice. Minneapolis: U of Minneapolis P, 2001.

Carter, Angela. *Nights at the Circus*. London: Vintage, 1994.

Chao, Lien. "Anthologizing the Collective: The Epic Struggles to Establish a Chinese Canadian Literature in English." *Essays on Canadian Writing* 57 (1995): 145–70.

———. *Beyond Silence: Chinese Canadian Literature in English*. Toronto: TSAR, 1997.

Cho, Lily. "Asian Canadian Futures: Diasporic Passages and Routes of Indenture." Spec. issue of *Canadian Literature* 199 (2008): 181–201.

Chong, Denise. *The Concubine's Children: Portrait of a Family Divided*. Toronto: Viking, 1994.

Choudry, Azia. "Brown Skins, White Masks." *Cultural and Pedagogical Inquiry* 3.1 (2011): 40–42.

Chow, Rey. "Ethnics after Idealism." *Ethics after Idealism: Theory—Culture—Ethnicity—Reading*. Bloomington: Indiana UP, 1998.

Choy, Wayson. *The Jade Peony*. Vancouver: Douglas & McIntyre, 1995.

———. *Paper Shadows: A Chinatown Childhood*. Toronto: Viking, 1999.

Chu, Garrick, et al., eds. *Inalienable Rice: A Chinese and Japanese Canadian Anthology*. Vancouver: Powell Street Review and The Chinese Canadian Writers Workshop, 1979.

Coleman, Daniel, and Donald Goellnicht. "Introduction: 'Race' into the Twenty-First Century. *Race* Sp. Issue of *Essays on Canadian Writing* 75 (2002): 1–35.

Coombe, Rosemary. "The Properties of Culture and the Possession of Identity: Postcolonial Struggle and the Legal Imagination." *Borrowed Power: Essays on Cultural Appropriation.* Ed. Bruce Ziff and Pratima Rao. New Brunswick: Rutgers UP, 1997. 74–96.

Clifford, James, and George E. Marcus. *Writing Culture: The Poetics and Politics of Ethnography.* Berkeley: U of California P, 1996.

Dabashi, Hamid. *Brown Skins, White Masks.* London: Pluto, 2011.

Dabydeen, Cyril. "Celebrating Difference." *Books in Canada.* September, 1994.

Danica, Elly. *Don't: A Woman's Word.* Toronto: McClelland and Steward, 1990.

Day, Iyko. "Must All Asianness Be American? The Census, Racial Classification, and Asian Canadian Emergence." *Asian Canadian Studies* Spec. issue of *Canadian Literature* 199 (2008): 45–70.

De Landa, Manuel. "Deleuze, Diagrams, and the Open-Ended Becoming of the World." *Becomings: Explorations in Time, Memory, and Futures.* Ithaca: Cornell UP, 1999. 29–41.

Derksen, Jeff. "Space Agent Wah." Count Me In: Writing Public Selves, SFU Writer-in-Residence Program. (Fred Wah in residence.) SFU Harbour Centre, Vancouver. 31 May 2007. Courtesy of the author.

Derrida, Jacques. *Specters of Marx: The State of Debt, the Work of Mourning, and the New International.* Trans. Peggy Kamuf. New York: Routledge, 1994.

Fanon, Frantz. *White Skins, Black Masks.* New York: Grove, 1967.

Fernandez, Sharon, et al., eds. *Awakening Thunder: Asian Canadian Women.* Spec. issue of *Fireweed* 30 (1990): 1–140.

Findlay, Stephanie, and Nicholas Köhler. "Too Asian?" *Maclean's.* 22 Nov. 2010: 76–81.

Foucault, Michel. *The Archeology of Knowledge.* New York: Pantheon, 1972.

———. *The History of Sexuality: An Introduction.* Trans. Robert Hurley. New York: Vintage, 1990.

Freud, Sigmund. *"The Uncanny."* In *The Standard Edition of the Complete Psychological Works of Sigmund Freud.* V. 18. Ed., Trans. James Strachey. London: Vintage, 2001. 217–52.

Fuss, Diana. *Essentially Speaking: Feminism, Nature and Difference.* New York: Routledge, 1989.

Fulford, Robert. "George Orwell, Call Your Office." *Globe and Mail.* 30 Mar. 1994.

———. "The Trouble with Emily." *Canadian Art* 10. 4 (1993): 35–41.

Gagnon, Monika. *Other Conundrums: Race, Culture and Canadian Art.* Vancouver: Arsenal, 2000.

Gagnon, Monika, and Richard Fung. *13 Conversations about Art and Cultural Race Politics.* Montreal: Artextes, 2002.

Garber, Marjorie. "'What's Past Is Prologue': Temporality and Prophecy in Shakespeare's History Plays." In *Renaissance Genres: Essays on Theory, History, and Interpretation.* Ed. Barbara Lewalski. Cambridge: Cambridge UP, 1986. 301–31.

Gilroy, Paul. *Against Race: Imagining Political Culture beyond the Color Line.* Cambridge: Harvard UP, 2000.

Givner, Joan. "Paper Shadows: A Chinatown Childhood." *Quill and Quire*. September 1999. Web. 27 Jan. 2014.

Glissant, Édouard. *Poetics of Relation*. Ann Arbor: U of Michigan P, 1997.

Goellnicht, Donald. "A Long Labour: The Protracted Birth of Asian Canadian Literature." *Essays in Canadian Writing*. 72 (2000): 1–41.

Gordon, Avery F. *Ghostly Matters: Haunting and the Sociological Imagination*. Minneapolis: U of Minnesota P, 1997.

Goto, Hiromi. "The Body Politic." *West Coast Line* 28.1–2 (1994): 218–19.

———. *Chorus of Mushrooms*. Edmonton: NeWest, 1994.

———. *The Kappa Child*. Calgary: Red Deer Press, 2001.

Grosz, Elizabeth, ed. *Becomings: Explorations in Time, Memory, and Futures*. Ithaca: Cornell UP, 1989.

Guillory, John. "Canonical and Non-Canonical: A Critique of the Current Debate." *ELH*. 54.3 (1987): 483–527.

———. *Cultural Capital: The Problem of Literary Canon Formation*. Chicago: U of Chicago P, 1993.

Haaken, Janice. "The Recovery of Memory, Fantasy, and Desire in Women's Trauma Stories: Feminist Approaches to Sexual Abuse and Psychotherapy." In *Women, Autobiography, Theory: A Reader*. Ed. Sidonie Smith and Julia Watson. Madison: U of Wisconsin P, 1998. 352–66.

Haraway, Donna. "A Cyborg Manifesto: Science, Technology and Socialist Feminism in the Late Twentieth Century." *Simians, Cyborgs and Women: The Reinvention of Nature*. New York: Routledge, 1991. 149–82.

Hardt, Michael, and Antonio Negri. *Empire*. Cambridge: Harvard UP, 2000.

Harvey, David. *A Brief History of Neoliberalism*. Oxford: OUP, 2005.

Hassan, Jamelie, and Jamila Ismail. *Jamelie-Jamila Project: A Collaborative Bookwork*. North Vancouver: Presentation House Gallery, 1992.

Hirsch, Marianne. "The Generation of Postmemory." *Poetics Today*. 29.1 (2008): 103–28.

ismail, jam. *sexions*. (Chapbook). kitsilano, canada (*sic*), 1984.

———. *from the diction air*. (Chapbook). No publication place or date listed.

Jakobsen, Janet. *Working Alliances and the Politics of Difference: Diversity and Feminist Ethics*. Bloomington: Indiana UP, 1988.

Jameson, Fredric. "Notes on Globalization as a Philosophical Issue." *The Cultures of Globalization*. Durham: Duke UP, 1998. 54–77.

———. "The Cultural Logic of Late Capitalism." *Postmodernism, or, The Cultural Logic of Late Capitalism*. Ed. Fredric Jameson and Masao Miyoshi. Durham: Duke UP, 1991. 1–54.

Jew, Anne. "Everyone Talked Loudly in Chinatown." *Many-Mouthed Birds*. Vancouver: Douglas and McIntyre, 1991. 22–27.

Jones, Lindsay, ed. *Encyclopedia of Religion. Vol. 3*. Detroit: Macmillan Reference USA, 2005.

Kamboureli, Smaro. *Scandalous Bodies*. Waterloo: Wilfrid Laurier UP, 2009.

Kang, Nancy. "Ecstasies of the (Un)Loved: The Lesbian Utopianism of Hiromi Goto's *The Kappa Child*." *Canadian Literature*. 205 (2010): 13–31.

———. "(Reading Closely) Calling for the Formation of Asian Canadian Studies." *Unruly Penelopes and the Ghosts: Narratives of English Canada.* Ed. Eva Darias-Beautell. Waterloo: Wilfrid Laurier UP, 2012. 43–76.

Keeshig-Tobias, Lenore. "Stop Stealing Native Stories." *Globe and Mail.* 26 Jan. 1990: A7. Reprinted in *Borrowed Power: Essays on Cultural Appropriation.* Ed. Bruce Ziff and Pratima Rao. New Brunswick: Rutgers UP, 1997. 71–73.

———. "For<e>ward." *Walking a Tightrope: Aboriginal People and Their Representations.* Waterloo: Wilfrid Laurier UP, 2005. xv–xvi.

Kennedy, George A. "Fenollosa, Pound and the Chinese Character." *Yale Literary Magazine.* 126.5 (1958): 24–36. Reprinted at <http://www.pinyin.info/readings/texts/ezra_pound_chinese.html>. Web. 29 Aug. 2013.

Khoo, Tseen-Ling. *Banana Bending: Asian-Australian and Asian-Canadian Literatures.* Hong Kong: Hong Kong UP, 2003.

Kim, Christine. "Rita Wong's *monkeypuzzle* and the Poetics of Social Justice." *SCL/ELC* 32.2 (2007): 59–74.

Kogawa, Joy. *Obasan.* Toronto: Penguin, 1983. (1981).

Kristeva, Julia. *Powers of Horror: An Essay on Abjection.* Trans. Leon S. Roudiez. New York: Columbia UP, 1982.

Lacan, Jacques. "The Mirror Stage as Formative of the Function of the I as Revealed in Psychoanalytic Experience." *The Norton Anthology of Theory and Criticism.* Ed. Vincent Leitch et al. New York: W. W. Norton, 2001. 1285–90.

Lai, Larissa. "Political Animals and the Body of History." *Asian Canadian Writing.* Spec. issue of *Canadian Literature* 163 (1999): 145–56.

———. "Corrupted Lineage: Narrative in the Gaps of History." *In-Equations: can asia pacific.* Spec. issue of *West Coast Line* 33.34/3 (2001): 40–53.

Lai, Larissa, and Jean Yoon. "Neither Guests Nor Strangers." *Yellow Peril: Reconsidered.* Vancouver: On Edge, 1990. 20–24. in fn ch 2.

Lai, Paul. "Autoethnography Otherwise." *Asian Canadian Writing Beyond Autoethnography.* Ed. Eleanor Ty and Christl Verduyn. Waterloo: Wilfrid Laurier UP, 2008. 55–70.

Lau, Evelyn. *Other Women.* New York: Hyperion, 1996.

———. *Runaway: Diary of a Street Kid.* Toronto: Harper Collins, 1989.

———. *You Are Not Who You Claim.* Vancouver: Beach Holme, 1994.

Lauter, Paul. "History and the Canon." *Social Text* 12 (1985): 94–101.

Lecker, Robert, ed. *Canadian Canons: Essays in Literary Value.* Toronto: U Toronto P, 1991.

Lease, Joseph. "'Progresive Lit.': Amiri Baraka, Bruce Andrews and the Politic of the Lyric 'I'." *African American Review.* 37.2/3 (2003): 389–98.

Lee, Christopher. "Enacting the Asian Canadian." *Canadian Literature* 199 (2008): 28–44.

———. *The Semblance of Identity.* Stanford: Stanford UP, 2012.

Lee, Sky. *Disappearing Moon Cafe.* Vancouver: Douglas & McIntyre, 1990.

Lee, Bennett, and Jim Wong-Chu. *Many-Mouthed Birds.* Vancouver: Douglas and McIntyre, 1991.

Lejeune, Phillippe. *Le Pacte Autobiographique.* Paris: Éditions du Seuil, 1975.

———. *Signes de Vie. Le Pacte Autobiographique 2.* Paris: Éditions du Seuil, 2005.

Lerer, Seth. "Medieval English Literature and the Idea of the Anthology." *PMLA* 118.5 (2003): 1251–67.

Levinas, Emmanuel. *Otherwise Than Being or Beyond Essence.* Trans. Alphonso Lingis. Pittsburgh: DuQuesne UP, 1998.

———. *Totality and Infinity: An Essay on Exteriority.* Trans. Alphonso Lingis. Pittsburgh: DuQuesne UP, 1969.

Lew, Walter, ed. *Premonitions: The Kaya Anthology of New Asian North American Poetry.* New York: Kaya Productions, 1995.

Li, Peter. *The Chinese in Canada.* Don Mills: Oxford UP, 1998.

Li, Xiaoping. *Voices Rising: Asian Canadian Cultural Activism.* Vancouver: U of British Columbia P, 2007.

Madison, Soyini D. *Critical Ethnography: Methods, Ethics, Performance.* Thousand Oaks: Sage Publications, 2005.

Manguel, Alberto. "Equal Rights to Stories." *Globe and Mail.* 3 Feb. 1990: D7.

Marx, Karl. *The Eighteenth Brumaire of Louise Bonaparte.* New York: International Publishers, 1963.

Mathur, Ashok, ed. *Race Poetry, Eh?* Spec. issue of *Prairie Fire* 21.4 (2001): 1–128.

McCarthy, Dermot. "Early Canadian Literary Historys and the Function of a Canon." *Canadian Canons: Essays in Literary Value.* Ed. Robert Lecker. Toronto: U of Toronto P, 1991. 30–45.

McCullough, Steve. "'Trust Me': Responding to the Threat of Writing in *Chorus of Mushrooms.*" *ESC* 29.1–2 (2003): 149–70.

McFarlane, Scott. "The Haunt of Race: Canada's *Multiculturalism Act*, the Politics of Incorporation, and Writing Thru Race." *Fuse Magazine.* 18.3 (1995): 18–31.

Medley, Mark. "Ling Zhang Addresses Gold Mountain Blues Plagiarism Allegations." *National Post.* 6 Oct. 2011. Web. 15 June 2012.

Miki, Roy. *Broken Entries: Race, Subjectivity and Writing.* Toronto: Mercury, 1998.

———. *In Flux: Transnational Shifts in Asian Canadian Writing.* Edmonton: NeWest, 2011.

———. *Surrender.* Toronto: Mercury, 2001.

———. "Why We're Holding the Vancouver Conference." *Globe and Mail.* 7 Apr. 1994.

Miki, Roy, and Fred Wah, eds. *Colour. An Issue.* Spec. issue of *West Coast Line* 28.1–2 (1994): 1–320.

Mookerjea, Sourayan. "Some Special Times and Remarkable Spaces of Reading and Writing Thru 'Race'." *West Coast Line.* 28.3 (1994–5): 117–29.

Moraga, Cherríe, and Gloria Anzaldúa. *This Bridge Called My Back.* New York: Kitchen Table, 1984.

Morrison, Toni. *Beloved.* New York: Penguin, 1988.

Mulvey, Laura. "Visual Pleasure and Narrative Cinema." *Media and Cultural Studies: Key Works.* Ed. Meenakshi Durham and Douglas Kellner. Malden: Blackwell Publishers, 2001. 342–52.

Newson, Janice. "Academic Feminism's Entanglements with University Corporatization." *Topia* 28 (2012): 41–63.

Ngai, Sianne. *Ugly Feelings.* Cambridge: Harvard UP, 2005.

Ong, Aihwa, 2006. *Neoliberalism as Exception: Mutations in Citizenship and Sovereignty*. Durham: Duke University Press.

O'Neill, Peter. "Feds Won't Fund Writers' Workshop That Bars Whites." *Vancouver Sun*. 9 June 1994.

Pearson, Wendy Gay. "'Whatever That Is': Hiromi Goto's Body Politic/s." *SLC/ELC* 32.2 (2007): 75–96.

Philip, Marlene Nourbese. *She Tries Her Tongue, Her Silence Softly Breaks*. Charlottetown: Ragweed Press, 1989.

Racial Minority Writers' Committee. *Writing Thru Race Final Report*. Toronto: Writers' Union of Canada, 1995.

Rajchman, John. "Diagram and Diagnosis." *Becomings: Explorations in Time, Memory, Futures*. Ed. Elizabeth Grosz. Ithaca: Cornell UP, 1999. 42–54.

Rak, Julie. "Doukhobor Autobiography as Witness Narrative." *Biography* 24.1 (2001).

Random House. *Margaret Atwood Page*. Web. 21 November 2003 <http://www .randomhouse.com/features/atwood/oryxandcrake/rg.html>.

Riley, Denise. *The Words of Selves*. Stanford: Stanford UP, 2000.

Said, Edward. *Orientalism*. New York: Vintage, 1979.

———. "Representing the Colonized: Anthropology's Interlocutors." *Critical Inquiry*. 15.2 (1989): 205–25.

Sakamoto, Kerri. *The Electrical Field*. Toronto: Knopf, 1998.

Samson, Natalie. "Plagiarism Case Heads to Court as Canadian Authors File Lawsuit Against Zhang, Penguin Canada." quillandquire.com. Web. 31 Oct. 2011. 26 July 2012.

Saul, Joanne. *Writing the Roaming Subject: The Biotext in Canadian Literature*. Toronto: U of Toronto P, 2006.

Schiller, Bill. "Literary Feud in China Puts Book in Limbo in Canada." *Toronto Star*. 1 Feb. 2011. n.p. Web. 28 July 2012.

Scott, Gail. "Red Tin + White Tulle: On Memory and Writing." *Spaces Like Stairs*. Toronto: Women's Press, 1989. 17–18.

Scott, Joan. "Experience." In *Women, Autobiography, Theory: A Reader*. Ed. Sidonie Smith and Julia Watson. Madison: U of Wisconsin P, 1998. 57–71.

Sedgewick, Eve Kosofsky. "Shame, Theatricality and Queer Performativity." *Gay Shame*. Ed. Daniel Halperin. Chicago: U of Chicago P, 2009. 49–62.

Sehdev, Robinder. *Anti-Racism and Public Spheres: An Examination of the Politicization of Anti-Racism at the Writing Thru Race Conference, 1994*. (M.A. Thesis.) Calgary: University of Calgary, 2002.

Shohat, Ella, and Robert Stam. *Unthinking Eurocentrism: Multiculturalism and the Media*. London: Routledge, 1994.

Silvera, Makeda, ed. *Piece of My Heart: A Lesbian of Colour Anthology*. Toronto: Sister Vision, 1991.

Silverman, Kaja. *The Threshold of the Visible World*. New York: Routledge, 1996.

Spivak, Gayatri. "Can the Subaltern Speak?" *Marxism and the Interpretation of Culture*. Ed. Cary Nelson and Lawrence Grossberg. Urbana: U of Illinois P, 1998. 271–316.

————. *In Other Worlds: Essays in Cultural Politics*. New York: Routledge, 1988.

————. *The Post-Colonial Critic: Interviews, Strategies, Dialogues*. Ed. Sarah Harasym. New York: Routledge, 1990.

Spivak, Gayatri, and Ranajit Guha. *Selected Subaltern Studies*. Oxford: OUP, 1988.

Stepto, Robert. *From Behind the Veil: A Study of Afro-American Narrative*. Urbana: U of Illinois P, 1979.

Surette, Leon. "Creating the Canadian Canon." *Canadian Canons: Essays in Literary Value*. Ed. Robert Lecker. Toronto: UTP, 1991. 17–29.

Tator, Carol, et al. *Challenging Racism in the Arts: Case Studies of Controversy and Conflict*. Toronto: U of Toronto P, 1998.

Taylor, Kate. "Can You Own a Tale? Canadian Authors File Plagiarism Suit." theglobeandmail.com. 4 Nov. 2011. Web. 15 June 2012.

The Telling It Book Collective. *Telling It: Women and Language Across Cultures*. Vancouver: Press Gang, 1990.

Todd, Loretta. "Notes on Appropriation/L'Appropriation." *Parallelogramme* 16.1 (1990): 24–33.

Tomkins, Sylvan. *Shame and Its Sisters: A Sylvan Tomkins Reader*. Ed. Ève Kosofsky Sedgewick and Adam Frank. Durham: Duke UP, 1995.

Trinh, Min-ha. *When the Moon Waxes Red: Representation, Gender and Cultural Politics*. New York: Routledge, 1991.

————. *Woman, Native, Other*. Bloomington: Indiana UP, 1989.

Ty, Eleanor. *The Politics of the Visible in Asian North American Narratives*. Toronto: U of Toronto P, 2004.

Valpy, Michael. "A Nasty Serving of Cultural Apartheid." *Globe and Mail*, Classroom Edition. 7 Apr. 1994.

Viswanathan, Gauri. *Masks of Conquest: Literary Study and British Rule in India*. New York: Columbia UP, 1989.

Wah, Fred. *Faking It: Poetics & Hybridity, Critical Writing 1984–1999*. Edmonton: NeWest, 2000.

————. *Waiting for Saskatchewan*. Winnipeg: Turnstone, 1985.

West, Cornel. "The New Cultural Politics of Difference." *Out There: Marginalization and Contemporary Culture*. Cambridge: MIT P, 1992. 19–37.

Wong, Paul. "Yellow Peril: Reconsidered." *Yellow Peril: Reconsidered*. Vancouver: On Edge, 1990.

Wong, Rita. "chaos feary." *Ribsauce*. Ed. Taien Ng-Chan et al. Montreal: Vehicule, 2001. 34.

————. *forage*. Gibson's Landing: Nightwood, 2007.

————. "Market Forces and Powerful Desires: Reading Evelyn Lau's Cultural Labour." *Essays in Canadian Writing* 73 (2001).

————. *monkeypuzzle*. Vancouver: Press Gang, 1998.

————. *Restless Bodies*. Vancouver: Simon Fraser U, 2006.

Wong, Tony. "Seeing Red over Gold Mountain Blues." Toronto.com. 23 Oct. 2011. Web. 14 June 2012.

Woodcock, George. "Old and New Oxford Books: The Idea of an Anthology." *Sewanee Review*. 82 (1974): 119–30.

Woods, Stuart. "Chinese Novel Alleged to Have Stolen from Canada's 'Literary Elite'." quillandquire.com. 1 Feb. 2011. Web. 26 July 2012.

Yee, Paul. *Salt Water City.* Vancouver: Douglas and McIntyre, 1988. mentioned in fn ch 2.

Young, James, and Susan Haley. "'Nothing Comes from Nowhere': Reflections on Cultural Appropriation as the Representation of Other Cultures." *The Ethics of Cultural Appropriation.* Ed. James O. Young and Conrad G. Brunk. Chichester: Wiley-Blackwell, 2009. 268–89.

Young, Robert J. C. *Colonial Desire: Hybridity, Culture and Race.* London: Routledge, 1995.

Yudice, George. Introduction. *Consumers and Citizens.* By Nestor Garcia Canclini. Minneapolis: U of Minneapolis P, 2001. ix–xxxviii.

Zantingh, Matthew. "When Things Act Up: Thing Theory, Actor-Network Theory, and Toxic Discourse in Rita Wong's Poetry." *Interdisciplinary Studies in Literature and the Environment* 20.3 (2013): 1–25.

Zen, Lillienne. "The Poetics of Offering: An Approach towards Chinese Canadian/ Indigenous Relations." Paper. 2013. Courtesy of Rita Wong.

Žižek, Slavoj. *The Sublime Object of Ideology.* London: Verso, 1989.

INDEX

201, 212, 239n9; social identity, 27, 94, 95, 110, 112
ideology, 5, 13, 27, 28, 49, 80, 82, 86, 95, 98, 109, 122, 178, 188, 192, 200, 210, 230n1, 235n1, 235n7
Imagining Asian and Native Women: Deconstruction from Contact to Modern Times (conference), 213–14
imperialism, 29, 66, 80, 113, 156, 162, 163, 165, 188, 189, 191
Inalienable Rice (anthology), 2, 6, 21, 91, 92, 99, 100, 101, 109, 110, 111, 115, 231n2
India, 19, 95
Indian Act, 222
Indians, "Indianness" (Canadian), 30, 31, 157, 229n10. *See also* Aboriginal; Indigenous; Inuit; Métis; Native
Indigenous, 15, 18, 19, 20, 22, 23, 27, 28, 29, 30, 31, 43, 91, 161, 168, 174, 229n3, 229n11, 234n6. *See also* Aboriginal; Indians; Inuit; Métis; Native
Industrial Revolution, 234n5 (chap 4)
In-Equations: can asia pacific (special issue of *West Coast Line*), 3, 65
Ingalls, Laura, 157
Inside Out (Lau), 48
Institute of Communication and Culture (University of Toronto), 66
Internet, 20, 195, 234n5 (chap 4), 235n3
internment of Japanese Canadians, 1, 40, 67, 69, 92, 137, 146, 222, 232n4
Into the Heart of Africa (exhibition), 3
Inuit, 229n3, 229n11. *See also* Aboriginal; Indians; Indigenous; Métis; Native
InVisible Colours (film and video festival), 2, 213, 232n3 (chap 2)
Iran-Contra scandal, 216
Iranian, 163
Iraq, 177, 208, 216; Iraq War, 208
Ireland, 19; Irish people, 116
ismail, jam, 12, 34, 161–68, 170, 173–78, 180, 226, 229n6; "Casa Blanca" (with Jamelie Hassan), 176; *from the diction air*, 180; Jamelie/Jamila Project, 176–77; "oolemma," 12, 185, 226; "Poeisis," 179; *scared texts*, 165; *sexions*, 173, 175, 180

Italian (language), 165
Italy, 204, 208
It's a Cultural Thing (conference), 2, 213, 226

Jade Peony (Choy), 19, 38, 53, 138
Jakobsen, Janet, 124
Jamelie/Jamila Project (ismail), 176–77
Jameson, Frederic, 187, 188, 192, 194, 195, 196, 197, 199, 200, 235n1; "Notes on Globalization as a Philosophical Issue," 187
Japan, 66, 174
Japanese (language), 143, 145
Japanese Canadian Citizens Association, 137
Japanese Canadian redress agreement, 72, 101
Japanese food, 149–50
Japantown (Vancouver), 18
Jasper (Alberta), 165
Jew, Anne, 2; *Everyone Talked Loudly in Chinatown*, 107
Jews, 141
John Rajchman, 72, 117, 133, 202; "Diagram and Diagnosis," 117
jook sing ("hollow bamboo"), 166
Joyce, James: *Ulysses*, 22
Justice in Our Time (Miki and Kobayashi), 72

Kadi, Joanna, 126, 127
Kali (Hindu goddess), 68, 69, 81
Kamboureli, Smaro, 2, 13, 16, 64, 76, 89–90, 94, 96, 97, 99–101, 109; "Sedative Politics," 13, 16, 109
Kang, Nancy, 155; "Cosmic Corporeality," 155
Kant, Immanuel, 95, 133
kappa (Japanese supernatural creature), 153, 154, 156, 157
Kappa Child (Goto), 34, 135, 152, 155, 156, 158, 159
Keeshig-Tobias, Lenore, 22, 23, 26, 27, 29, 30, 31, 221, 229n11
Kennedy, George, 163
Kim, Christine, 168
kin, kinship, 68, 191, 203, 208, 232n4

Books in the TransCanada Series
Published by Wilfrid Laurier University Press

Smaro Kamboureli and Roy Miki, editors
Trans.Can.Lit: Resituating the Study of Canadian Literature / 2007 / xviii + 234 pp. /
ISBN 978-0-88920-513-0

Smaro Kamboureli
Scandalous Bodies: Diasporic Literature in English Canada / 2009 / xviii + 270 pp. /
ISBN 978-1-55458-064-4

Kit Dobson
Transnational Canadas: Anglo-Canadian Literature and Globalization / 2009 / xviii
+ 240 pp. / ISBN 978-1-55458-063-7

Christine Kim, Sophie McCall, and Melina Baum Singer, editors
Cultural Grammars of Nation, Diaspora, and Indigeneity in Canada / 2012 / viii +
276 pp. / ISBN 978-1-55458-336-2

Smaro Kamboureli and Robert Zacharias, editors
Shifting the Ground of Canadian Literary Studies / 2012 / xviii + 350 pp. / ISBN
978-1-55458-365-2

Kit Dobson and Smaro Kamboureli
Producing Canadian Literature: Authors Speak on the Literary Marketplace / 2013 /
xii + 208 pp. / ISBN 978-1-55458-355-3

Eva C. Karpinski, Jennifer Henderson, Ian Sowton, and Ray Ellenwood, editors
Trans/acting Culture, Writing, and Memory / 2013 / xxix + 364 pp. / ISBN
978-1-55458-839-8

Smaro Kamboureli and Christl Verduyn, editors
*Critical Collaborations: Indigenity, Diaspora, and Ecology in Canadian Literary
Studies* / 2014 / viii + 288 pp. / ISBN 978-1-55458-911-1

Larissa Lai
*Slanting I, Imagining We: Asian Canadian Literary Production in the 1980s and
1990s* / 2014 / xii + 262 pp. / ISBN 978-1-77112-041-8